ANGLO-SAXON
SCHOLARSHIP

the first three centuries

A
Reference
Publication
in
Literature

ANGLO-SAXON SCHOLARSHIP

the first three centuries

Edited by

Carl T. Berkhout

and

Milton McC. Gatch

G.K.HALL &CO.

70 LINCOLN STREET, BOSTON, MASS.

Library of Congress Cataloging in Publication Data
Main entry under title:

Anglo-Saxon scholarship, the first three centuries.

  Papers presented at the 13th Conference on Medieval
Studies, Western Michigan University, Kalamazoo, May 1978
  Bibliography: p. 183
  Includes index.
  1. Anglo-Saxon philology—Congresses. 2. Anglo-Saxon
philology—History—Congresses. I. Berkhout, Carl T.,
1944-   . II. Gatch, Milton McCormick. III. Con-
ference on Medieval Studies (13th : 1978 : Western
Michigan University)
PE103.A5   429   82-959
ISBN 0-8161-8321-X   AACR2

This publication is printed on permanent/durable acid-free paper
MANUFACTURED IN THE UNITED STATES OF AMERICA

Contents

Contributors

Carl T. Berkhout, who studied at Benedictine College, Marquette University, and the University of Notre Dame, has taught at Marquette and Notre Dame and is presently on the faculty of the University of Dallas. His publications on Old English language and literature have appeared in Mediaeval Studies, Neuphilologische Mitteilungen, English Language Notes, and other journals. Palaeography and bibliography are among his scholarly interests.

Milton McC. Gatch holds degrees from Haverford College, the Episcopal Theological School, and Yale University. He was a Professor of English at the University of Missouri (Columbia) before he became Academic Dean of Union Theological Seminary in New York City and has published widely on Old English prose sermons and other medieval religious writings. Recently, he has studied English collectors of manuscript fragments, c. 1700.

Gretchen P. Ackerman, a graduate of Radcliffe, University of Toronto, and Harvard resides in Walpole, New Hampshire. With her late husband, Robert W. Ackerman, she wrote Sir Frederic Madden: A Biographical Sketch and Bibliography.

Peter Stuart Baker studied at Columbia and Yale Universities and teaches at Emory University. He has edited works and letters of James Boswell, but his central interest is the writings of Byrhtferth of Ramsey, whose Ehchiridion or Manual he is editing with Michael Lapidge.

Ronald E. Buckalew was educated at the College of Wooster and the University of Illinois. He teaches at the Pennsylvania State University and has twice been an associate of Clare Hall, Cambridge. He is preparing an edition of Ælfric's Glossary and has written articles on the Glossary and other topics in medieval English literature and historical linguistics.

Sarah H. Collins, Professor of Language and Literature at The Rochester Institute of Technology, is a graduate of Centre College and Indiana University. In addition to several studies on Elizabeth Elstob, she has published on children's literature and technical writing.

Sandra A. Glass works in development at the Claremont University Center and teaches English in the Graduate School at Claremont. She studied in Claremont at Pomona College and the Graduate School. She has written about the Sutton Hoo ship burial as well as the revival of Anglo-Saxon studies.

M. Sue Hetherington has published several papers on the history of Old English lexicography. She holds degrees from the Universities of Missouri (Columbia), Houston, and Texas and taught at Lamar University before assuming her present post at the College of Charleston.

Shaun F. D. Hughes studied at Victoria University, Wellington, New Zealand, and the University of Washington. He has taught at Purdue University since 1978 and has published papers on aspects of the history of language and Icelandic studies.

Theodore H. Leinbaugh is a member of the English faculty at the University of North Carolina at Chapel Hill. He has published reviews in Speculum and The Review of English Studies and has worked on a critical edition of the liturgical sermons in Ælfric's Lives of Saints. An undergraduate alumnus of Yale, he holds advanced degrees from Oxford and Harvard Universities.

Michael Murphy was born in Ireland and has studied at Birkbeck College in the University of London and at the University of Pittsburgh. Since becoming a member of the faculty of Brooklyn College of the City University of New York, he has published several papers on early modern Anglo-Saxon studies.

Richard C. Payne, a major in the United States Army Reserve, holds degrees from the University of Virginia and Princeton. He has taught at the University of Chicago, where he was also associated with "The Linguistic Atlas of the North-Central States," and has published papers on historical linguistics and Old English poetry.

Introduction

Serious students of Anglo-Saxon literary history, perhaps more than scholars in other areas of medieval studies, constantly encounter their predecessors in the field. Consequently, they need to understand and to evaluate both the motivations of the early scholars for studying the Anglo-Saxons and the achievements of their research.

The literary accomplishments of the English before the Norman Conquest were little appreciated from the twelfth through the fifteenth century. Indeed, the nostalgic Arthurian literature that flourished throughout the later Middle Ages tended implicitly to denigrate the Anglo-Saxons by glorifying the cause of the Britons, whom they had defeated and displaced. With the replacement of a Saxon by a Norman nobility, the English language had, of course, also changed radically; and very few later medieval readers of English could understand the literary remains of the Saxon period.

The revival of interest in the English writings of the Anglo-Saxons coincided with the dissolution of the monasteries and the reformation of the church in England. Not only did the new owners of the manuscripts of the monastic establishments evince interest in manuscripts containing Old English, but they also imagined that the ecclesiastical ideas of the Anglo-Saxons might help to justify what were regarded by some as the innovations of the reformers, notably the principle that the crown might exercise leadership in the church. Thus, for example, Matthew Parker, Elizabeth I's archbishop of Canterbury, used the Saxon writings, which he and his followers had begun to study, to justify the independence of the national church from the papacy and to claim antiquity for their departures from the consensus of late medieval theology in such matters as the nature of Christ's presence in the Eucharist. Although it seems to us in retrospect that the points the Parker group wanted to make were in fact difficult to sustain, the use of "antiquarian" Anglo-Saxon studies for apologetic and polemical purposes became standard and endured throughout the seventeenth century. Grammatical and lexical studies of Old English were, for the most part, handmaidens to the larger purpose of justifying the policies of the English state church and its reformed doctrine.

It remains unclear when the apologetic-polemical motivations of Anglo-Saxon scholarship were broken by a scholarship of more disinterested motives. Certainly the work of George Hickes and Humfrey Wanley at the turn of the seventeenth and eighteenth centuries set standards in grammatical and paleographical study that scholars today can ignore only at their peril. But Hickes, a complex and little-understood man, was a non-juring clergyman and was consecrated a bishop by the party of churchmen who refused to take the oath to William and Mary after the deposition of James II. In view of Hickes's centrality to Saxon antiquarianism in his time and the frequency of non-juring connections among his fellow scholars, some contemporary apologetic concern remained important in the study of Old English language and literature.

Certainly the theological and legal writings of the Anglo-Saxons were the texts that most interested scholars until the middle of the eighteenth century. With the rise of the romantic movement and the appearance of such works as Macpherson's Ossian and Percy's Reliques, the way opened to greater interest in the poetry of the Saxon period. The great change, which still influences strongly the study of Old English language and the editions of Old English texts, occurred with the importation from Germany of the discipline of Germanistic philology. Ostensibly a "scientific" discipline, Germanistik also sought to rediscover the ethos of the Germanic peoples; and when this pursuit implied the pure and original character and the religious impulses of those peoples (among whom, of course, the Anglo-Saxons were numbered), it sometimes developed unfortunate, new apologetic tendencies.

The importance of understanding this scholarly history is almost universally recognized, but surprisingly few works attempt to trace its progress. The most important of these, a synoptic history of the subject, is Eleanor N. Adams's Old English Scholarship in England from 1566-1800, volume 55 of the Yale Studies in English series, first published in 1917 and reprinted in 1970. Since the publication of Adams's dissertation, a number of studies on special aspects of the subject have appeared. Perhaps the single most distinguished and stimulating contribution, focused on the seventeenth and eighteenth centuries and concerned primarily with historical studies broader than simply the Saxon period, is David C. Douglas's English Scholars: 1660-1730 (London: Eyre and Spottiswoode, 1939; 2d ed. 1951), a book especially notable for its discussion of George Hickes and the reasons he has not yet attracted a biographer.

The purpose of this volume of essays is to stimulate new research in the history of Anglo-Saxon scholarship. The book had its origin in two sessions arranged by the editors for the Thirteenth Conference on Medieval Studies of Western Michigan University at Kalamazoo in May 1978, with the encouragement and support of Professor Otto Gründler, Director of the Medieval Institute at Western Michigan. Two papers have since been added to the original group: Michael Murphy's general survey of the entire volume's subject and Theodore H. Leinbaugh's discussion of reformation Saxonists on Ælfric's sermon on the eucharistic presence. Although we have attempted to gather a set of papers of uniformly acceptable scholarly quality and character, no effort has been made to impose uniformity of methodology or style upon the contributors. On the contrary, the collection is intended to reflect the range of interests and approaches in current Anglo-Saxon scholarship and to provide samples of scholarly styles ranging from the discursive essay to the highly technical textual analysis. When a new history of modern Anglo-Saxon scholarship is written, it will depend upon the work of students running the full range of these approaches and styles.

Just as no effort has been made to make these papers uniform in method, style, or level of difficulty, so also no attempt has been made to make this volume a history of Anglo-Saxon or even Old English scholarship. Many important figures are untouched or barely touched: Matthew Parker, Francis Junius, Humfrey Wanley, and Benjamin Thorpe leap to mind. Partly to cover these lacunae and to indicate some of the work on the subject published since the appearance of Adam's monograph, we have supplied a selective bibliography of more recent studies of early modern Anglo-Saxon scholarship. The bibliography emphasizes particularly secondary studies on scholars and issues discussed by the contributors to this volume. Further references can be found in Stanley B. Greenfield and Fred C. Robinson's monumental Bibliography of Publications on Old English Literature to the End of 1972 (Toronto: University of Toronto Press, 1980). Together, we hope our collection of essays and these bibliographical aids may renew interest among contemporary scholars in the work of earlier Saxonists.

To our contributors and our publisher, for their able efforts and tolerance of the editors' malingering ways, we are most grateful. We also wish to record our thanks to Professor Stanley B. Greenfield for a thoughtful and helpful reading of the entire typescript and to Professor J. R. Hall for a careful reading of the proofs.

Antiquary to Academic:
The Progress of Anglo-Saxon Scholarship

Michael Murphy

Hardly more than a century after Chaucer's death, John
Skelton complained about the inability of his contemporaries to read the great poet:

> And now men would have amended
> His englisshe whereat they barke . . .
> Chaucer that famous clarke
> His termes were not darke.
> ("Phillip Sparrow," ca. 1507)

If the language of late medieval England was dark to many
people in the early sixteenth century, Old English was
effectively a dead language, and its literary remains
less accessible than those of ancient Greece and Rome,
which were beginning to enjoy a renaissance themselves.
If the Italian Renaissance stimulated Englishmen to a
renewed and deeper acquaintance with the Greek and Roman
classics, it was, to a sizable degree, the reformation in
religion that encouraged a look at the ancient language
of England itself. Indeed, in the case of England, it is
artificial to separate the Renaissance and the Reformation, for they went very much hand in hand.

There were two strong feelings operating simulta-
neously: a deep reverence for a past golden age; and a
determination to move forward to something totally new
which was nevertheless seen, or at least presented, as a
return to better times. The beginning of Anglo-Saxon
studies in the sixteenth century is a good example of the
amalgamation of these two forces. In the ecclesiastical
field, for example, the reformed church, led by Matthew
Parker, Queen Elizabeth's first archbishop of Canterbury,
appealed to the doctrine and practice of an older English

church to justify a complete break with medieval Catholicism. It contended that the pre-Conquest Ecclesia Anglicana had been a Church allied to but independent of the church of Rome, and that one of its established practices was to propagate the word of God in the vernacular. The Reformation was, therefore, supposed to be a "revolution" in the sixteenth-century sense of the term: a turn of the wheel back to the beginning, although modern scholars point out that the Anglo-Saxon church was one of the most vigorous supporters of the papacy. How much the reformers knew their movement to be a revolution in the modern sense of a complete overthrow of the past is another matter.

Reformation was not to be confined to the ecclesiastical field, for similar feelings were evident in the literary world which we think of more commonly as the Renaissance. While there was indeed a renewed respect for the ancient classics, the spirit of nationalism was active too. Literary men and educational theorists began to feel that England had a language, if not yet a literature the equal (or nearly) of anything that Greece or Rome had produced; others were not so sure. The argument was settled largely by a host of translators who poured out a flood of English versions of the classics.[1] Not least in importance among the translations were versions of the Bible. Thus the literary and ecclesiastical worlds supported each other in their efforts to bring to literate Englishmen, who had small Latin and less Greek, the words of the great poets and philosophers, and the word of God in their own tongue. Latin remained, of course, the language of scholarship for those writers who wished to reach a European audience. For all other purposes English was felt to be more than adequate. By the time that Sidney could say in 1583, "for the uttering sweetly and properly the conceit of the minde, which is the end of speech, English hath it equally with any other tongue in the world," the matter had been firmly settled in favor of English.

Renaissance and Reformation went beyond the ecclesiastical and literary fields. Even in Elizabeth's time there were signs that these movements would not be complete until the political system too had been revamped. Effort in this direction remained somewhat quiescent until the old queen died in 1603, and it came to full life only under the Stuart monarchs. When it did, the call of the common lawyers who led the movement was the same as that of their clerical counterparts: there should be a "revolution" back to an immemorial law and constitution that was not the creature of monarchs.

Archbishop Parker (1504-1575), as we know, took up the
challenging task of directing research into the distant
past of the English church. Vernacular manuscripts that
had escaped the destruction of the monasteries would have
to be collected; and someone would have to buckle down,
learn Old English, and sort through the collection for
useful material. Parker scoured the cathedral libraries
and other available sources of manuscripts, and assembled
the fine collection that rests today in Cambridge. He
organized his household, including his son John and his
secretary John Joscelyn, into a kind of school of Anglo-
Saxon. One of the chief results of this cooperative
scholarly effort was the first book ever printed in Old
English, A Testimonie of Antiquitie (1566/7).[2] It reproduced a sermon of Ælfric's on the sacrament of the
Eucharist, which appeared to favor the reformer's view of
that much-debated subject. Actually, it was a small haul
from the large corpus of available Ælfrician material,
but it was also a very astute choice: the sermon dealt
with one of the areas of fundamental difference between
Catholics and Protestants in a fashion that has given
disputants room for discussion ever since. It has been
endlessly reproduced either in the original or in translation. Even in the middle of the nineteenth century
Ælfric's sermon was at the center of a vitriolic scholarly debate between John Lingard and Henry Soames; and as
late as 1963 C. L. Wrenn found its theology worth another
look.[3]

Another somewhat different fruit of the Parker
group's researches was an edition of the Anglo-Saxon
Gospels (1571) published over the name of John Foxe, the
martyrologist.[4] Why Foxe, who was no scholar of Old
English, was chosen to put his name to the edition can
only be a matter for speculation. He had just published
the second English edition of his very popular Book of
Martyrs (1570), and perhaps it was felt that the use of
his name could only help the wider distribution of a very
different kind of book. The main aim of this edition was
undoubtedly to demonstrate in a very concrete and visual
way that the work of Parker and his colleagues in publishing the Bishops' Bible in the vernacular (1572) had
an ancient and venerable tradition in England: the Bible
had been available in the vernacular before the Normans
introduced their continental corruptions into the true
Ecclesia Anglicana. The verse from Jeremiah cited on the
title page of A Testimonie sums up perfectly the purpose
of the whole enterprise: "Goe into the streetes, and
inquyre for the olde way: and if it be the good and
ryght way, then goe therein, that ye may finde rest for
your soules. But they say: we will not walke therein."

It is easy to account for an ecclesiastical interest
in Old English material that might be of polemical use in
the 1560s. It is not so easy to explain a deep interest
at the same time in pre-Conquest law written in the vernacular. There were, indeed, some stirrings of unrest
with the political system, but the violent argument that
led to civil war and regicide in the following century
under a new royal house must have been impossible to
foresee, even vaguely, in the 1560s when Laurence Nowell
was teaching himself the language and studying the Anglo-
Saxon laws. Moreover, Nowell was a "servant" in the
house of William Cecil, the queen's chief minister; the
autocratic minister of an autocratic monarch probably
would not have encouraged (as he clearly did) any study
possibly subversive of the English crown. Nowell's work
became a favorite with the common lawyers at the end of
the sixteenth and the beginning of the seventeenth century, but one cannot read back into it any intention to
produce the effect for which they used it.

Let us defer for the moment a consideration of the
importance of Nowell's work as a polemical document in
the hands of later constitutional lawyers in order to
reflect on the considerable achievement it represented in
another respect. Clearly Nowell had acquired a remarkable, if incomplete knowledge of a dead language without
the aid of a grammar or dictionary, and had even passed
some of his competence on to his friend William Lambarde.
Nowell probably had a good deal to do with the skill in
Old English achieved by John Joscelyn, the archbishop's
secretary. Nowell was even confident enough in his own
ability (and no doubt in the ignorance of his readers) to
compose Old English himself in order to fill inconvenient
gaps in his sources; and he did it well enough to avoid
detection until very recent years.[5]

How did Nowell and his contemporaries go about learning the language without the aid of printed texts, dictionary, and grammar--all the tools we take for granted?
I have tried elsewhere to outline his probable method as
far as it can be reconstructed.[6] It may be briefly re-
stated as follows. In Anglo-Saxon England young monks
needed to be taught Latin, and Ælfric had written a
grammar and a glossary for the students in his monastery.
These works were still available in the sixteenth century, and could be used in precisely the reverse way by
scholars who knew no Old English but were very familiar
with Latin. Available also were some separate manuscript
Latin-Old English glosses; versions of large parts of the
Bible, some of them glossed interlinearly; and the Latin
originals of the Alfredian translations such as the

Orosius, Boethius, and Bede. There was even an early
Latin version of some of the Anglo-Saxon laws. Manuscript material for learning Old English was, therefore,
not lacking, but it took a remarkably determined student
to deal with it and to extract from it the kind of command of the language that Nowell achieved.[7]

Let us now return to the political importance of
Nowell's work. His edition of the Anglo-Saxon laws, entitled Archaionomia, appeared in 1568 under the name of
William Lambarde. This editorial arrangement was not
quite the same as that which Parker's household had with
Foxe; for Lambarde did indeed know the Old English he had
learned from Nowell, and he provided the Old English text
with a Latin translation and some additional material
from his own collection. Moreover, Nowell had gone
overseas for some reason, leaving the publication of
the book to Lambarde. The work is, therefore, known as
Lambarde's, though a fairer and more accurate reference
to the authorship would be to Nowell-Lambarde.

The influence of their published work was as per-
vasive if not as long-lasting as the publications of
their ecclesiastical counterparts.[8] For when the common
lawyers, led by Sir Edward Coke, argued their constitutional case against James I and Charles I, the
Archaionomia became an important weapon. A constitutional historian assures us that it was "one of the key
books of the common law interpretation," which held that
"the common law, and with it the constitution, had always
been exactly what they were now, that they were immemorial: not merely that they were very old, or that they
were the work of some remote and mythical legislators,
but that they were immemorial in the precise legal sense
of time beyond memory--beyond, in this case the earliest
historical records that could be found."[9] Since the
Anglo-Saxon laws were indeed historical records, it is
difficult for the layman to understand how they were used
to bolster such an argument. But in disputes of this
kind perhaps logic or consistency is not at a premium.
In any case Coke "was able to make very extensive use of
Lambarde's book to prove that institutions which had in
fact been introduced by the Normans formed part of the
immemorial law."[10] What Nowell and Lambarde would have
said about Coke's use of their book we can only conjecture.

What does this use of the Archaionomia say of real
knowledge of Old English in the earlier seventeenth century? Not much, probably. The book may have been used
extensively, but its readers were not obliged to learn

Old English, because Lambarde had provided a Latin
translation. Indeed, a reading of standard works like
Pocock's Ancient Constitution and Samuel Kliger's The
Goths in England confirms the impression that most
Jacobean and Caroline constitutional lawyers were much
more at home with Tacitus than they were with the Anglo-
Saxon.[11] John Selden was one exception to this rule; he
did have a knowledge of Old English, but only someone
well acquainted with the legal issues could say how important to his legal studies was his undoubted knowledge
of the language. There is no doubt, however, even for
the layman, that Sir Henry Spelman, another eminent
jurist, made much use of his knowledge of Old English.
In fact he became aware that any serious study of constitutional history or ancient civil and ecclesiastical law
in England required mastery of Old English, and he made a
serious effort to see that permanent instruction in the
language and culture of Anglo-Saxon England should be
available at a university. He paid Abraham Wheelock,
Professor of Arabic at Cambridge, to study and teach the
language and history of Anglo-Saxon England, to provide
him with transcripts of manuscripts that he needed in his
work, and to check his translations, for Sir Henry never
felt complete master of the language. But this arrangement between Wheelock and Spelman--never a perpetual en-
dowment--did not begin until 1638. By then Sir Henry was
an old man and Wheelock was just beginning the study of
Old English, so that except for supplying some transcripts, he was not of much use to Spelman before the
latter's death in 1641. At that date Spelman was still
the master, and the "professor" was still very much the
pupil. Wheelock progressed fast enough, however, to
publish the Old English version of Bede's Historia
Ecclesiastica (1643) for the first time, together with
an edition of the Anglo-Saxon Chronicle, which he also
translated into Latin. A reissue in 1644 added a somewhat augmented edition of the Archaionomia. Here all the
major interests and motivations for the early study of
Old English met in one volume. The Historia and the
Chronicle are, of course, essential sources for the study
of England's early history, and any edition of Anglo-
Saxon law has a historical relevance beyond the polemical
purposes for which the Archaionomia was sometimes used.
But Bede's work was an ecclesiastical history; and
Wheelock, in the tradition of Parker and his group, lost
few opportunities in his abundant annotations to use it
for ecclesiastical polemic. His position was the same as
Parker's: the church of Bede was not a Roman but an
English church to which the reformers had returned.

In spite of faults apparent even to seventeenth-
century scholars, Wheelock's book became an essential
source for every student of early English history for the
rest of the century and even later. One student was John
Milton, who commented dryly on Wheelock's Latin version
of the poem commemorating the battle of Brunanburh, em-
bedded in the Chronicle at the year 937.[12] Milton's comment reveals one serious inadequacy in the study of Old
English at this point, namely an ignorance of the rules
and vocabulary of Old English verse. Wheelock acknowledged his deficiency by an embarrassed note to his translation of the poem. His ignorance is hardly surprising,
given the way in which the knowledge of the language was
acquired. Nowell, Lambarde, Joscelyn, Parker, and a
number of others since had acquired a considerable mastery of Old English prose, but none of them made much
effort to come to terms with the verse. This reluctance
arose, apparently, from two causes. The poetic idiom was
"perantiquum et horridum," as Wheelock put it, and was
much more difficult than the prose. Furthermore, insofar
as it was understood, it had no "practical" value; that
is, it could not be used to make profitable points in the
discussions of legal, constitutional, or ecclesiastical
issues. There was, therefore, less impetus in the period
to study the poetry.[13]

Indeed there had been no real advance since Nowell's
time in the availability of tools to learn even Old
English prose. There was still no published grammar or
dictionary, although Nowell had made a manuscript glossary and Joscelyn had made an even more extensive one
based on Nowell's, but neither of these was available
to the only "professor" of the language in the country.
Wheelock's frequent correspondent Sir Simonds D'Ewes did
have a copy of Joscelyn's, but he was very jealous of
his own plan to produce the definitive dictionary of Old
English. Apparently he never made his copy available to
Wheelock. Joscelyn had also made a grammar, though it
did not survive even in manuscript, and Nowell probably
made one in order to teach Lambarde. This painfully
acquired knowledge was not passed on in a sensible way,
so that Wheelock was compelled to learn the language by
using the published editions and translations of his
predecessors and the Old English manuscripts at Cambridge
that had Latin versions available, such as the Bede.
Inevitably he, too, started a glossary and a grammar.
The scraps of his glossary that survive are inferior to
Nowell's dictionary, but William Somner thought well
enough of his grammar to print a version of it later in
his own Dictionarium (1659).[14]

Wheelock seems to have attracted no more students to Old English than he did to Arabic. Indeed it is hard to see how he could have induced young students to such an arcane study without the usual aids of a published grammar and dictionary. In any case his lectureship seems to have become largely a research post, and he left no body of students trained in the language and history of Anglo-Saxon England, as Spelman had hoped he would. After the reissue of the Bede volume with some additions, Wheelock apparently concentrated once more on his Oriental studies. Fortunately, other scholars had been pursuing Old English studies independently. After Wheelock's death in 1653 the Spelman endowment was transferred to one of them, William Somner, who produced a full-scale dictionary by 1659.

Partly for technical reasons Somner's dictionary was published at Oxford rather than Cambridge; for many years thereafter Oxford was to take the lead in Anglo-Saxon study. Not until the mid-nineteenth century was Cambridge to have an endowed professorship of Anglo-Saxon. The publication of Somner's dictionary at Oxford probably encouraged the surge of interest in Old English study there in the latter half of the seventeenth century, when Oxford became known as a "nest of Saxonists." The nest included John Fell, the bishop of Oxford; Francis Junius, an anglicized Dutch scholar; his friend William Marshall, who became Rector of Lincoln College; George Hickes, a fellow of the same college; William Elstob, Arthur Charlett, and Humfrey Wanley, all connected with University College; and William Nicolson, Edmund Gibson, and Edward Thwaites, all of Queen's College. Fell was a genuine patron and promoter of Anglo-Saxon studies, Charlett more a "pretender." The others were active in the field.[15]

Marshall had become a fellow of Lincoln in 1668, three years after he and Francis Junius had co-edited the Old English Gospels[16] on the Continent, where Marshall was chaplain to a company of English merchants. From that point until after the end of the century, there was almost no break in the line of scholars at Oxford who studied and published Old English. Junius joined his friend in Oxford about 1675, a couple of years before his death. By then he was a very old man; but his learning was widely known and deeply respected, and he received a constant stream of visitors. His presence, conversation, and publications spurred Englishmen to pursue the study to which he had devoted so much of his life. He was one of the first continental scholars to develop a mastery of early English philology greater than their English

counterparts--a situation that was to become particularly
galling in the nineteenth century.

William Nicolson was one of Junius's visitors.
Whether or not Junius influenced his decision, Nicolson
certainly took up the study of Old English and even
taught it for a while at Queen's College between 1679
and his departure from Oxford in 1681. Unfortunately we
know nothing of his students or his methods of teaching.
Even more unfortunately the teaching seems to have
lapsed after Nicolson left to go on eventually to high
ecclesiastical office. He must have contributed to a
tradition in the pursuit of Old English study at his own
college, however, for both Edmund Gibson and Edward
Thwaites, who both arrived there in the 1680s, became
prominent contributors to the field.

The rapid rise in interest in Old English during the
late seventeenth century and the early eighteenth was not
solely because of the teaching of Nicolson, the presence
of Junius, or the publication of Somner's dictionary. In
the year that Thwaites arrived at Oxford (1689) the university press published the first grammar of Old English,
the Institutiones Grammaticae of George Hickes. Hickes
was a remarkable man in many respects; it is unfortunate
that we do not have a thorough study of his full and
painful career as cleric, scholar, and controversialist.[17]
Here we can only touch on the most relevant points.

Hickes was a man of great intellectual energy, un-
shakeable principle, and powerful personality. He and
Marshall had been fellows of Lincoln together, and no
doubt it was there that Hickes acquired an interest in
Old English. But he did not take up the study in earnest
until he went to Worcester as dean of the cathedral in
1683. By then he had had a fairly turbulent career as a
staunch supporter of church and crown against sundry op-
ponents--in spite of his own assessment he loved controversy. His years at Worcester, however, were serene
enough to allow him to pursue his other passion, scholarship. There he took up the study of Old English in
earnest, and by 1689 he had produced the Institutiones, a
far cry from Wheelock's skimpy effort. Political events,
however, had overtaken Hickes; King James II had fled and
William of Orange was on the English throne. Hickes de-
tested James's Catholicism like most Protestants, but he
did not deny James's divine right to the throne of
England. He refused to take the oath of allegiance to
William, and from that point on his career as cleric of
the Church of England was finished. Even while his book

was in press he was suspended from office, and shortly thereafter he was ejected from his deanery. For the next ten years or so he was a man without a profession or a permanent home, forced to use a false name and various addresses. During that time he decided on a new edition of his grammar, an aim he achieved without access to books and libraries. What is perhaps the most remarkable part of this achievement is how he got other scholars to give him the help he needed to finish his work. Some of these men, Nicolson and Gibson for example, were clerics who had no quarrel with the oath of allegiance and who heartily disagreed with Hickes's non-juring principles. Nevertheless, they gave their help generously, as did a large number of other collaborators.

One of the most important of these was Edward Thwaites, who may have met Hickes when he came incognito to Oxford to begin arrangements for a revision of his grammar. Certainly a short time after Hickes's visit he was corresponding with him about the revision, and in a very short time, was himself preparing an edition of the Old English Heptateuch for publication. He supplied Hickes with transcripts and eventually became business manager for the large operation into which the revised edition of the grammar evolved.[18] Most interesting, perhaps, is that he now began to teach Old English at Queen's College, as Nicolson had done before him. Here we have more information than we do about the labors of either Wheelock or Nicolson. Theoretically at least Thwaites's position as a teacher was much easier than that of his predecessors, for he had available both a published dictionary and a grammar. But the dictionary and grammar were large and expensive books not totally suitable for teaching young and often impecunious students. At one point Thwaites had as many as fifteen students, and he complained that they had to share the one available copy of Somner among them. Thwaites took prompt and sensible action: he and a number of his students made a condensed version of Somner, which was published under the name of Thomas Benson, one of the students who presumably did most of the work. "It will not exceed 3d price, I hope," wrote Thwaites before publication, showing a commendable concern for the thin purses of his students. Perhaps there were more copies of Hickes's grammar available, for a similar condensation of that work did not appear until 1711, the year of Thwaites's death.[19]

In the meantime the revised version of Hickes's grammar proceeded with painful slowness, but the famous Thesaurus finally appeared between 1703 and 1705.[20] It

was a much larger book than its predecessor. Besides the
grammar of Old English there were grammars of Old Icelandic and Gothic, an essay on numismatics, a lengthy
"Dissertatio Epistolaris" which was largely an Ars
Diplomatica directed to Anglo-Saxon charters, an essay
on the usefulness of the study of Northern languages,
dedications, prefatory essays, and finally a catalog of
Anglo-Saxon manuscripts. It was an unwieldy book bound
in large volumes, and unsuitable for the average student,
not least in its price. It was a monumental work and unfortunately, like most monuments, it was admired rather
than actually used.

The part of it that remains of most value was not,
ironically, by Hickes himself, but was the work of his
collaborator Humfrey Wanley. This was the great
Catalogus of manuscripts, the third essential aid, after
a grammar and dictionary, to the study of Anglo-Saxon
culture. Most of the materials of interest to Saxonists
were still in manuscript, and Hickes had determined to
provide students with the best possible guide to their
contents and whereabouts. He was in no position to do
this work himself, and he chose the best man in England
to do the job, Humfrey Wanley, a sub-librarian at the
Bodleian with talent as a bibliographer and paleographer.
Hickes engaged him to do the catalog and paid him what he
could afford for the labor. But what Hickes could afford
could never have repaid Wanley for the work he put into
the project. Hickes was well aware of this, but in a
paternally relentless way he pushed Wanley to complete
the work through years of disappointment and drudgery.
Disabused of hopes of promotion at Oxford, Wanley had
moved to London where he was also disappointed in his
hopes of becoming Keeper of the Cotton Library. In the
meantime he became assistant secretary to the Society for
the Promotion of Christian Knowledge, a post which provided him a salary and a prodigious amount of uncongenial
work. Through it all he continued, prodded by Hickes and
Thwaites, with the work of the catalog. Wanley's trou-
bles caused the delay in publishing the Thesaurus. But
he was a perfectionist, and the result of his stubborn
slowness was a work that has never really become obso-
lete. His Catalogus, the second part of the Thesaurus,
was not replaced until 1957 when Neil Ker produced his
Catalogue of Manuscripts Containing Anglo-Saxon. In the
preface to his book Ker, the man most qualified to pay
Wanley tribute, said that even now the Catalogus "is a
book which scholars will continue to use, or neglect at
their peril."21

With the publication of the Thesaurus the study of
Anglo-Saxon should, theoretically, have taken an upward
turn, but this was not the case. Hickes's book was
daunting, as has already been remarked, and Thwaites
tried to make the Old English part of it more accessible
to his students by producing a condensed version, still
with Latin apparatus (1711). Elizabeth Elstob, the sister of one of Hickes's Oxford collaborators and a fine
Saxonist herself, attempted the same for less academic
students, using English explanations (1715).[22] Her book,
however, remained a curiosity rather than a text. After
Thwaites's death in 1711 interest in Old English at
Oxford lapsed once more. His Old English teaching had
always been an unofficial affair. (His university posts
were Professor of Greek and Reader in Moral Philosophy,
about as far removed from his Anglo-Saxon interests as
Wheelock's Arabic professorship had been.) He had
trained a number of young men in the discipline; a couple
of them had even produced work in Old English under his
direction. Another, George Smith, had finished his
father's work on an edition of the Old English Bede
(1722), but we hear no more of any of them as Old English
scholars.

The rest of the eighteenth century was not a total
wasteland for early English philology,[23] but the most
notable achievement in the period was the successful
effort to direct attention to the more literary products
of ancient England. Ironically, the first effective consideration of early English poetry as poetry was the work
of amateur enthusiasts like Thomas Percy and Thomas Gray,
neither of whom was a genuine student of Old English.
They were not interested in scholarly rigor; indeed,
Percy earned the justified wrath of Joseph Ritson for his
tampering, in the interests of "smoothness" and completeness, with the Middle English texts that he published.
Although for Percy the "barbarism" that had repelled literary men like Swift now became "gothic" and romantic,
he felt correctly that contemporaries, like himself, pre-
ferred their Ossian Macphersonized. In the seventeenth
century the term "gothic" had conveyed notions of freedom, political and ecclesiastical, which controversial-
ists derived from their (largely imaginary) ancestors as
portrayed by Tacitus. For Percy and Gray, less interested in political and ecclesiastical disputes, "gothic"
also meant free from the literary restrictions of Augustan theme and form and displaying a certain "wildness"
that was especially attractive to those reacting against
Augustan restraints.

The sneers that Pope and Swift had directed at the labors of editors of medieval texts like Thomas Hearne unfortunately continued. Even Thomas Warton, who had so much to do with the revival of interest in medieval lit- erature, scorned the earlier scholars for "reviving ob- scure fragments of uninstructive morality or uninterest- ing history." But in 1774 he said this unfortunate state of affairs had changed and "the curiosity of the anti- quarian is connected with taste and genius, and his researches tend to display the progress of human manners, and to illustrate the history of society."[24] This con- descension was understandable if unfortunate. Warton was, after all, interested in "literature," and espe- cially in poetry; and the pioneer Saxonists had done little to excite interest in the more literary produc- tions of Anglo-Saxon England, least of all in the poetry of that period. Percy and Gray may not have known as much early English or Icelandic as Hickes, but they suc- cessfully directed attention for the first time to the literature of early England.

Warton, Percy, and Gray produced their work in the 1760s and 1770s. In 1755 Richard Rawlinson had already endowed a chair of Anglo-Saxon at Oxford. Surely this was the perfect opportunity for the marriage of amateur enthusiasm and professional scholarship; but again it was not to be. Rawlinson had set so many restrictions upon the tenure of the chair that nobody occupied it for the first 45 years. The first holder of the chair, Charles Mayo, knew little about Old English. The second and third occupants, James Ingram and John Josias Conybeare, however, did apply themselves with some success to the study of Old English, though they remained very much in the antiquarian tradition, with little awareness of com- parative philology. In his inaugural address, for exam- ple, Ingram still repeated without much change the old Parkerian and Lambardian ideas on the importance of Old English for proof of the antiquity and Englishness of the civil and ecclesiastical establishment.[25] Conybeare's popular Illustrations of Anglo-Saxon Poetry, the first book of its kind, was published posthumously in 1826. It consisted largely of selections from Old English poetry in the original with literal Latin translations and "versions" in English, often in Conybeare's best romantic verse.[26]

But the days of the old-fashioned, gentlemanly ap- proach to the study of English philology quickly waned. In the very year that Conybeare's book was published, Benjamin Thorpe went to Copenhagen to study with Rasmus Rask, the distinguished Danish scholar who had published a revolutionary grammar of Anglo-Saxon almost ten years earlier. A few years later John Kemble went to Germany, possibly meeting Grimm, who had produced independently a similar grammar at about the same time.[27] The 1830 publication of Thorpe's translation of Rask's grammar marks the change from the enthusiastic to the "scientific" in Anglo-Saxon studies in England. Shortly thereafter Kemble returned from the Continent with a respect for Rask, Grimm, and Thorpe matched only by his unbounded and openly expressed contempt for the Saxonists of the older school, especially for the occupants of the Rawlinson chair at Oxford. He created bad blood by his vigorous attacks on the university men, which was probably why he was not offered an academic position. Indeed, neither he nor Thorpe ever held academic posts, but their publications, carefully edited and abundantly glossed, revolutionized the study of Germanic philology in England. Nevertheless, the new philology caught on very slowly in the universities. It was many years before the Germanic philology taught in England was held in as high esteem as the scholarship in German universities.[28] Many American scholars, for example, went to Germany rather than to England for their philological training in the later nineteenth and earlier twentieth centuries.

The dilatoriness of the universities was compensated for, in part, by the learned societies in England: the Philological Society, the Society of Antiquaries, and the Early English Text Society whose members, mostly untrained by the universities, carried the weight of promoting philological study and publishing texts. It had taken 300 years and the rigor of continental scholars to force an appreciable number of Englishmen to form an organization to promote the study of the early language and culture of their own island.

Notes

1. For an excellent short account of the controversy see Julia Ebel, "Translation and Nationalism in the Elizabethan Era," Journal of the History of Ideas 30 (1969): 593-602. Another account can be found in Albert Baugh's A History of the English Language (New York: Appleton-Century-Crofts, 1957), pp. 240-305.
2. The full title expresses the intent of the edition clearly: A Testimonie of Antiquitie shewing the ancient fayth in the Church of England touching the sacrament of the body and bloode of the Lord, here Publikely preached and also received in the Saxons tyme, above 600 yeares agoe.

3. John Lingard, Antiquities of the Anglo-Saxon
Church, 2 vols. (London: E. Walker, 1806); and Henry
Soames, The Bampton Lectures (Oxford: Rivington,
1830); and The Anglo-Saxon Church (London: J. W.
Parker, 1835). Lingard's 1845 edition of his original
work was almost an entirely new book, incorporating
the work of Thorpe and Kemble which had appeared since
the first edition. The revision was also used to
answer Soames, whose further reply came in The Latin
Church during Anglo-Saxon Times (London: Longman's,
1848), and The Romish Decalogue (London: Longman's,
1852). Wrenn's article, "Some Aspects of Anglo-Saxon
Theology," appeared in Studies in Language, Literature, and Culture, ed. E. Bagby Atwood and A. A. Hill
(Austin: University of Texas Press, 1969), pp. 182-
192. See also the article of Theodore H. Leinbaugh in
this volume.
4. The Gospels of The Fower Evangelistes translated in
the olde Saxons tyme out of Latin into the vulgare
toung of the Saxons, newly collected out of the
Auncient Monumentes of the sayd Saxons and now published for the testimonie of the same (London: John
Daye, 1571).
5. For a full account of Nowell's "forgery," see
Kenneth Sisam, Studies in the History of Old English
Literature (Oxford: Clarendon Press, 1953), pp. 232-
258.
6. Michael Murphy, "Methods in the Study of Old
English in the Sixteenth and Seventeenth Centuries,"
Mediaeval Studies 30 (1968): 345-350.
7. An enjoyable demonstration of Nowell's skill in
translation can be found in The Principal Navigations
Voyages Traffiques & Discoveries of the English
Nation by Richard Hakluyt, more commonly known as
Hakluyt's Voyages (Glasgow: MacLehose, 1903), 1:11-16.
8. The Archaionomia was reissued with some additions
by Wheelock in his 1644 issue of Bede's Historia. It
remained the only collection of Anglo-Saxon laws until
that of Wilkins in 1721.
9. J. G. A. Pocock, The Ancient Constitution and the
Feudal Law (Cambridge: Cambridge University Press,
1957), p. 36.
10. Ibid., p. 43.
11. Ibid., esp. chapters 3-5. The Goths in England
(Cambridge, Mass.: Harvard University Press, 1952),
passim.
12. "The Saxon Annalist wont to be sober and succinct
. . . now labouring under the weight of his argument,
and over-charg'd, runs on sudden into such extravagant
fansies and metaphors, as bare him quite beside the
scope of being understood." Cited in The History of

Britain, ed. French Fogle, in The Com lete Prose Works
of John Milton, (New Haven: Yale University Press,
1971), 5: 308-09, 323 n34.
13.   The most detailed account of Wheelock so far is in
the Dictionary of National Biography. His name is
variously spelled, but a review of his MS correspondence indicates that he himself seems to prefer
Wheelock. For some commentary on his Old English work
see David Douglas, English Scholars, 2d ed. (London:
Eyre and Spottiswoode, 1951), esp. pp. 68-70; Michael
Murphy, "Abraham Wheloc's Edition of Bede's History in
OE," Studia Neophilologica 39 (1967):46-59. I am preparing an article which will give a more thorough
account than the Dictionary of National Biography
entry of his life and negotiations to establish both
the Arabic Professorship and the Old English lectureship.
14.   For an account of early Old English dictionary-
making, see Mary Sue Hetherington's article in this
book.
15.   For details of the work of these scholars, see
Eleanor Adams, Old English Scholarship in England from
1566-1800 (1917; reprinted ed., Hamden, Conn.: Archon
Books, 1970), pp. 42-114 and "Chronological Table";
and J.A.W. Bennett, "A History of OE and ON Studies in
England from the Time of Francis Junius till the End
of the Eighteenth Century" (Ph.D. diss., Oxford University, 1939). Both are still indispensable.
16.   William Marshall and Francis Junius, eds., Quatuor
D.N. Jesu Christi Evangeliorum Versiones Perantiquae
Duae scil. et Anglo-Saxonica (Dordrecht: Published by
the Authors, 1665).
17.   The best account of Hickes is that by David Douglas
in English Scholars. There is also a Ph.D. dissertation by W. B. Gardner, "Life of George Hickes"
(Harvard University, 1946).
18.   See J. A. W. Bennett, "Hickes's Thesaurus: A Study
in Oxford Book Production," Essays and Studies, n.s. 1
(1948): 28-45.
19.   George Hickes, Grammatica Anglo-Saxonica ex
Hickesiano Thesauro Excerpta (Oxford: Oxford University Press, 1711).
20.   Hickes, Linguarum Veterum Septentrionalium
Thesaurus Grammatico-Criticus et Archaeologicus
(Oxford: Oxford University Press, 1703-05).
21.   N. R. Ker, Catalogue of Manuscripts Containing
Anglo-Saxon (Oxford: Clarendon Press, 1957). For
accounts of Wanley, see Douglas, English Scholars;
Kenneth Sisam, Studies in the History of Old English
Literature (Oxford: Clarendon Press, 1935); C. E.
Wright, "Humfrey Wanley: Saxonist and Library Keeper,"

Proceedings of the British Academy 46 (1960):99-129.
An edition of Wanley's collected correspondence is in
preparation by Professor Peter Heyworth of the University of Toronto.

22. Elizabeth Elstob, *Rudiments of Grammar for the
English-Saxon Tongue* (London: Bowyer, 1715). The
best account of the Elstobs is Sarah H. Collins,
"Elizabeth Elstob: A Biography" (Ph.D. diss.,
Indiana University, 1970).

23. For some account of the lexicographical work of
Edward Lye and his influence on Percy see T. A.
Birrell, "The Society of Antiquaries and the Taste for
Old English 1705-1840," *Neophilologus* 50 (1966):
107-117.

24. Cited by Arthur Johnstone, *Enchanted Ground*
(London: Athlone Press, 1964), p. 221.

25. James Ingram, *Inaugural Lecture on the Utility of
Anglo-Saxon Literature* (Oxford: Oxford University
Press, 1807). Ingram also published an edition of the
Anglo-Saxon Chronicle in 1823.

26. The *Illustrations* is readily available again in a
reprint by Haskell House (New York, 1964). The point
of Kemble's attack on Conybeare is partially blunted
by the statement of John Earle, perhaps the first
really distinguished scholar to hold the Rawlinson
chair. The *Illustrations*, says Earle, "had a great
effect in calling the attention of the educated, and
more than any other book in the present century has
served as the introduction to Saxon studies." *Anglo-
Saxon Literature* (1884; reprinted ed., New York: AMS,
1969), p. 45.

27. Rasmus Rask, *Angelsaksisk Sproglaere* (Stockholm:
Wiborg, 1817); Jakob Grimm, *Deutsche Grammatik*
(Göttingen: Dieterich, 1819; 2d ed. 1822).

28. For an account of the New Philology in England see
Hans Aarsleff, *The Study of Language in England 1780-
1860* (Princeton: Princeton University Press, 1967).

Nowell, Lambarde, and Leland:
The Significance of Laurence Nowell's
Transcript of Ælfric's *Grammar and Glossary*

Ronald E. Buckalew

The sixteenth century marks the beginning of Anglo-Saxon scholarship and the study of the Old English language. The dissolution of the monasteries in 1536-39 put many medieval manuscripts into circulation, only some of which ended up intact in libraries. Among those that were used as scrap, some ultimately returned to library shelves in the bindings of other books, but these were exceptional. Large numbers of manuscripts were ultimately lost.[1] While this great upheaval in monastic book collections led to the loss, destruction, and dismemberment of many old manuscripts, the fresh circulation and sudden availability of many such manuscripts also aroused new interest in their contents. This interest was part of a growing curiosity at the time about the political, religious, and nationalistic significance of the entire span of England's British, Anglo-Saxon, and Norman past-- its people and places, battles and beliefs, and lineage and laws.

The small number of surviving Old English manuscripts was especially subject to these contrary effects. On the one hand, the many changes in language and script over the centuries made them virtually unreadable and thus particularly likely to be scrapped. On the other hand, their documentary evidence of early English history, law, and religion both stimulated and helped to satisfy the emerging interest in England before the Conquest. This special value not only promoted concern about the fates of these Anglo-Saxon manuscripts, but also spurred some men to collect and copy manuscripts and even to attempt to read and study them.

Among those who took up this challenge were two pioneer groups. The first consisted of people like John Leland (ca. 1503-52), Sir John Prise (ca. 1502-52), John Bale (1495-1563), Robert Recorde (d. 1558), and Robert Talbot (ca. 1502-58).[2] The lives of most of these figures remain relatively obscure. But the two most important of this first group for the study of Old English were Talbot and Leland.

How and why Robert Talbot became competent in Old English are not completely clear, but his underlinings, notes, and cross-references in the manuscript of Ælfric's Grammar and Glossary now in the Cambridge University Library (Hh. 1. 10) show that he studied it carefully. By using the Latin examples as glosses to their Old English translations, thereby reversing the original purpose of the Grammar from teaching Latin to learning Old English, Talbot could make the Grammar his basic Old English textbook, as a number of others did after him. Besides evincing a special interest in names, particularly place names, Talbot's extensive annotations here and elsewhere indicate a good working knowledge of the language and his use of at least ten and probably eleven of the surviving Anglo-Saxon manuscripts.[3] Besides Ælfric's Grammar, these manuscripts contain the Old English versions of Bede, Orosius, the Hexateuch, the Gospels, and computistica, as well as Old English sermons and laws, the Anglo-Saxon Chronicle, and Archbishop Wulfstan's handbook. Especially important to Old English scholarship was Talbot's assistance in making accessible to others both the manuscripts and the Old English language which they contained. Among such beneficiaries of Talbot's help and his success in learning Old English were Robert Recorde, John Bale, and John Leland.

John Leland's interest in learning Old English may well have begun as he traveled around England noting its points of interest and antiquities in his Itinerary. The Anglo-Saxon items in his Commentarii de Scriptoribus, his notes on library contents, and the excerpts and transcriptions from manuscripts in his Collectanea suggest both his interest and progress in learning Old English.[4] In his book lists in the Collectanea, Leland noted eight Old English manuscripts that he had seen in the libraries of Abbotsbury, Christchurch (Hampshire), Glastonbury, Pershore (an unidentified copy of Ælfric's Grammar-- perhaps British Library MS Cotton Faustina A. x), Southwick, and Wells.[5] Two of these he also cited in his Commentarii de Scriptoribus, where he refers to the transcript of the Anglo-Saxon laws that he had seen at Christchurch: "vidi et multo cum labore legi" (p. 14).

Two other manuscripts Leland used contained the Old
English poem known as "Bede's Death Song" in the otherwise Latin text of the eighth-century Epistola Cuthberti
de Obitu Bedae. One of these manuscripts, Trinity College, Cambridge, R. 7. 28 (Ker, Catalogue, no. 88), was
the Chronicon Fani Sancti Neoti, which Leland annotated
and later cited in his Commentarii (p. 152); the other,
British Library MS Arundel 74, provided him with the
source of some of his transcriptions, including the complete text of the Epistola (fol. 99). While transcribing
the Epistola, Leland made a careful copy of the West
Saxon version of "Bede's Death Song" in it. From this
and other manuscripts Leland copied bits and pieces of
Old English which must have stimulated his curiosity
about Anglo-Saxon places and names, as well as the language in general. From a "Vita S. Oswini," for example,
Leland quoted such passages as "Eadwine, id est, beatus
vir" and "Oswine, i.e., fortitudo amici, vel latitudo
charitatis" (Hearne, ed., Collectanea, 4:43). From an
early fourteenth-century copy of Leges Anglorum Londoniis
s. xiii in Collectae (Quadripartitus), Corpus Christi
College, Cambridge, MS 70, Leland copied numerous passages: "Wita, id est, foris factura," "Geneat, id est,
villanus," "Mundbreche, id est, infractio pacis," sometimes retaining Old English letters as in "Cþydeleas, id
est, intestatus" (Collectanea, 3:212-13). With his
thorough knowledge of Latin and French and his general
interest in older tongues, seen for example in his extensive extracts from Jean Lagadeuc's Old Breton Catholicon
(Collectanea, 4:2-6), no doubt Leland was intrigued by
such early English words, passages, and texts.[6]

Leland's efforts to read Old English may be seen in
his use of the annotated manuscripts Talbot lent him and
in his excerpts from Ælfric's Glossary. Leland used
Talbot's computistica manuscript (St. John's, Oxford,
MS 17 [Ker, Catalogue, no. 360]), from which he transcribed the Old English days of the week (Collectanea
4:99), and his historical manuscript (British Library
MS Cotton Tiberius B. i [Ker, Catalogue, no. 191]) containing the Old English Orosius, Menologium, Maxims II,
and the C-text of the Anglo-Saxon Chronicle. From this
Leland took brief excerpts from the Orosius and more extensive ones from the Chronicle (Collectanea, 4:121-25);
he worked all the way through the manuscript, following
Talbot's underlinings and annotations as his guide.
Apparently independent of Talbot were Leland's numerous
extracts from a manuscript of Ælfric's Latin-Old English
topical Glossary. Talbot used the Grammar and Glossary
manuscript which Archbishop Parker gave to Cambridge University Library in 1574 (Hh. 1. 10 [Ker, Catalogue,

no. 17]), but I have shown elsewhere that the manuscript Leland studied and transcribed was none of those extant or otherwise known today.[7] Thus Leland's interest in Old English has preserved for us part of another text of Ælfric's Glossary, which attests to the original popularity of Ælfric's Grammar and Glossary, contributes to the modern study of the text of that work, and testifies to the great importance of the Grammar and Glossary in the founding of Anglo-Saxon studies in the sixteenth century and of that work to present research in Old English.

A few years after Leland and Talbot died, another group of Anglo-Saxonists became active. Whereas the earlier work dated primarily from the 1540s, this new wave began in earnest in the 1560s. Laurence Nowell and his pupil, collaborator, and successor, William Lambarde, initiated this new phase; they were soon joined by John Joscelyn and the rest of the Parker circle. This group, however, was linked with the older scholars both in goals and in materials. For example, Nowell and Lambarde were clearly inspired by Leland's topographical work. Moreover, by this time William Bowyer, keeper of the Tower of London, possessed books belonging formerly to Talbot, such as the MS Cotton Tiberius B. i, which had served Leland and Talbot well and was now to be used by Nowell and Lambarde.

We now know much about Lambarde, thanks to Retha M. Warnicke's recent biography, but for the same reason rather less about Nowell than was formerly thought. Warnicke found evidence that the antiquary Laurence Nowell (whom she calls Laurence Nowell of London) was in fact not the dean of Lichfield.[8] Much of what has been written about him is consequently inapplicable. What remains certain about Laurence Nowell of London is that his thoroughgoing pursuit of Anglo-Saxon led to a mastery of the language unparalleled in his time and to the transcription of a number of texts. This general scholarly activity seems to have begun as early as 1561, with the bulk of the Anglo-Saxon work coming in the years 1564 to 1567 when Nowell left England for France, not to be heard from again after 1569.[9]

As yet without textbooks for learning Old English, Nowell like his predecessors turned to that most convenient of tools, Ælfric's Grammar and Glossary. But going far beyond Talbot's annotations and underscoring in the Cambridge University Library manuscript and Leland's transcript of part of the Glossary, Nowell prepared an annotated transcript of almost the whole Grammar and Glossary, which he gave Lambarde in 1565.[10] Since the

gift was made early in the period of their intense collaboration, this transcript appears to have been intended
as a practical text for Lambarde as he sought to learn
the language, while the process of compiling it no doubt
enhanced Nowell's own knowledge of Old English.

The transcript is of particular interest not only as a
manifestation of this pioneering activity in Anglo-Saxon
studies, but also for the contributions it makes to current work in Old English. In this study, I shall consider the nature and possible exemplar of the transcript,
its use by Nowell and Lambarde, the exemplar's possible
fate, and the present-day implications of what we learn
from this inquiry. It is significant that the transcript preserves most of the text of a now-lost manuscript; this transcript was one of the major sources of
Nowell's Anglo-Saxon dictionary, to which Somner's
Dictionary of 1659 and subsequent printed ones are
heavily indebted.[11]

Nowell's transcript, now Westminster Abbey MS 30, is a
vellum-covered quarto volume of 112 paper pages, 105
written, in which Nowell copied a substantial portion of
the Grammar and Glossary. It includes the English preface, covers the full span of the Grammar, and contains
most of the Glossary, lacking at the end the equivalent
of what may have been on a folio lost from the end of the
exemplar. The absence of the Latin preface is consonant
with Nowell's general treatment of the Latin portion of
the text: he usually omits it when the Old English could
be understood without it. Even the Old English tends to
be abridged--the transcript retains much more of the text
at either end than in the middle. Thus quires at the beginning and end of the transcript each contain material
corresponding to about a dozen pages of Zupitza's edition, whereas one of the central quires of the same size
(eight pages) covers in abridged form the equivalent of
forty-five pages of Zupitza.[12] The verb paradigms, especially the Latin ones, and the linguistic descriptions in
the central section are substantially reduced. Even when
Nowell was copying the text more completely, he sometimes
omitted words and explanatory statements, to judge from
other manuscripts of the Grammar and Glossary. Nowell
wrote the whole transcript, however, in an imitation
Anglo-Saxon insular script, and this practice makes reading it and interpreting its forms straightforward. Present in Nowell's, and occasionally Lambarde's, small
Elizabethan script are underlining and indexes and occasional comments in the margins. In spite of the high
frequency of the nasal bar over vowels, omission of ic
with most of the first person verbs, and frequent etcs

to indicate deletion of portions of paradigms and lists, the transcript conveys the impression of a conscientiously copied text, especially by Elizabethan standards. The impression of care and completeness is much stronger at the ends than it is in the center section. Not only does Nowell omit material in the verb sections, but occasionally he apparently alters and even compresses the Old English, as other texts and the ungrammatical nature of some Old English sentences suggest.[13] These features contrast sharply, however, with most of the work, which accords closely with forms found elsewhere in most or all of the manuscripts. The numerous corrections especially attest to Nowell's care. For example, in a list of ordinals (Nowell MS, p. 85; Zupitza 282) he wrote seofonta, apparently as the form of seventh that he expected (under the influence of the preceding fifta and sixta); he then corrected it to seofoþa, the form which presumably stood in his exemplar. Several similar corrections occur in the same passage, each producing a form which we would expect from the evidence of the other manuscripts.[14]

How important, however, is Nowell's accuracy here? Is this transcript like the four other sixteenth- and seventeenth-century transcripts of the Grammar (two with the Glossary) which are each copies of different extant manuscripts? Or is it like the copies (one of them Leland's) of three different nonextant manuscripts of the Glossary? If it is based on a nonextant manuscript, it could be of considerable importance. Of the fourteen extant manuscripts of the Grammar, three are fragmentary and others lack large portions. Three are also abridged, two drastically. In the early medieval abridgments it is the Old English text that is usually sacrificed, just the opposite of Nowell's practice.[15] If Nowell has indeed preserved for us another copy, it would be a valuable adjunct to the texts of Ælfric's Grammar and Glossary, particularly since the spellings in his copy are typical of manuscripts of the early eleventh century written soon after the composition of the combined work. His transcript would then be not only a further manifestation of interest in and use of the Grammar and Glossary in the sixteenth century, but also a means to our establishing a sounder text of that work.

This question can be answered through a careful comparison of Nowell's text with each of the twenty others to establish those significant divergences which would rule it out as his exemplar. Nowell's text itself shows no signs of conflation or use of more than one exemplar in its production, such as the occurrence of alternative forms or spellings. Such variants occur in the Glossary

transcript in British Library MS Cotton Vitellius C. ix,
for instance, where the two fragments the sixteenth-
century scribe was copying overlap. Although extant
manuscripts sometimes have two glosses for one lemma,
they never give variant spellings. Yet the Vitellius
scribe writes, for example, "Fannus reoche, vel rihche,"
where other evidence reveals that the first variant de-
rives from one copy and the second from the other. The
absence of such variants in Nowell's transcript is strong
evidence that he had access to only one manuscript of the
Grammar when making his transcript.

For ease of reference in the discussion that follows,
the manuscripts and important transcripts of the Grammar
and Glossary are listed below with the sigla by which
they will be identified here and in the new critical
edition which I am preparing for the Early English Text
Society:

I. The fourteen extant manuscripts of the Grammar, and
    often the Glossary*, arranged in approximately
    chronological order, according to the dating by Ker
    in his Catalogue (see note 3). Unless otherwise
    indicated, sigla are those used by Zupitza (see
    note 12).
    O* Oxford, St. John's College 154, fols. 1-160
        (Ker, Catalogue, no. 362); s. xi in.
    S   Preserved only in the following two fragments:
        Sh London, British Library, Harley 5915,
            fols. 8-9, bifolium (Ker, Catalogue,
            no. 242); s. xi¹; not used by Zupitza.
        Si Bloomington, Indiana University, Lilly
            Library, Add. 1000, binding strip (Ker,
            Catalogue, no. 384); s. xi¹ formerly
            Sigmaringen, Hofbibliothek Hs. Nr 6.
            (Zupitza's S)
    D   Durham, Cathedral Library B. III. 32,
        fols. 56-127 (Ker, Catalogue, no. 107B);
        s. xi¹.
    P   Paris, Bibliothèque Nationale, Anglais 67 (Ker,
        Catalogue, no. 363); s. xi¹; bifolium.
    C* Cambridge, Corpus Christi College 449,
        fols. 42-96 (Ker, Catalogue, no. 71); s. xi¹.
    Y   London, British Library, Harley 3271,
        fols. 7-90 (Ker, Catalogue, no. 239); s. xi¹.
        (Zupitza's h)
    H* London, British Library, Harley 107,
        fols. 1-71v (Ker, Catalogue, no. 227); s. xi
        med.

A   Preserved only in the following two fragments:
 Ar London, British Library, Royal 12 G. xii,
      fols. 2-9 (Ker, Catalogue, no. 265); s. xi
      med. (Zupitza's r)
 Aa Oxford, All Souls College 38, fols. 1-12
      (Ker, Catalogue, no. 265); s. xi med.
      (Zupitza's A)
J* London, British Library, Cotton Julius A. ii,
      fols. 10-135 (Ker, Catalogue, no. 158); s. xi
      med.
F* London, British Library, Cotton Faustina A. x,
      fols. 3-101 (Ker, Catalogue, no. 154A); s. xi^2.
R   London, British Library, Royal 15 B. xxii,
      fols. 5-70v (Ker, Catalogue, no. 269); s. xi^2.
U* Cambridge, University Library Hh. 1. 10,
      fols. 1-93 (Ker, Catalogue, no. 17); s. xi^2.
 Uj John Joscelyn's extracts from now-lost
      fols. 94 and 95 of U in London, Lambeth
      Palace MS 692, fols. 9v-11v; not used by
      Zupitza.
T   Cambridge, Trinity College R. 9. 17, fols. 1-48
      (Ker, Catalogue, no. 89); s. xi/xii.
W* Worcester, Cathedral Library F. 174, fols. 1-63
      (Ker, Catalogue, no. 398); s. xiii^1.

II. Excerpts from the Grammar or Glossary (mainly the
    latter) in medieval manuscripts, and early modern
    transcripts of now-lost manuscripts, chiefly of
    parts of the Glossary. None of these was used by
    Zupitza.
B   Oxford, Bodleian, Barlow 35 (Ker, Catalogue,
      no. 298); s. xi in. (Alcuin on Genesis, etc.).
K   Oxford, Bodleian, Bodley 730 (Ker, Catalogue,
      no. 317); s. xii/xiii (Cassian, Collations).
N   London, Westminster Abbey 30 (Ker, Catalogue,
      p. li, n. 3); 1565. A somewhat abbreviated
      transcript by Laurence Nowell of a now-lost,
      probably eleventh-century manuscript of the
      Grammar and Glossary; 105 pp.
L   A Glossary manuscript known only from John
      Leland's extracts in vol. 3 of his Collectanea,
      Oxford, Bodleian Library, Top. gen. c. 3,
      pp. 222-27; about 1545.
Q   A large portion of the Glossary in a manuscript
      of Bede acquired by François Pithou at Oxford
      in 1572 (Ker, Catalogue, no. 405), now lost and
      known only from
 Qv Virtually complete transcript (but damaged
      in the fire of 1731) in London, British
      Library, Cotton Vitellius C. ix,
      fols. 208-13v; s. xvi ex.

Ql Extracts by Friedrich Lindenbrog in
    Hamburg, Staats- und Universitätsbibliothek,
    Cod. philol. 263, fols. 16-19; before
    1648

Qb Extracts by Jacques Bongars in Bern,
    Bürgerbibliothek 468, art 14, 4v; before
    1612

Qlh Transcript of Ql by or for J. G. Eccard in
    Hanover, Niedersächsische Landesbibliothek,
    IV. 495, fols. 574-80; before 1730

Qlv Transcript of Ql by Jan van Vliet in
    London, Lambeth Palace 783, fols. 248-53;
    1659

V   A large portion of the Glossary and a small
    portion of the Grammar in a manuscript of
    Augustine acquired by Marcus Welser of Augsburg
    in the late sixteenth or early seventeenth cen-
    tury (Ker, Catalogue, no. 406), now lost and
    known only from

    Vv A virtually complete transcript in London,
        British Library, Cotton Vitellius C. ix,
        fols. 210v-15; s. xvi ex.

    Vl Extracts by Friedrich Lindenbrog in
        Hamburg, Staats- und Universitätsbibliothek,
        Cod. philol. 263 (Berlin), fols. 32-36;
        before 1648

    Vlh Transcript of Vl by or for J. G. Eccard in
        Hanover, Niedersächsische Landesbibliothek,
        IV. 495, fols. 581-88r; before 1730

III. A version of most of the Glossary, known as the
     Vocabularium Cornicum, in which the Latin lemmas
     have been retained, but the Old English glosses
     have been replaced by their Old Cornish equivalents.
     X   London, British Library, Cotton Vespasian A.
     xiv, fols. 7-10r; s. xii; not used by Zupitza

It is first necessary to consider the extant manuscripts which may easily be eliminated as Nowell's exemplar because of their physical state or linguistic features. One manuscript, A, was already scattered in
various fifteenth-century bindings by Nowell's time; and
two others, B and K, consist only of brief excerpts in
tenth- and twelfth-century books. The Middle English
version from Worcester can be ruled out on the basis of
language, as can the Old Cornish one, X, which contains
only the Glossary. In a similar fashion we can eliminate
a nonextant or lost manuscript, V, for which two transcripts, both made within a century after Nowell's work,
have survived. Consisting at that time of only part of
the Glossary and excerpts from the Grammar, it is unique

in having several Scandinavian glosses in place of the
usual Old English ones, such as þingman for þen, glossing
minister (Zupitza 315/11) and rote for wyrtruma, glossing
radix (Zupitza 312/7). Nowell's copy has none of these
Scandinavian forms, not even for very uncommon Old
English words such as wandewurpe 'mole' for which he
could hardly have provided all the native forms himself.

Large portions missing from two manuscripts, H and C,
in Nowell's time suffice to eliminate them, although they
can also be ruled out on the basis of significant variants. The first, H, lacked the text-equivalent of two
quires when it was copied, quires which presumably were
missing from its exemplar; they do not correspond to the
ends of quires or leaves in H. Given the damage to the
first leaf of the second, C, it had lost its first third
well before it was filled out from R and repaired under
the auspices of Archbishop Parker, Nowell's contemporary.
Two of the three abridged texts have already been ruled
out on the grounds of language (W) and missing portions
(H). The third, T, especially omits so much of the Old
English material which Nowell favors that it is easily
weeded out also. We have thus eliminated as Nowell's
exemplar nine of the twenty other known manuscripts.
These nine in the order of our discussion above are A, B,
K, W, X, V, H, C, and T.

Other now fragmentary manuscripts might in Nowell's
time have been more complete; they and other extant manuscripts of the eleven not already eliminated--D, F, J, L,
O, P, Q, R, S, Y, and U--consequently have to be tested
on different grounds. There are two chief remaining
tests of whether any of the other manuscripts might have
served as the exemplar for Nowell's transcript. One is a
manuscript's lack of words or sentences that are none-
theless in Nowell's copy; the other is the occurrence of
a variant in Nowell's copy which clashes with the form in
the manuscript in question in such a way that anyone out-
side the Old English period, and perhaps even many of
those in it, would not be reasonably able to supply it on
his own. Particularly telling are types of evidence, in
conjunction with that already reviewed, such as language
or incomplete text, distributed over both the Grammar and
Glossary in those manuscripts which have both parts.

Examples of material omitted from a text, yet in N,
are the specific heading of the Glossary as a whole
(Nomina multarum rerum anglice) and of its first large
section (Nomina membrorum--used both for parts of the
body and, presumably under Pauline influence, for occupa-
tions). The first is omitted not only from X and W,

already ruled out, but also J and F. The second heading
is likewise missing from J and F as well as U and two
already eliminated, C and X. Another important omission
from the Glossary is shared by U and C. This is the
gloss to poeta, namely sceop oððe leoðwyrhta, with its
following lemma mimus vel scurra (Zupitza 302/8-9; N,
p. 94).[16] What may be either an omission or a marginal
addition incorporated in the main text is the Glossary
entry "mastruga crusene oððe deorfellen roc" (Zupitza
315/5; N, p. 101). Although Zupitza mentioned it only in
his textual notes as an item restricted to two manuscripts, O and J, and occurring at two different places
even in them, it occurs in six--O, J, Q, V, X, and N--
of the nine manuscripts which have the Glossary or this
portion of the Glossary among the larger number of texts
now known. In four of the six this entry also occurs at
the same place in the sequence of entries with the fifth,
N, just one item away.[17] The absence of this entry from
C, F, and W provides further evidence against them as N's
exemplar.

Similar omissions from all these texts can be found in
the Grammar portion. In the transcription of the passage,
"pariter samod. simul manducant samod hi etað. pariter
ambulant æt gædere hi gað" (Zupitza 229/5-6), for example,
the eye of a scribe at one point skipped from the first
pariter to the second, causing the omission of the entry
in between. Unlike a missing portion of a paradigm, this
loss could hardly be recovered, much less discovered by
a subsequent scribe. This omission is shared by manuscripts C, F, and U but not by N (p. 71). Of the same
kind are discursive comments on the months October,
November, and December, missing from J, T, and W but
present in N (pp. 24-25). Of the manuscripts not previously eliminated, omissions from both the Grammar and
the Glossary show that F, J, and U could not have been
Nowell's exemplar.

Some manuscripts furnish evidence of this kind only
from the Grammar, although they may have other kinds as
well. While the most significant omission in the Glossary of O (Zupitza 321/4) is in the portion missing from
N--the very few other omissions from the Glossary of O
are shared by N--the Grammar of O omits significant items
present in N, such as "abscondo ic behyde" (Zupitza
182/1; N, p. 61) at the end of a list, an omission shared
with H. D, Y, and R have in common the absence of the
Glossary as a whole, one of the reasons in itself for
doubting them as N's possible source, since Nowell would
have had to obtain his Glossary elsewhere. Yet no copy
of the Glossary known which has its beginning intact

exists apart from the Grammar (except X, a special case), and we have seen that there is indeed a positive lack of evidence that Nowell had access to more than one copy of the Grammar. D, Y, and R, however, also exhibit significant omissions in the Grammar which are not shared by N. D, for example, lacks with C and U a sequence of two entries: "comprimo ic samod ofðrycce, compressi, compressum; exprimo ic geswutelige oððe swutelice secge" (Zupitza 170/4-5). Yet these are present in N (p. 58) and are a particular combination of Latin and Old English which Nowell could not have duplicated exactly on his own. Another instance is the entry "patior ic þrowige" (Zupitza 254/10; N, p. 77) which is part of a larger omission unique to D. Nowell would have had no basis for providing this where he did had it not been present in his exemplar, which therefore cannot have been D.

Both Y and R are extraordinary for the small number of omissions in their texts.[18] Y has fewer than fifty and R only about twenty, compared with those of other manuscripts of the Grammar (excluding the Glossary), such as D (about two hundred), O (about three hundred), J (over five hundred), and H (over six hundred); the nearest to Y and R is F with well over a hundred. When this circumstance is compared with Nowell's tendency to abridge his text in certain sections, our discovery of significant material omitted from them but present in N is much less likely. Evidence of this kind is available from both, however, which cumulatively and in conjunction with our evidence of other kinds, such as variant forms, rules out these two manuscripts as candidates for Nowell's exemplar. For example, Y lacks the vocative singular in the paradigm of citharista, the first noun paradigm in the Grammar. It is very unlikely that Nowell would have known at this point to place the vocative case form between the accusative and ablative cases or that the form the Old English translation should take was "eala þu hearpere" (Zupitza 22/2; N, p. 14). Moreover, its presence in the transcript shows no signs of hesitation or subsequent insertion. Even more conclusive is an omission from Y among the denominatives (Zupitza 17/19; N, p. 12). Where Ælfric provides mæden and mædenlic as glosses to both puella/puellaris and virgo/virginalis, the scribe of Y skipped the Latin and Old English of the second set. Yet N has both puella and virgo with the Old English.

The evidence of omissions from R consists entirely of single words, but there are at least five which individually are significant and cumulatively conclusive. These are the hit of "hit rinþ" (Zupitza 128/16; N, p. 49); the me of "poenitet me" (Zupitza 207/11; N, p. 65)—the first

of these omissions is shared with J and the second with
O; pytt as an alternative gloss to scrobs (Zupitza 66/10;
N, p. 32); the þam in the phrase "nytendum þam weard-
mannum" (Zupitza 272/1; N, p. 82); and the and of "vah
getacnaðgebysmrunge, and racha . . ." (Zupitza 279/17;
N, p. 84)--these last three are unique to R.

In addition to the three manuscripts just ruled out,
D, Y, and R, which contain only the Grammar, are three
fragmentary manuscripts of the Grammar: A, P, and S.
These may once have included both the Grammar and the
Glossary, but they are now too fragmentary for us to
tell. Of these three, A, now twenty flyleaves in two
fifteenth-century manuscripts, is by far the largest.
The amount of text on the extant leaves suggests that
about one quarter of the original Grammar manuscript
survives. A was ruled out earlier as Nowell's exemplar
on the basis of its having already been used for binding
purposes about a century before Nowell's time. Should
the dating of the bindings be wrong, however, significant
omissions also rule it out. Two passages lacking uniquely from A (Zupitza 135/18-136/2, 143/19) are present in
N (pp. 51, 53), although the first was subject in part to
Nowell's abridgment. The other two manuscript fragments
are so brief, a total of two bifolia and a binding strip,
that only one omission of any kind occurs in the extant
portions, and that is in P. The ic of the sentence "Eala
gif ic æte" is lacking from P yet present in N (p. 64;
Zupitza 200/16).

Of two manuscripts, V and Q, not even one original
fragment apparently survives. Yet we have more extensive
evidence of their contents than we have of fragments like
P and S. V and Q represent lost manuscripts of large
portions of the Glossary. These lost originals, especially Q's, may have once been a portion of the same
manuscript as one of our fragments. But lacking a sample
of the scribal hand and format, we are unable to determine this. We are fortunate, however, in having more
than one copy of each--and rather full copies at that.
An anonymous Elizabethan scribe apparently copied both
completely (Qv and Vv), except for the section where they
overlap (Zupitza 308/5-315/15), for which he sometimes
drew on either; where they differed, he usually copied
both. The two manuscripts were also copied on the Continent by Friedrich Lindenbrog (1573-1648), who omitted
some items found in the earlier copy but still transcribed most of both texts, Q1 and V1. Wherever entries
or groups of entries are lacking from the text of the
Elizabethan scribe, they are also missing from Lindenbrog's copies, as well as from a third set of extracts

from Q (Qb) made by Jacques Bongars (1546-1612). This
consistency of agreement, even in sequences of entries
where the copies otherwise are complete, strongly suggests that these gaps represent omissions in the originals. We have already ruled out MS V on the basis of
language, because its Scandinavian glosses are not found
in N. It also has ten omissions, some extensive (e.g.,
Zupitza 317/17-20, twenty-four words), in the portion of
the Glossary it shares with N. N has none of these. MS
Q has fewer omissions, but besides numerous variants not
shared by N, it has three omissions, one of eight words
(Zupitza 306/10-11--"aestivus dies . . . hærfestlic dæg"),
where N always has the expected text. The quality and
strength of the evidence definitely eliminate V and Q.

To summarize: the evidence so far has ruled out conclusively as Nowell's exemplar at least seventeen of the
twenty manuscripts for which we have texts or transcripts,
leaving only P, S, and L to be tested by our second important criterion.

The second criterion for manuscripts not eliminated by
linguistic or physical considerations is what may be
called the extraordinary variant. Such a variant is
demonstrated, for example, where the context requires the
ordinal seofoðe ("seventh") in the phrase "seo seofoðe
præteritum" (Zupitza 180/1); where most texts have it,
Nowell's (p. 61) and two others, C and H, have feorþe
("fourth").[19] Those with the expected reading (seofoðe)
are thus eliminated: D, Y, F, R, and U. This and many
similar examples which could be cited in both the Grammar
and the Glossary buttress conclusions reached on other
grounds. Where other kinds of evidence are lacking or
sparse, as for MSS P, S, or L, the testimony of variants
may be crucial.

Of the three manuscripts not yet rejected as Nowell's
exemplar are two, P and S, which are now just small fragments of manuscripts of the Grammar used in early bindings; whether they were in that condition by Nowell's
time we do not know. As already noted, the brevity of
omissions not matched by V restricts the evidence, but
there are still a number of differences in each case,
such as a reading swa swa (Zupitza 199/4; N, p. 64) which
Nowell shares with most other manuscripts against the
single swa shared by the fragment P and by four manuscripts: C, D, U, and T.

Although the portion of the Grammar in S corresponds
to a section in N which is heavily abbreviated, it still
offers a few variants which cumulatively are regarded as

persuasive if not absolutely conclusive. Nowell not only
uses an abbreviation g̅lufod where S does not (e.g.,
Zupitza 142/2; N, p. 53), but he also uses the abbreviation in several places in this section, whereas the
scribe of S never does in the portions of his manuscript
that survive. The fact that this abbreviation is sporadic and exceptional in N and is characteristic of other
eleventh-century manuscripts of the Grammar, indicates
that Nowell was following his exemplar when he used it.
If so, that exemplar could not be S. Similar but less
distinctive is N's þon for S's þonne at Zupitza 142/7.
Here Nowell presumably omitted the abbreviatory bar over
þon, since this abbreviation occurs elsewhere in S--even
later in the same paradigm (Zupitza 142/8; Sh, fol. 8r,
1.14)-- as well as in other manuscripts. A more perva-
sive difference is the predominant use of the spelling
gyf in Nowell's transcript where S consistently has gif.
Analyses of Nowell's transcription practice with extant
manuscripts have shown that whereas Nowell often replaces
y with i, he almost never changes i to y.[20] The contrast
in the spelling of gif would thus argue against S as
Nowell's exemplar. Finally, and perhaps most significant,
neither S nor P uses the error of unbegungen for unbegun-
nen (Zupitza 201/9; N, p. 64) shared by Nowell's transcript and two other extant manuscripts, Y and F.

The remaining text to be compared is a special case.
This is John Leland's Glossary transcript, L, which, I
have previously established, is based on a nonextant
manuscript (see note 7). But that was before Nowell's
copy came to my attention. The question here is not
whether Leland's transcript served as Nowell's exemplar,
when in fact Nowell's is far more extensive than Leland's,
but rather whether both Leland and Nowell used the same
nonextant manuscript in making their transcriptions. All
extant manuscripts have already been eliminated as potential exemplars, including ones used by associates of
Leland and Nowell. Such a manuscript is U, which Leland's
friend Talbot annotated a couple of decades before it
came into the hands of Matthew Parker, a close friend of
William Cecil, Lord Burghley, who shared Parker's and
Nowell's interest in manuscripts and in whose house in
London Nowell lived and worked. It has also been established that neither Leland nor Nowell used any other
manuscript now known to survive only in modern transcript.
Therefore they must have used either two other lost manuscripts or the same one. If they used the same Grammar
and Glossary from which Nowell made an extensive transcript, then Leland must have extracted fewer than two
hundred Glossary entries and nothing from the Grammar.

If they used two different manuscripts, then it is possible that Leland's contained only the <u>Glossary</u> or was at least fragmentary.

There are a number of ramifications to this question of the independence of L and N. If they stem from two different exemplars, this fact would increase the evidence that in the late Anglo-Saxon period these works of Ælfric's were very popular and often copied. The same fact would also challenge the general validity of Flower's hypothesis that a chain of manuscript transmission led from Leland through Nowell and Lambarde to Cotton.[21] The only <u>Grammar</u> manuscript in the Cotton collection until the eighteenth century (when F was acquired) was J, and I have already demonstrated that this manuscript could not have been the exemplar of either L or N. If these two transcripts both derive from a common exemplar, however, they would attest to the link between Leland and Nowell (though not with Cotton); they would provide a check on each other textually; and they would reinforce the value of N as a textual witness--one that is more extensive, especially for the Old English portions, than several of our extant manuscripts, such as S, P, A, and T.

The nature of the evidence, however, makes this issue virtually impossible to resolve with confidence. Complicating the relationship between L and N is the fact that Leland's copy, unlike Nowell's, is a series of extracts rather than a relatively full transcript.[22] Even if Leland had made a more complete transcript, doubt would remain whether any single omission common to both Leland's and Nowell's versions was a reflection of their exemplars or was merely the result of coincidental omission by them. A number of common omissions would be very persuasive. But Leland only recorded, on the average, one of every three or four <u>Glossary</u> entries in his original. Thus, shared omissions can mean nothing, and we must rely totally on variant forms or spellings to indicate whether their exemplars were the same or not. In this situation the reliability of the transcripts becomes a crucial question. For early modern transcripts of the two other lost or nonextant manuscripts of the <u>Glossary</u>, Q and V, there are at least two independent copies which serve to confirm each other. For Leland's transcript there is only the occasional self-confirmation of his corrections. For Nowell's there are no known independent copies, even if we have as a possible check on his work both his own corrections made while he was copying and his use of the <u>Grammar and Glossary</u> elsewhere. For both Leland and Nowell evidence also exists of other transcripts they made from extant manuscripts of other works. Thus, before the issue of whether Leland and Nowell copied from the same Old English manuscript of the Grammar and Glossary or from a different nonextant codex can be resolved, we must address ourselves to two important questions: (1) Does Nowell's Grammar and Glossary material elsewhere represent transcription from another manuscript, or use of the transcript under review? and (2) How reliable are Leland's and Nowell's transcriptions?

To answer the first question one must establish where, in addition to making his transcript, Nowell can be shown to have used Ælfric's Grammar and Glossary. At least three of his works contain evidence of such use: his dictionary of Old English known as the Vocabularium Saxonicum; the glossary in the margins of a copy of the first edition (1552) of Richard Huloet's Abcedarium Anglico Latinum (which James Rosier has dubbed "Nowell upon Huloet"); and some portions of the Anglo-Saxon laws which Nowell concocted in pseudo-Old English for the Archaionomia (1568) to fill gaps in his texts where extant Latin versions attested to the loss or absence of the corresponding Old English.[23]

Nowell's dictionary is important not only as the first modern compilation of the Old English vocabulary, but also as the foundation of subsequent Old English dictionaries, including William Sommer's of 1659, the first to be printed. The Vocabularium Saxonicum was compiled about 1565, the year Nowell gave his Grammar transcript to Lambarde. It was first printed, however, only about thirty years ago in Albert H. Marckwardt's edition. In his introduction Marckwardt noted, "By tracing the sources of the words that are defined and the citations that are employed in the dictionary, we are able to determine with a considerable degree of accuracy the precise documents upon which the Vocabularium was based" (Vocabularium, p. 7). In countering Eleanor Adams's position that Nowell's dictionary was compiled primarily from the Anglo-Saxon laws and Ælfric's Glossary,[24] Marckwardt concluded that "the Vocabularium Saxonicum is based upon a remarkably wide range of prose materials, much wider in fact than anyone has hitherto suspected or suggested" (Vocabularium, p. 7). Yet in an attempt no doubt to correct what he rightly felt was Adams's distorted view of the dictionary, Marckwardt went too far in playing down the contribution that Ælfric's Grammar and Glossary made to Nowell's dictionary.

That Marckwardt underestimated the extent of this contribution stems primarily from his ignorance of Nowell's
transcript and secondarily from his faulty knowledge of
the contents and texts of the Grammar and Glossary. For
the entry aBroðene (p. 41), for example, Nowell gives as
a definition "Degener, nugas." In a footnote to nugas,
Marckwardt says, "Read nugar." But nugas occurs with
abroðen(e) at Zupitza 51/5, just as degener does at
32/10; and in both places in N (pp. 28, 20) abroðen(e) is
underlined. This particular definition of the word,
moreover, is peculiar to Ælfric's Grammar. Likewise,
where Lambarde added "Ælfric, Grammat." after Nowell's
entry "Hold A carion, a deadbodie," Marckwardt comments
in a note, "I have not been able to locate this word in
Ælfric's Grammar." (p. 100). But besides its usual occurrence as the gloss to cadaver in the Glossary (Zupitza
319/17; N, p. 105, the last), it also occurs uniquely in
N in the Grammar (p. 25--where the entry "cadaver hold
oððe lic" replaces the usual "hoc iter ðis siðfæt"
Zupitza 44/2), and there it is underlined. In addition
to noting the many words in the dictionary which are
known only from the Grammar and Glossary, such as forðwif
(glossing matrona, Zupitza 301/1; N, p. 93), hleapestre
(glossing saltatrix, Zupitza 302/10; N, p. 94), sandhricg
(glossing syrtis, Zupitza 75/8; N, p. 34), and sceaðig
(or scæððig, glossing sons, Zupitza 63/15; N, p. 32) and
the several references to the Grammar by name, Marckwardt
claimed that nineteen citations in the dictionary were
drawn from it. But I have noted well over a hundred such
citations, demonstrating with other evidence that Ælfric's
Grammar and Glossary was indeed one of the major sources
Nowell used in compiling his Vocabularium.

Had Marckwardt been fortunate enough to have known of
Nowell's transcript of this work, he would not have decided, "Because of the number of manuscripts of this work
[Ælfric's Grammar] and the brevity of some of the citations, it is impossible to arrive at any satisfactory
conclusion about the particular manuscript or manuscripts
Nowell may have used."[25] He would also not have claimed
later (Vocabularium, p. 34) that certain entries prove
Nowell used the glossary in MS Cotton Julius A. ii, which
Marckwardt treats as a separate work rather than as a
manuscript of Ælfric's Glossary. Marckwardt, like many
others both before and since, was obviously misled both
here and in his confusion of the Antwerp-London Glossary
(Ker, Catalogue, no. 2) with Ælfric's by their treatment
in Wright and Wülcker's Anglo-Saxon and Old English
Vocabularies.[26] The entry words peculiar to Julius A. ii
are in fact in other manuscripts of the Glossary, all of
them occurring in Nowell's transcript as well.

Not only can we now demonstrate that Nowell made extensive use of the Grammar and Glossary in compiling his dictionary, but also that Nowell's transcript (or text N) was the manuscript he used. Throughout the transcript Old English words are underlined, often several to a page, and they regularly turn up in the dictionary, sometimes with the corresponding Latin lemma in the definition, sometimes with part of the context used as a citation. On page 25 of N, for example, seven words are underlined and all seven appear in the dictionary. Five are used as headwords and given English definitions which correspond to the meanings of the Latin lemmata in the Grammar. For N's "sequester. syma" (Zupita 43/16), the sixth, the dictionary simply has "Syma. Sequester," a kind of direct borrowing from the Grammar and Glossary found frequently in the Vocabularium, sometimes with an English definition as well. The seventh item underlined on page 25 of N, "Degener. welboren 7 [sic] yfelegeþogen" (Zupitza 45/4-5), is used in a citation in the entry "geþogen on mægen. Mactus virtute; welboren. Yfel geðogen. Degener." (Vocabularium, p. 193), where the portion preceding welboren is also from Ælfric's Grammar (Zupitza 251/5; N, p. 76). The forms of these words as well as the underlining links them with N: the spelling syma is found in N and five other manuscripts which have the word (D, Y, H, F, and R), but D, H, and F have deneger for degener and R has geboren for welboren. N's forms regularly accord with those in the dictionary.[27]

Because Nowell's exemplar does not survive, it is uncertain how he used it. It seems unlikely, however, that he underlined the same items there, too, and used it as well as the transcript in compiling the dictionary. That N was the text Nowell used for his dictionary, however, is clear from the occurrence of forms in the dictionary that are known only from N. In every manuscript but N, pyrata is glossed flotmann. In N it is mistakenly lotman, and this lotman shows up as an entry in the dictionary glossed "pyrate." To the entry "Nugelā & Nulā" Marckwardt added the following note: "All the manuscripts of Ælfric's Grammar, the Old English source for these interjections, write the component parts as separate words, nu ge la." But in N (p. 70) both of these occur as compound words with accents over the a's, as in the dictionary. Similar is the entry Wlite with its citation, "Priscianus is ealra lædensþrece wlit[e] 7 lareowe." N alone has "7 lareowe" (p. 41), whereas all other manuscripts read "gehaten" here (Zupitza 94/4). Some entries and some references to Ælfric's Grammar in Nowell's entries are in Lambarde's hand. That Lambarde, too, used N is shown, for example, by his peculiar entry "Græt.

Waspe." Where the lemma scinifes is glossed "gnæt" in N
(p. 97) as in all other manuscripts (Zupitza 308/2), the
n of the gloss closely resembles an r, thereby accounting
for Lambarde's ghost-word græt.

That Nowell used N as a major source in compiling his
Vocabularium Saxonicum is indisputable. Can one, how-
ever, assume that he used no other manuscripts of the
Grammar and Glossary? Four manuscripts of the Grammar,
C, U, R, and T, eventually passed through Archbishop
Parker's hands, but none may yet have been in Parker's
possession, just as the chronicle which came to bear his
name was not. A book of Anglo-Saxon laws, Corpus Christi
College, Cambridge, MS 70, was used by both Leland and
Nowell, and was probably in Parker's possession. But in
spite of this connection, no evidence exists that any of
the Grammar and Glossary manuscripts other than N was
used for the dictionary. In fact, words like leoðwyrhta,
lacking from C and U, for example, nevertheless occur in
the dictionary; and all words and citations in the dictionary from Ælfric's Grammar and Glossary also occur in
N. Although an omission in a passage in N nevertheless
shows up in the Vocabularium, it is simply one of three
related Latin phrases. Since Nowell had the other two
Latin phrases in N and the Old English translation for
all three, he could easily have reconstructed the missing
Latin phrase.[28]

Clearly then Nowell made extensive use of Ælfric's
Grammar and Glossary in compiling the Vocabularium Saxonicum, and the manuscript he used was N. On the basis of
this discovery, a clearer understanding of Nowell's technique in compiling the dictionary is possible. Besides
the entries based on words unique to Ælfric's textbook,
many other words which are common to a variety of Old
English works can be understood to have entered this
first Old English dictionary from Nowell's transcript of
the Grammar and Glossary when they are underlined there.
Text N can thus be recognized as a foundational manuscript in the inauguration of Anglo-Saxon studies. In
the absence therefore of any significant Grammar and
Glossary material in the dictionary not also in Nowell's
transcript, no basis exists for believing that Nowell
used any other text of the Grammar in compiling it. The
last words of the Grammar itself, for example, as they
occur in N are "fif peningas gemaciað ænne scylling and
þrittig penegas ænne mancus" (p. 90, Zupitza 296/15-16).
The form peningas is patently unhistorical, however; all
extant manuscripts have penega(s) not only here but all
five times this word occurs with a third syllable.[29] The
penegas after þrittig elsewhere also does not have a

final s. We may attribute these features to Nowell, who
cites this passage twice in his Vocabularium. When he
gives the whole passage under mancus, he uses peningas
both times. Under scylling Nowell cites only the first
clause; and this time he uses penegas, which had not
occurred with scylling either of the other two times he
gave the passage. But we cannot assume that this correct
form derived from Nowell's exemplar; it occurs in N immediately below the incorrect one and in the last line of
the page, where it is quite conspicuous. Both of these
citations in the dictionary, therefore, are derived most
likely from N rather than N's exemplar. Had the citations in the dictionary been correct in their forms of
penegas where the spellings in N had been incorrect, we
could assume that Nowell went to his exemplar for the
correct dictionary forms rather than resorting to the
transcript. In that case, the citations would represent
independent evidence of the exemplar. In fact, however,
everywhere else the plural of pening is used, the transcript has the correct form while the dictionary has the
unhistorical form.[30] This suggests that Nowell was less
concerned about the accuracy of forms when he compiled
his dictionary than he was in his transcription. One
reason for this was that he took his citations from the
transcript rather than directly from a manuscript. On
the basis of evidence of this kind, the Vocabularium did
not contain any material transcribed directly from N's
exemplar and therefore is not an independent witness to
the text that would help us evaluate or validate the
forms in N. Nowell's dictionary, potentially the chief
complement to N, turns out to be fully derivative; thus
it is of no apparent use in our attempt to determine the
relationship between N and L.

There is evidence that Nowell also used N in his
other Old English projects. These include the Nowell-
upon-Huloet glossary and his work on the Archaionomia.
The Huloet glossary like the dictionary contains entries
which are otherwise unique to Ælfric's Grammar and Glossary, such as gegymmod (Zupitza 257/6; N, p. 77). It
also contains forms peculiar to N, such as sculeged
"squint eyed" (Zupitza 36/12; N, p. 22); the spelling of
the Huloet glossary matches that of N exactly and differs
only slightly from that in the dictionary (sculeaged),
whereas the other manuscripts have sceolegede or
scylegede. Moreover, the absence of the final -e is more
likely Nowell's modification in N than a variant in his
exemplar. In other instances the form in the Huloet
glossary is that of N, such as fotwylm "sole" (Zupitza
299/4; N, p. 91), but the form in the dictionary differs
from it slightly (fotwylma). It may be assumed, at

least occasionally, that Nowell was more conscientious about the Huloet entries than those of the Vocabularium. Nevertheless, N was clearly his source here, too, for entries taken from the Grammar and Glossary. Again there seems to be no evidence that any other manuscript was used nor that the exemplar of N was used rather than the transcript. Such evidence might consist of words or phrases present in the Grammar and Glossary generally but lacking from Nowell's transcript. Further study of this matter, however, is needed.

The same can be said of the relationship between N and Nowell's work on certain parts of the Archaionomia. Sisam has made a strong case for believing that Nowell himself fabricated portions of the Old English text of the Anglo-Saxon laws. He also cogently suggested that Nowell used Ælfric's Grammar on occasion to supply him with phrases. The examples Sisam cites (Studies, p. 254, note) are found accordingly in N (pp. 4, 45), although they could be from any of several manuscripts of the Grammar. Further analysis might turn up more instances, but that information is unavailable and would be difficult to provide. On the basis of the evidence, Nowell's transcript seems to be the primary and perhaps sole witness to the medieval manuscript upon which it is based.

Without direct means of confirming the accuracy of the forms in N, one must consider both Nowell's practice in other transcripts and the plausibility of the forms in N. Those who have studied Nowell's practice in his transcriptions from extant manuscripts differ in their evaluations of his accuracy. The differences stem partly from varying emphasis on Nowell's departures from his exemplar or on his agreements with it. Sisam concluded (Studies, p. 51, note 1) that Nowell's transcription "shows a mixture of mechanically accurate and careless copying, which makes close consideration of its abnormal forms and spellings unprofitable." Grant's detailed study in Anglo-Saxon England, volume 3, of Nowell's transcript of Cotton Otho B. xi purported to show that Nowell is "far from reliable in detail" (Laurence Nowell's Transcript, p. 124). Yet the evidence Grant gives, as Torkar and Lutz recently pointed out in Anglia (1976 and 1977--see note 14 above), demonstrates that Nowell is accurate far more often than not. Except for interchange of þ and ð and e and æ, his deviations, when they can be checked against extant manuscripts, are usually at less than one percent. Each variation must be separately considered and weighed to determine the accuracy of Nowell's transcriptions.

The general agreement of Nowell's forms with those
found in our best manuscripts lends support to those who
defend his accuracy. The omission or addition of an
occasional final -e, such as Nowell's wold for wolde in
the opening words of the English preface, is the chief
kind of difference to be attributed to him. The completeness of his text varies, however, with the portion
of the Grammar and Glossary being copied. It is very
full in the early part of the Grammar and also toward the
end of the Glossary. Where Nowell was abbreviating and
condensing, he was also less faithful to his text. His
freedom appears in occasional sentences which as a whole
have no counterpart in any other text of the Grammar, the
same signs of Nowell's invention that Sisam challenged in
the Archaionomia, such as a lack of concord between an
article or a demonstrative and its noun (this lack of
concord usually consisting of masculine determiners with
feminine nouns) and modern instead of Old English idiom
(see note 13). Although these sentences can be ascribed
to Nowell, other variations are less certain. Whereas
praeteritum is regularly used with feminine endings on
the article and on the modifying ordinal number in our
other texts, it is consistently used with masculine endings in Nowell's. That such a divergence is not found
with conjugatio indicates that it is not simply the result
of Nowell's predilection for the masculine forms. Given
the mass of Old English material in N (over a hundred
pages) and the rarity of the divergences from the standard
forms in the majority of the manuscripts, any particular
form is probably genuine and accurate, at least if it is
paralleled elsewhere in Old English.

From this survey of Nowell's further use of items from
the Grammar and Glossary and of the evidence of his accuracy, the two questions posed earlier may now be answered.
First, Nowell's use of Grammar and Glossary material
elsewhere does not seem to represent transcription from
a manuscript, either N's exemplar or another, but rather
to depend upon the transcript of N itself. Second,
Nowell's transcript is on the whole quite reliable.

Leland's forms in his transcript, L, seem slightly
less dependable than Nowell's, but this is truer of his
early entries, as he was becoming accustomed to the language and text, than of his later ones. Leland's putative divergences are of several types and easily accounted
for. Unhistorical final es are common at first, as are
certain modernizations such as th for þ or ð and ch for c
(e.g., foster child as gloss to alumnus). Apparent
interchange of e and æ is also not surprising. His own
corrections reveal a tendency to omit a letter here and

there, some of which omissions he seems not to have
caught, such as the f from his hledige "lady" and the h
from his writa "wright."

In light of this discussion of Nowell's and Leland's
transcripts of a manuscript or manuscripts of the Glossary no longer extant, we may now review the evidence of
their differences to see if we can reasonably decide
whether they used different exemplars or both transcribed
from the same one. Some of the fifty-nine spelling differences between the two transcripts may be instances of
the kinds of variation we have noted, such as the addition or omission of final e. Others, however, seem more
significant. As the gloss to comes (Zupitza 300/15),
Nowell has "ealdormann oþþe gefera oþþe gerefa," where
Leland has "ealdorman oðóe gereua." Neither of these is
matched exactly by any extant manuscript. All others
have "ealdormann oðóe gerefa," except O, which for gerefa
has the error gefera. N's exemplar must have been related
to a manuscript similar to O, but one which contained
both forms. Leland, on the other hand, never uses u for
f except in his gereua; but this substitution is paralleled occasionally in Anglo-Saxon manuscripts, including
those of the Grammar and Glossary. An especially pertinent example is found in F where this same word is likewise spelled gereua, but where the word glosses prae-
positus six items after comes. The form in L thus
appears genuine. Another contrast is N's þegn versus L's
þegen. N's form is matched by J's, while L's is corrected from þegan and thereby surely accurate, especially
since the resulting þegen is the usual spelling here.
Among other potentially significant differences between
N and L are the following:

N incantator: galdere	--	L (and all others) incantator: galere (Zupitza 303/9)
N (and others) pictor: metere; pictura: meting	--	L pictor: mytere; pictura: metyng (Zupitza 304/9)
N fannus: hreohche	--	L fannus: hreoche (Zupitza 308/6)

When all of these and similar differences are considered,
they suggest strongly, if not conclusively, that Nowell
and Leland used two different exemplars for transcripts
of Ælfric's Glossary.

It appears that Nowell did not transcribe the same Old English manuscript of Ælfric's Glossary that Leland did, and the supposed links between them are not as strong as some have thought. The number of manuscripts of the Grammar and Glossary produced from the eleventh to the thirteenth century, especially in the eleventh, still in existence in the sixteenth century, is probably greater than we had realized. Both N and L are independently available for textual study, and if used with appropriate caution may help us determine the text of the Glossary. Each appears from its spelling to represent an early manuscript; these two usually agree with each other and with the majority of manuscripts, thus adding weight and confidence to our critical text. As fewer manuscripts of the Glossary survive than of the larger Grammar, this added testimony is welcome.

To determine the independence of N and L from any extant manuscript, I have in this and in a previous study contrasted them with all the other texts as well as with one another. Even if they are not simply transcripts of other existing copies of the Grammar and Glossary, their textual affinities and positions among the extant texts must be ascertained. A more complete answer must await the collation of all the manuscripts and transcripts. The relatively full text of N promises a much clearer picture than is possible for L. Even now, however, the general outlines are apparent. Neither shows a very close affinity to any other text; and on the basis of our limited transcription material, the two are probably closest to each other. Some of the manuscripts show very clear affinities: U descends from C, approximately the first third of H from D, and X from Q and W from J--the last chain being also fairly close to O. N's and L's links with other manuscripts cut across various sub-groupings, but N seems to agree most often with Y and F (as in unbegungen [Zupitza 201/9] and other variants, such as those at Zupitza 14/21, 25/8, 25/12 and 84/2). Y lacks the Glossary, however, in contrast to N. N and L both often stand opposed to F, as in their conservative forms of cynehelm and cystig (shared with C and J), where F, like O and Q, has kynehelm and cysti (Zupitza 303/15, 305/11). The generally conservative or early spellings in N and L and the central but nonderivative character of their textual relations make them valuable witnesses to the text of the Grammar and Glossary. That N was an early manuscript is also suggested by its use of feorþe for seofoðe, discussed above, an error only early manuscripts preserve and later ones apparently have corrected. N's preservation of the mastruga entry and

others lacking from various manuscripts further attests
to its importance.

N represents a copy of a virtually complete manuscript
of the Grammar and Glossary that is no longer extant;
this fact raises the question of its exemplar's fate.
Nowell seems to have used only his transcript in his
lexicographical work, probably because he did not possess
the exemplar. Unlike most of the other manuscripts he
used, it was not preserved in a major collection. Just
as Nowell is known to have annotated the Exeter Book,
even though it has remained at Exeter, so too he may have
copied his Grammar and Glossary text from a manuscript
which was available to him only briefly. Of course, not
all manuscripts which passed through the hands of the
sixteenth-century antiquaries have survived intact. A
recently discovered binding fragment has proved to be
from a manuscript of Bede's lost Liber Epigrammatum that
was annotated and excerpted by John Leland.[31] N's exemplar may have suffered a similar fate or even a worse
fate.

Whatever the fate of this Anglo-Saxon manuscript,
there may be two widely separated traces of it besides
Nowell's transcript. One is an entry in MS Cotton Otho
E. i (Ker, Catalogue, no. 184). This manuscript, se-
verely damaged in the fire of 1731, contains a copy of
the glossaries in MS Cotton Cleopatra A. iii (Ker,
Catalogue, no. 143), to which were added a number of
other entries, many of them from a copy of Ælfric's
Glossary. These entries were added about the year 1000,
soon after the composition of the work and contemporary
with the oldest extant manuscript of the Grammar and
Glossary, O. One such entry is "fannus hreohche." The
only other manuscript to have this particular form of
that entry is N; it is possible that the exemplar of N
was the source of the Ælfrician material in Otho E. i.
The other possible trace of the original manuscript comes
from early seventeenth-century Germany. Ker notes
(Catalogue, pp. 470-71) that Friedrich Lindenbrog (1573-
1648) compiled a collection of Old English material which
included, among other things, a copy of Joscelyn's Old
English dictionary, extracts from a copy of Ælfric's
Grammar, and a copy of the Glossary based on more than
one source, presumably including manuscripts Q and V
which Lindenbrog transcribed elsewhere. Unique to these
Glossary materials, and indeed to Old English texts, is
the entry "compater godsib," following "amita faðu"
(Zupitza 300/8). Yet in the margin of page 92 of N
there stands opposite "amita faðu" the addition

"godsib.compater" in Nowell's hand. The exact relationship between Nowell's marginal entry in N and Lindenbrog's
citation is a mystery. The manuscript Nowell transcribed
may have been among those which, like Q and V, were taken
to the Continent in the sixteenth and seventeenth centuries, only to disappear later. Even Lindenbrog's compilation has since suffered a similar fate: Hamburg
Staats- und Universitätsbibliothek Cod. Germ. 22, the
librarian writes, "seit dem Zweiten Weltkrieg als ver-
schollen gilt."

   Fortunately, Nowell's transcript has come down through
his friend William Lambarde as both evidence of a lost
Anglo-Saxon manuscript and testimony to the industry and
enthusiasm of scholars like Laurence Nowell and John
Leland. Their work and interest in Old English manuscripts, texts, and antiquities should encourage modern
scholars to preserve, use, and better comprehend their
legacy.[32]

Notes

1. The lamentable story of the evidence for the losses
is well summarized in two articles by C. E. Wright,
"The Dispersal of the Monastic Libraries and the Be-
ginnings of Anglo-Saxon Studies," Transactions of the
Cambridge Bibliographical Society I (1949-53):208-37;
and "The Dispersal of the Libraries in the Sixteenth
Century," in The English Library before 1700, ed.
Francis Wormald and C. E. Wright (London: Athlone
Press, 1958), pp. 148-75. See further, Helmut Gneuss,
"Englands Bibliotheken im Mittelalter und ihr Unter-
gang," in Festschrift für Walter Hübner, ed. Dieter
Riesner and Helmut Gneuss (Berlin: Schmidt, 1964),
pp. 91-121, esp. 112-21 ("Das 16. Jahrhundert" and
"Die Verluste"). Gneuss cites Leland's report of
Canterbury monks using leaves of old Latin and Greek
manuscripts for shelf paper in their library. Against
this we may set Karl Strecker's conclusion in his
Introduction to Medieval Latin, trans. and rev.
Robert B. Palmer (Dublin: Weidmann, 1967), p. 124:
"An enormous number of manuscripts has been lost, and
yet that not more have disappeared is for the most
part due to the circumstance that the Renaissance
brought with it a great zeal for manuscript collect-
ing."
2. For Leland, especially the date of his birth, see
T. D. Kendrick, British Antiquity (London: Methuen,
1950), pp. 45-64. For Prise, see N. R. Ker, "Sir John

Prise," The Library, 5th ser. 10 (1955): 1-24. Otherwise, pertinent biographical and bibliographical information is available in Wright's and Gneuss's articles, cited in note 1, as well as the Dictionary of National Biography.

3. N. R. Ker, Catalogue of Manuscripts Containing Anglo-Saxon (Oxford: Clarendon Press, 1957), pp. 1, 567; R. I. Page, "Anglo-Saxon Texts in Early Modern Transcripts," Transactions of the Cambridge Bibliographical Society 6, pt. 2 (1973): 79.

4. Lucy Toulmin Smith, ed., The Itinerary of John Leland, 5 vols. (London: 1906-10); John Leland, Commentarii de Scriptoribus Britannicis, ed. Antonius Hall, 2 vols. (Oxford: Oxford University Press, 1709); and Thomas Hearne, ed., Joannis Lelandi Antiquarii de Rebus Britannicis Collectanea, 6 vols. (Oxford: Oxford University Press, 1715).

5. Ker, Catalogue, pp. xlv-xlviii; and Hearne, Lelandi Collectanea, 4:148-49, 154-155, and 160.

6. Michael Swanton, "Une version perdue du Catholicon de Jean Lagadeuc," Études celtiques 15 (1978): 599-605.

7. Ronald E. Buckalew, "Leland's Transcript of Ælfric's Glossary," Anglo-Saxon England 7 (1978): 149-64.

8. Retha M. Warnicke, William Lambarde: Elizabethan Antiquary, 1536-1601 (Chichester, Sussex: Phillimore, 1973), esp. p. 23; and her "Note on a Court of Requests Case of 1571," English Language Notes 11 (1974): 250-56. A subsequent article by Pamela M. Black, "Laurence Nowell's 'Disappearance' in Germany and Its Bearing on the Whereabouts of His Collectanea, 1568-1572," English Historical Review 92 (1977): 345-53, shows no awareness of Warnicke's conclusions, though it is based on the same primary documents. The author assumes the existence of only one Laurence Nowell and does not seem to consider Warnicke's solution. The convoluted argument which results provides (unintentionally) strong confirmation of Warnicke's position that the antiquary was not the dean of Lichfield.

9. Warnicke, Lambarde, p. 23; and Robin Flower, "Laurence Nowell and the Discovery of England in Tudor Times," Proceedings of the British Academy 21 (1935): 46-73, esp. p. 59.

10. Attested to by a note in Lambarde's hand at the top of page one of the manuscript: "Gulihelmi Lambarde, ex dono Laurentii Noelli 1565. wille ham lamwyrhte." The "signature" was written in an imitation Anglo-Saxon hand. An illustration of this signature may be seen in plate 1 in Warnicke, Lambarde, facing p. 32, from the manuscript of Lambarde's Perambulation of Kent.

11. Albert H. Marckwardt, ed., <u>Laurence Nowell's</u>
<u>"Vocabularium Saxonicum"</u> (Ann Arbor: University of
Michigan Press, 1952); William Somner, <u>Dictionarium</u>
<u>Saxonico-Latino-Anglicum</u> (Oxford: G. Hall, 1659);
and Albert H. Marckwardt, "Nowell's <u>Vocabularium</u>
<u>Saxonicum</u> and Somner's <u>Dictionarium</u>," <u>Philological</u>
<u>Quarterly</u> 26 (1947): 345-51. Marckwardt, however,
had no knowledge of Nowell's transcript of the <u>Grammar</u>
<u>and Glossary</u>.

12. Julius Zupitza, Ælfrics Grammatik und Glossar
(1880; reprinted Berlin: Weidmann, 1966), with a
foreword by Helmut Gneuss. The central quire referred
to is the eighth of fourteen (pp. 57-64) and corresponds in extent to Zupitza, pp. 158/7-203/14 (numbers
after the virgule refer to lines).

13. On page 51 of N are two sentences which correspond
to the beginnings of pages 136 and 137 of Zupitza re-
spectively; but the two sentences in between, which
replace a considerable portion of text, have no
counterpart in Zupitza or any text he uses. They contain ungrammatical forms here like <u>þysne</u> (masculine,
accusative demonstrative with a feminine genitive
noun) and <u>cumð</u>: "Se forma preteritum þysne geþeodnysse
sceal geendian in <u>avi</u> and he cumð of þam oðran had þæt
is <u>amas</u>. Gyf þu dest aweg <u>s</u> and setst þærfore <u>vi</u>."

14. Nowell's accuracy in his transcriptions has recently
been the subject of some controversy. The last two of
the following three studies have defended his general
accuracy and reliability against the criticism of the
first: Raymond J. S. Grant, "Laurence Nowell's Transcript of BM Cotton Otho B. xi," <u>Anglo-Saxon England</u> 3
(1974): 111-24; Angelika Lutz, "Zur Rekonstruktion der
Version G der Angelsächsischen Chronik," <u>Anglia</u> 95
(1977): 1-19; and Roland Torkar, "Zu den <u>ae</u>. Medi-
zinaltexten in Otho B. xi und Royal 12 D. xvii," <u>Anglia</u>
94 (1976): 319-38.

15. The two drastically abridged copies are the Trinity
College, Cambridge, MS (R. 9. 17) of about A.D. 1200
and the Worcester Cathedral MS (F. 174), the latter
a Middle English translation of about 1225 which N. R.
Ker has attributed to the famous scribe with the
"tremulous" hand. The third, with over 200 omissions
shared with at least one manuscript and about 400
unique to this copy, is British Library MS Harley 107.

16. The evidence for U here comes from Uj that preserves extracts from two leaves which in the sixteenth
century still followed what is now the last extant
leaf of U. For a full discussion, see Buckalew,
"Leland's Transcript," pp. 158-59.

17. The <u>mastruga</u> entry may have originated as a marginal
gloss and been incorporated in the main text early in

its transmission. This is suggested by its location in N one item further on, and in O fourteen items further on than in the four other manuscripts which have it. But Nowell sometimes goes back to an item he skipped, and the scribes of O were quite erratic. Thus, the possibility arises that this item was part of the original Glossary text and that omission through eyeskip rather than addition accounts for its limited distribution.

It is to be understood that whenever X is cited, Old Cornish rather than Old English is the language of the gloss.

18. R is noteworthy, furthermore, in having most of the Old English translations of the Latin exemplar entered above the main lines of text instead of continuously on the same line with the Latin. On the contrary, Nowell's transcript sometimes has the Latin lemmata entered above the line, presumably where Nowell decided, perhaps as an afterthought, that the Old English could not be fully comprehended without them.

19. Nowell's form actually ends in -a rather than the expected -e, but that spelling of feorþe (p. 61) may be his rather than the exemplar's. O's seo foðe for seo seofoðe appears to represent the starting point for the error in C, H, and N, a circumstance which raises a number of interesting questions about textual relations.

20. Lutz, "Zur Rekonstruktion," pp. 6-7, esp. note 24.

21. Flower, "Laurence Nowell," p. 52.

22. Although Nowell clearly abbreviated portions of his transcript, the Glossary--the only portion represented in L--appears to be a virtually complete transcript of the Old English glosses with most of the Latin lemmata, as well.

23. James L. Rosier, "A New Old English Glossary: Nowell upon Huloet," Studia Neophilologica 49 (1977): 289-94; Kenneth Sisam, "The Authenticity of Certain Texts in Lambard's Archaionomia 1568," Studies in the History of Old English Literature (Oxford: Clarendon Press, 1953), pp. 232-58; and note 11 above.

24. Eleanor Adams, Old English Scholarship in England from 1566-1800, Yale Studies in English, no. 55 (New Haven, Conn.: Yale University Press, 1917), p. 56.

25. Albert H. Marckwardt, "The Sources of Laurence Nowell's Vocabularium Saxonicum," Studies in Philology 45 (1948): 30.

26. Thomas Wright and Richard Paul Wülcker, eds., Anglo-Saxon and Old English Vocabularies, 2d ed., 2 vols. (London: 1884; reprinted Darmstadt: Wissenschaftliche Buchgesellschaft, 1968), glossaries nos. 4, 5, 10, and 13. The first two are based on

Junius's transcript of the Antwerp-London Glossary;
the last two are based on manuscripts J and W of
Ælfric's Glossary. For an excellent explication of
the confusion surrounding the Antwerp-London Glossary,
see C. A. Ladd, "The 'Rubens' Manuscript and Archbishop Ælfric's Vocabulary," Review of English Studies
n.s. 11 (1960): 353-64.

27. When they differ, the dictionary form is paralleled
in few if any of the manuscripts. Cf. the discussion
of pening below and in note 30. Geongman and geon-
gling, furthermore, occur together in the dictionary
out of alphabetical order, but juxtaposed as they are
in the manuscripts and N (p. 93). All of the manuscripts of the Glossary, however, except C and Uj,
have jungling for the second word. Like Nowell's
treatment of pening, this difference appears not to be
a true variant reflecting a different manuscript--we
never have two different spellings of one word together. Rather there appears to be a tendency in the
dictionary to "standardize" certain Old English words.

28. The passage in question occurs as a citation in the
dictionary under mot: "Ic mot. I may; mihi licet.
We moton. We may; nobis licet. þu mostest. Tibi
licuit." Zupitza 264/7-8 is the same but without the
modern translations. N (p. 80) lacks the nobis licet.
Because scholars like Nowell knew Latin far better
than Old English, it is a basic methodological principle to treat purely Latin omissions and variants as
less significant than Old English ones where the Latin
is recoverable or possibly the result of standardiza-
tion.

29. Ælfric regularly has peni(n)g in the singular
(Zupitza 50/14, 264/18, 316/13) and penenga(s) in the
plural (Zupitza 102/1, 202/13, 285/3, 296/15, 296/16).
See A. Campbell, Old English Grammar (Oxford:
Clarendon Press, 1959), p. 190. But Campbell's rule--
ing to -ig-, -eg- after a nasal--does not match
Ælfric's pattern, in which the second nasal is always
lacking in the plural.

30. There are actually two such instances, in one of
which the Vocabularium has a plural for what in N and
the manuscripts is a singular (under eala, Zupitza
264/18, N, p. 80). Of two others in the Grammar, one
(Zupitza 285/3) is omitted from both N and the
Vocabularium and the other is in N only (Zupitza 120/1;
N, p. 44). The other one of the two in the Vocabularium, however, follows N with the sentences cited in
reverse order, as well as the alteration of penegas to
peningas. Nowell must have felt the latter a sort of
canonical form of this word.

The dictionary passage is noteworthy: "Wana.
Lacke. Me synd wana peningas. I lacke money. Me is

feos wana. Idem. Wana sie. Absit; God forbidde"
(cf. Zupitza 202/12-13; N, p. 64).
31. The verses from this work preserved by Leland in
his Collectanea are edited and discussed by Michael
Lapidge, "Some Remnants of Bede's Lost Liber Epigrammatum," English Historical Review 90 (1975): 798-820;
and the surviving bifolium of Leland's manuscript by
Luitpold Wallach, "The Urbana Anglo-Saxon Sylloge of
Latin Inscriptions," in Poetry and Poetics from
Ancient Greece to the Renaissance: Studies in Honor
of James Hutton, ed. G. M. Kirkwood, Cornell Studies
in Classical Philology, no. 38 (Ithaca, N.Y.: Cornell
University Press, 1975), pp. 134-51.

32. This study is indebted to numerous institutions and
individuals, including the following libraries and
their librarians: The Pennsylvania State University
Library; the University Library, Trinity College
Library, and the Parker Library of Corpus Christi
College, Cambridge; the Bodleian Library, All Souls
College Library, and St. John's College Library,
Oxford; and the British Library and Westminster Abbey
Library, London. Thanks are due especially to the
editors of the Dictionary of Old English, Toronto, for
the use of their concordance, to the editors of this
volume for their patience, and to my research assis-
tants, Marilyn L. Sandidge and Joseph G. Queen, and my
typists, Jill Smith and Victoria Music, for their hard
work and skill. The research on which this study is
based was supported by grants from the College of the
Liberal Arts and the Institute for the Arts and Human-
istic Studies of the Pennsylvania State University,
the American Philosophical Society, the American Coun-
cil of Learned Societies, and the National Endowment
for the Humanities, to all of which I am most grateful.

Ælfric's *Sermo de Sacrificio in Die Pascae:*
Anglican Polemic in the Sixteenth
and Seventeenth Centuries

Theodore H. Leinbaugh

"Difference in opinions," says the narrator of
Gulliver's Travels, "hath cost many millions of lives;
for instance, whether flesh be bread, or bread be flesh;
whether the juice of a certain berry be blood or wine."
Gulliver refers, of course, to the eucharistic controversies which so bitterly divided Europe, which caused
the flow of so much ink and so much blood, from the
Reformation and Counter-Reformation periods through
Swift's own day. Protestants of the "flesh as bread"
school, represented at one extreme by Zwingli, believed
in a figurative or spiritual understanding of Christ's
presence in the host, and rejected notions of a carnal,
corporeal, or Capernaitic presence. Catholics of the
"bread as flesh" school favored a literal or metabolic
interpretation of Christ's presence in the Eucharist.
Ælfric's Sermon on the Sacrifice on Easter Day, the first
and most controversial text ever printed in Old English,
came to play an important role in the eucharistic debates
of the Elizabethan period, and consequently spurred the
growth and development of Anglo-Saxon studies. Anglican
theologians seized upon Ælfric's sermon as ancient evidence against the doctrine of transubstantiation, even
though several passages in the sermon describe Christ's
eucharistic presence in vividly corporeal terms. In the
sixteenth century, reformist editors cut, trimmed, and
annotated these passages in such a way that a false
textual tradition was established, a tradition that made
Ælfric's eucharistic beliefs more acceptable to Lutheran,
Calvinist, and even Zwinglian opinion. In this essay I
shall trace the development of this tradition, a tradition persisting until the middle of the nineteenth century, that portrayed Ælfric as a remarkably early
apologist for Protestant thought.[1]

Archbishop Matthew Parker, Queen Elizabeth's new primate at Canterbury, introduced this faulty textual tradition by suggesting that passages in Ælfric describing Christ's literal presence in the Eucharist were interpolations. In 1566 Parker published Ælfric's sermon, together with letters to Wulfsige and Wulfstan, in a polemical treatise designed to demonstrate the continuity between the religious beliefs of the Protestant reformers and the Anglo-Saxons: A Testimonie of Antiquitie, shewing the auncient fayth in the Church of England touching the sacrament of the body and bloude of the Lord here publikely preached, and also received in the Saxons tyme, above 600 yeares agoe.[2] Parker and his associates-- his learned secretary John Joscelyn, the printer John Day, Laurence Nowell, and other advisors-- believed that Ælfric's writings upheld Anglican eucharistic belief as outlined in the Thirty-Nine Articles of 1563: "The body of Christ is given, taken, and eaten, in the Supper, only after an heavenly and spiritual manner."[3] Remarks in the preface, marginal comments, and instances of apparently deliberate mistranslation in the Testimonie enforce the Anglican viewpoint in matters concerning both religious doctrine and practice. Subsequent reformist editors followed Parker's lead, altering Ælfric's work until it conformed to their own interpretation of Anglican belief.

While Parker endorsed Ælfric's eucharistic beliefs, or rather what he took to be Ælfric's beliefs, his attitude toward the sermon as a whole was somewhat ambiguous. Parker conceded that the sermon contained material "of some reprehension," and he imputed the intrusion of this material to the fact that Ælfric was "an earnest lover and a great setter forwarde of monkerye."[4] "Monkerye," a byword for Roman Catholic belief, was anathema to the Anglican editors of the Testimonie, so much so that they considered even the Danish invasions of England as acts of divine retribution directed against the monks. The preface of the Testimonie rebukes King Edgar for his part in helping to

> set up of newe the religion or rather superstition and hipocrisie of monkes, after that the same had been a longe tyme, by the juste judgement of God, utterlye abolished, the Danes spoyling them, and cruelly burning them up in there houses, as is at large, and plentifullye confessed in the historyes of their owne churches. (fol. 6v)

Though many errors in the Testimonie resulted from a
simple inability to translate Old English, other errors
originated in the editors' desire to rid Ælfric's text
of "monkish" material and the "blindnes and ignoraunce"
that they thought corrupted the "church, when Ælfricke
him self lived" (fol. 16v). Errors of the first sort,
simple mistranslations, came about for several reasons.
The editors of the Testimonie had difficulty distinguish-
ing certain grammatical categories. Singular and plural
forms of verbs, adjectives, and nouns are often confused
--frumcennedan cild (fol. 25v), for example, is translated "first borne childe"--and occasionally verb tenses
are misconstrued.[5] Though Nowell and Joscelyn had begun
work on dictionaries and glossaries, Old English lexicography, still in its infancy, could not meet the needs
of the early editors. For example, evidently confusing
the verb ehtan with an inflected form of the noun æht,
the editors mistranslated a phrase describing Pharaoh's
pursuit of the people of Israel across the Red Sea--ðe
heora ehton--as "with their possessions" (fol. 23) rather
than as "who had pursued them."[6] A phrase referring to
the apostles and heora æftergencgan, "their successors,"
is also mistranslated through confusion of noun and verb
forms and difficulties in word-division. The editors of
the Testimonie divided the noun æftergencgan into two
words, æfter and gencgan, took these fragments as a
preposition and a verb, and translated "since their departure" (fol. 29). A more striking indication of the
difficulties involved in these first attempts to resur-
rect the Old English language appears in a passage in the
Testimonie that describes Christ as "a lambe, and a lyon,
and a mountayne" (fol. 31). Ælfric makes no mention of a
mountain, writing instead that Christ is symbolically or
typologically called lamb, and leo, and gehu elles, "a
lamb, and a lion, and in every other way."

Other inaccuracies in the Testimonie's translation
seem more tendentious. It is conceivable that a simple
editorial oversight allowed the word "holy" to slip from
a phrase which ought to have read "at the holy mass"
(fol. 46). The very next sentence does contain the
phrase "holy masse," but that sentence also contains an
error that seems much less likely to have been an oversight: the Old English reads forði fremað seo halige
mæsse micclum ge þam lybbendum ge ðam forðfarenum, and is
translated, "Therefore that holy masse is profitable both
to the lyving, and to the dead" (fol. 47). The word
micclum is not translated; the sentence ought to read
"that holy masse is greatly profitable. . . ." This
omission may be designed to weaken the Roman Catholic
assertion that the mass is efficacious for the living

and the dead. The adverb <u>micclum</u>, accurately translated elsewhere in the <u>Testimonie</u>, gives Ælfric's statement an emphasis which the editors thought undesirable, and a marginal note declares: "This doctrine with praying to images and to the dead bodies of men at their tombes tooke his beginning of the avarice of monkes unto whom it was gainfull" (fol. 47).[7]

Other marginal notes challenging the scriptural authority for such practices as making the sign of the cross and mixing water with wine also reveal the Anglican bias of the editors. But the most important annotation concerns the two miracle stories that fall at the center of the sermon. These stories contradict the theory that Ælfric believed only in a spiritual or figurative eucharistic presence. It is hardly coincidental that the editors of the <u>Testimonie</u> decided that the stories had been interpolated: "These tales seme to be infarsed placed here upon no occasion" (fol. 39). This cavalier attitude toward the integrity of Ælfric's text springs from the stories' vivid portrayal of Christ's corporeal presence in the Eucharist:

> We rædað on ðære bec ðe is gehatan <u>Vitae</u>
> <u>Patrum</u> þæt twegen munecas bædon æt Gode sume
> swutelunge be ðam halgan husle, and æfter
> ðære bene gestodon him mæssan. Ða gesawon
> hi licgan an cild on ðam weofode þe se
> mæssepreost æt mæssode, and Godes engel stod
> mid hand-sexe, anbidiende oðþæt se preost
> þæt husel tobræc. Þa toliðode se engel þæt
> cild on ðam disce, and his blod into ðam
> calice ageat. Eft, ðaða hi to ðam husle
> eodon, ða wearð hit awend to hlafe and to
> wine, and hi hit ðygedon, Gode ðancigende
> þære swutelunge. Eac se halga Gregorius
> abæd æt Criste, þæt he æteowode anum
> twynigendum wife embe his gerynu micele
> seðunge. Heo eode to husle mid twynigendum
> mode, and Gregorius begeat æt Gode þærrihte,
> þæt him bam wearð æteowed seo snæd þæs
> husles ðe heo ðicgan sceolde, swilce ðær
> læge on ðam disce anes fingres lið eal
> geblodgod: and þæs wifes twynung wearð ða
> gerihtlæced.

These lurid descriptions of the Eucharist transformed into a bloodied child lying on the altar, and into a bloody finger about to be served to a communicant, were an embarrassment to the editors of the <u>Testimonie</u>. They chose to emphasize instead those sections of Ælfric's

sermon more in keeping with Anglican belief. An accurately translated passage bearing the marginal note "No
transubstantiation" declares,

> Muche is betwixte the invisible myghte of
> the holye housell, and the visible shape
> of his proper nature. It is naturally
> corruptible bread, and corruptible wine:
> and is by mighte of Godes worde truely
> Christes bodye, and his bloude: not so
> notwithstanding bodely, but ghostly.
> (fols. 34-35)

Another passage, with its sentences chopped into phrases
for added emphasis, states, "That housell is temporall,
not eternall. Corruptible, and dealed into sondrye
partes. Chewed betwene teeth, and sent into the bellye"
(fol. 37). The passage with its glancing reference to
the Stercoranist heresy is also annotated to call attention to the difference between "Christes naturall body,
and the Sacrament therof" (fol. 35).

Out of context, these passages seem to express contra-
dictory eucharistic beliefs. Modern scholars, however,
have suggested that Ælfric reconciles "the symbolist with
the carnal interpretation of the Eucharist," and that
Ælfric's doctrine is "mi-spirituelle, mi-réaliste."[8] In
order to understand how Ælfric creates this synthesis it
would be necessary to trace his relationship to the
ninth- and tenth-century eucharistic controversies on the
Continent. It must suffice here to note that Ælfric
draws on two distinct schools of patristic thought concerning the Eucharist represented by the writings of two
ninth-century theologians, Ratramnus and Paschasius
Radbertus. Ratramnus provided a source for the passages
favorably cited by Parker and and later Anglican editors,
while the writings of Paschasius influenced those portions of Ælfric's sermon that supported a literal interpretation of Christ's presence in the Eucharist.

In his eucharistic treatise, De Corpore et Sanguine
Domini, Ratramnus argues in favor of a figurative interpretation of Christ's presence in the Eucharist, contend-
ing that the bread and wine on the altar are not Christ's
body and blood in veritate but in figura.[9] During the
tenth and early eleventh centuries his ideas were increasingly viewed as highly independent and even unorthodox. By the middle of the eleventh century his
treatise on the Eucharist, by then wrongly attributed to
John Scotus Erigena, was condemned at a synod in Vercelli.
His teaching appealed, of course, to the proponents of

Reformation, and his eucharistic treatise was printed in
Cologne, Geneva, Basel, and Leiden throughout the sixteenth century. An English edition appeared as early as
1548.[10]

Although Parker knew that Ælfric relied on Latin
sources, he was unable to identify Ælfric's significant
borrowings from Ratramnus. Had Parker been able to do
so, he would have better understood his endorsement of
Ælfric's eucharistic teaching: eucharistic doctrine
taken from Ratramnus was sound Anglican doctrine. The
eucharistic miracle stories, on the other hand, had an
altogether different source, and Parker spoke with some
accuracy when he dismissed the two "vayne miracles, which
notwithstanding seeme to have been infarced for that they
stand in their place unaptly, and without purpose, and
the matter without them, both before and after, doth
hange in it selfe together most orderly" (fols. 76-76v).
Whether the miracles are "vayne" or whether they "stand
in their place unaptly" is a matter of opinion, but it is
not surprising that the "matter without" appealed to
Parker, or that it seemed to "hange . . . together": the
material on either side of the miracle stories comes directly from Ratramnus's De Corpore et Sanguine Domini.[11]

The next major edition of the sixteenth century follows the textual precedents set by Parker and gives
Ælfric's sermon an even stronger Anglican bias. Published by the martyrologist John Foxe in 1570, the edition appears in his massive Ecclesiastical History containing the Acts and Monuments, commonly known as "Foxe's
Book of Martyrs."[12] A section of this work confutes the
Six Articles of 1539, which were promulgated to check the
spread of Reformation doctrine and practice. Ælfric's
sermon is the final document in a long series collected
to challenge the claims of transubstantiation:

> And thus I suppose, it standeth cleare and
> evidently proved by course of all these ages
> afore recited, from the tyme of Tertullian
> and Austen, unto the dayes of this Ælfricus
> above mencioned, and after hym, that this
> newcome miracle of transubstantiation was
> not yet crept into the heads of men, nor
> almost came in any question amongest learned
> men, nor was admitted for any doctrine in
> the Churche, at least for any general doc-
> trine of all men to be receaved, til a
> thousand yeare complete after Christ, that
> is, till that Sathan began to bee let at
> large. Apocal. 20. (p. 1310)

Satan, however, must have been unleashed upon Ælfric's
text at an even earlier date. Clearly acting upon
Parker's editorial comments, Foxe felt compelled to
delete Ælfric's eucharistic miracle stories in an attempt
to keep the sermon free from the taint of transubstantiation. There is no indication in Foxe's edition that material has been omitted, and Bromwich's harsh but accurate judgment that Foxe's edition is "plagiarized and
tendentiously abbreviated" must stand.[13] Foxe reproduces
virtually word for word Ælfric's text as it appears in
Parker's Testimonie, often duplicating the same mistranslations (ðe heora ehton remains "with their possessions," and gehu elles is still "a mountain"). And following Parker's marginal notes, Foxe alters or "abbre-
viates" the text when it swerves too closely toward Roman
Catholic doctrine or terminology.

Foxe's methods of abbreviation can be observed in the
passage immediately preceding the eucharistic miracle
stories. At first Foxe carefully reproduces Parker's
text. The passage, an adaptation of chapters 88 and 60
from Ratramnus's De Corpore, interprets the Eucharist as
a pledge and a figure (Old English wedd and hiw translating the Latin pignus . . . et species), which the faithful are said to hold mystically until they come to the
truth itself. The Eucharist is described as Christ's
body and blood in a spiritual sense, and the section ends
with the admonition, Ne sceole ge smeagan hu hit gedon
sy, ac healdan on eowerum geleafan þæt hit swa gedon sy.
Foxe, however, balks at printing this last sentence, and
omits it from both his text and translation. Presumably
the call to unquestioned faith sounded dangerously popish
to Foxe, particularly when coupled in Ælfric's original
with the eucharistic miracles.

The section on the efficacy of the mass, which elic-
ited adverse comment in the Testimonie, also disappears
without trace in Foxe's edition. And to an apparently
innocuous reference to the mass--("hereof syng Gods
servantes at every Masse")--Foxe adds somewhat snappishly,
"Thys Masse was not then lyke to these our popishe and
blasphemous masses now" (p. 1308). Foxe chafes too at
the use of the word "mass" in the following passage from
the Testimonie: "Truely the bread and the wine whyche by
the masse [OE mæssan] of the priest is halowed, shewe one
thyng without to humayne understanding and an other thing
they call [OE hi clypiaþ] within to beleving mindes"
(fol. 32). Foxe alters the word "mass" to "supper" and
eliminates altogether the words "they call," with their
suggestion of a corporeal, speaking presence in the host.
Foxe's revised version of the passage reads, "Truely the

bread and the wyne, whiche in the supper by the priest is halowed, shewe one thyng without to humane understanding, and an other thyng within to beleving mindes" (p. 1309). Throughout, changes introduced by Foxe subtly alter the theological implications of Parker's translation. Where the Testimonie speaks of baptismal water's "holowing mighte" (fol. 34; translating OE halwende mihte), which suggests a certain efficacy or salutary power, Foxe refers in more neutral tones to the water's "wholesome vertue" (p. 1309).

Not every change in Foxe's text, however, is designed to make the Easter sermon conform to Anglican belief. In several places mistranslations from the Testimonie have been corrected, although these corrections are not necessarily the work of Foxe.[14] Thus, heora æftergencgan is amended from "since their departure" to "their successors" (p. 1309). Forðfarenra, mistranslated "of those pilgrimes," is corrected to "of men departed thys lyfe" (p. 1310). Finally, where the Testimonie inadvertently skips over the phrase gif hi ne beoð mid leahtrum ofsette, the Ecclesiastical History accurately translates "if they be not oppressed with sinne" (p. 1310).

For a brief period in the years immediately following the Puritan ascendancy under the Protectorate, the doctrine of transubstantiation was believed suppressed, so much so that several bishops at the Savoy Conference argued against restoring the "Black Rubric" to the Book of Common Prayer, maintaining that the world was "in more danger of profanation than idolatry."[15] But this appears to have been the minority opinion. Protestant divines feared the spread of idolatry at this time as well as at the end of the century, when James II, an avowed Catholic, assumed the throne and eased the prohibitions against the practice of Catholicism and the dissemination of Roman Catholic doctrine.

Anglicans, Puritans, and Roman Catholics debated both the nature of Christ's presence in the Eucharist and the terms used to describe that presence throughout the seventeenth century, and it is not surprising that Ælfric's Sermon on the Sacrifice on Easter Day was printed in at least six separate editions in this century of eucharistic debate. Following the false textual tradition established by Parker and Foxe, Ælfric's editors continued to believe that the sermon provided ancient testimony against the doctrine of transubstantiation, and a growing spirit of nationalism made this testimony all the more valuable because its author was an Englishman. Furthermore, critical studies from such scholars as James

Ussher, archbishop of Armagh, William Hopkins, and
William Cave, confirmed the view put forward in the editions that Ælfric's writings conformed to Anglican belief.

The first quarter of the seventeenth century saw two
editions of Ælfric's Easter sermon. The first, a reprint
of A Testimonie of Antiquitie, was appended to William
L'Isle's A Saxon Treatise concerning the Old and New
Testament.16 William Guild published the next edition in
Three Rare Monuments of Antiquitie.17 Guild closely follows Foxe's text, printing only an English translation of
Ælfric's sermon. There is no reason to suppose that
Guild himself knew any Old English, and his few altera-
tions of Foxe's translation only serve to fit the sermon
more securely into a Procrustean bed of Protestant belief.
Guild does not amend any of the omissions or mistransla-
tions of the earlier editions.

In his preface, Guild condemns the Roman Catholics,
"our Adversaries," who "shameleslie . . . raze out of
Auncientes whatsoever maketh against them." He adds that
"they may well blot out the letters, but the fayth they
shall never abolish."18 Guild, however, is himself
guilty of blotting out several passages, including those
sections on the eucharistic miracle stories and the efficacy of the mass that had been suppressed by Foxe. In
these omissions, Guild may have been misled by Foxe's
edition, but Guild's own editorial bias may be detected
in those places where he deviates from the translation
found in the Ecclesiastical History.

An explanatory subtitle in Guild's edition labels
Ælfric's sermon "Convincing the late Errour now-a-dayes
of Trans-substantiation." Guild edits Ælfric's text to
fit this subtitle and to remove material offensive to
Calvinist belief. Two examples may clarify Guild's editorial procedures. Guild read the following passage on
the sign of the cross in Foxe's edition, "And we ought to
marke our foreheades, and our bodyes with the token of
Christes roode, that we maye be also delivered from destruction, when we shall be marked both on forehead, and
also in harte with the bloud of our Lordes suffering"
(p. 1308). Foxe disapproved of the practice of making
the sign of the cross by saying, "We must beare with the
ignoraunce of that tyme." And a marginal note, appended
to the passage in Foxe declares, "That onely crosse is it
wherwith we are marked, that S. Paule speaketh of Eph. 2.
Christ reconciled both to God in one body through hys
crosse" (p. 1308). Guild, in sympathy with these comments, condenses Ælfric's text and omits altogether the
reference to the "token of Christes roode": "And we

ought to marke our Fore-heads and our Heartes, with the
Bloode of our Lordes Suffering."19

Guild makes more subtle textual revisions in a passage
dealing directly with transubstantiation. Foxe reads,
"Without they bee sene bread and wyne both in figure and
in tast, and they be truly after their halowing, Christes
body and his bloude through ghostly misterye" (p. 1309).
A more accurate translation of the Old English would give
greater emphasis to the idea of a change in the eucharistic elements. Ælfric uses the adversative ac (ac hi
beoð soðlice, æfter ðære halgunge . . .), and the translation ought to read "but they are truly, after the consecration, Christ's body and blood. . . ." Through a
strategic insertion of the word "so," a change in punctuation, and the addition of the word "but" in a position
not authorized by the Old English text, Guild deftly
alters the sense of the passage, placing even greater
emphasis on the preservation of the elements of bread and
wine after consecration: "With-out, they are seene bread
and wine, both in figure, and taste: and they bee so
truelie after their hallowing: But Christes bodie and
blood, by ghostlie mysterie."20

In 1624, the same year in which Guild's Three Rare
Monuments of Antiquitie appeared, Ussher published An
Answer to a Challenge made by a Jesuite in Ireland.21
The eucharistic theology in Ussher's treatise is essen-
tially Calvinistic. Ussher argues against the "corrupt
doctrine of the carnall presence" and praises the work of
Ratramnus. Ussher found support for his eucharistic beliefs in the "Saxon Homily" of "Ælfrick," and also made
the important discovery that Ælfric used Ratramnus's De
Corpore as a source for the Easter sermon: "His resolution is not onely the same with that of Ratrannus [sic],
but also in manie places directly translated out of
him."22

Although Ussher was able to demonstrate the close
relationship between Ælfric's sermon and the writings of
Ratramnus, his documentation nevertheless includes a
serious omission. In An Answer, Ussher prints eight passages from Ælfric's sermon, and compares these to corresponding sections in Ratramnus's treatise. In seven of
the eight passages, Ussher prints consecutive lines from
the sermon, but in the sixth passage, Ussher prints only
the lines which precede and follow the eucharistic miracle
stories without indicating that material has been deleted.
Because Ussher relies on the Testimonie for his translation of Ælfric, he clearly knew of the existence of these
stories. It is also clear that Ussher was aware of the

doctrinal distance between these stories and the eucharistic teaching of Ratramnus. A few pages before his
discussion of Ælfric, Ussher condemns these same stories
--though found in the Latin writings of another author--
as examples of the "grosse conceit of the gutturall
eating and drinking of the bodie and blood of Christ."[23]

The miracle stories discussed by Ussher appear in a
late version of a eucharistic treatise originally composed in 831 by Ratramnus's superior at Corbie, Paschasius
Radbertus. In his treatise, Paschasius defends the literal interpretation of Christ's presence in the Eucharist,
and defines this presence as the flesh born of Mary, which
had suffered on the Cross and had risen again. The eucharistic teaching of Paschasius offended Ussher, who remarked that the doctrine of Paschasius "since the time of
Satans loosing, obtayned the upper hand."[24] Ussher sum-
marizes the miracle stories found in chapter fourteen of
Paschasius Radbertus's eucharistic treatise; the first
tells of "a Romane Matron, who found a piece of the
sacramentall bread turned into the fashion of a finger,
all bloodie, which afterwards, upon the prayers of S.
Gregory, was converted to his former shape againe."[25]
The second relates the story of the "little childe" who
"was seene upon the Altar and an Angell cutting him into
small pieces with a knife, and receiving his blood into
the Chalice, as long as the Priest was breaking the bread
into little parts."[26]

Ussher might have readily identified Paschasius
Radbertus as a possible source for the miracle stories
in Ælfric. Either Parker's suggestion that the stories
were interpolated and therefore unworthy of consideration, or the fear that printing the stories would under-
mine Ælfric's credibility as an opponent of transubstantiation, caused Ussher to remain silent. The stories do
little to advance the opening thesis of Ussher's treatise:
"We are therefore here put to prove, that Bread is bread,
and Wine is wine: a matter (one would thinke) that
easily might be determined by common sense."[27]

Later in the seventeenth century L'Isle published
another edition of the Testimonie in his Divers Ancient
Monuments in the Saxon Tongue, but no significant changes
in the presentation of the text or translation of
Ælfric's sermon were made until Abraham Wheelock's edition of the Historiae Ecclesiasticae Gentis Anglorum.[28]
Printed in that edition simply as an appendix to Bede's
description of Easter observances in Britain, the sermon
was nevertheless edited with great care. After comparing
the earlier editions of Parker, Foxe, and L'Isle,

Wheelock collated L'Isle's first edition against Cambridge
University Library MS Gg.3.28. The result was an un-
expurgated text that included a Latin translation far
superior to the available modern English translations.

Wheelock's edition, though not entirely free from
error, is nevertheless a remarkable scholarly achievement
for the early years of Anglo-Saxon studies. In several
places it corrects mistakes that had plagued all previous
editions of Ælfric's sermon. The phrase ðe heora ehton,
mistranslated by Parker, Foxe, Guild, and L'Isle,
Wheelock accurately translates illos persequebatur.
Wheelock also rectifies confusions between singular and
plural noun forms; Ælfric's frumcennedan cild, misconstrued as a singular form in Parker, Foxe, and L'Isle, is
corrected to primogenitos . . . pueros. He also rids
Ælfric's text of the spurious "mountain" raised by earlier
editors desperately trying to make sense of the trouble-
some Old English phrase gehu elles; Wheelock accurately
interprets this as adeoque alias.[29]

Despite these corrections of the text and translation
of Ælfric's sermon, Wheelock shared the desire of his
predecessors to mold Ælfric's sermon into an Anglican
document. Following the example set by Parker and Foxe,
Wheelock is guilty of printing misleading or inaccurate
annotations. Phrases which speak of Christ's spiritual
presence in the Eucharist are marked Non per praesentiam
corporalem, sive transubstantiationem or ergo non per
transubstantiationem.[30] And Ælfric's eucharistic miracle
stories presented Wheelock with difficulties similar to
those which confronted previous Anglican editors. Wheelock ascribes these stories to the ignorance of the age
that produced them (Isti aetati ignoscendum, visiones
flagitanti), but nevertheless struggles to find evidence
against transubstantiation even within these narratives.[31]
In the gory account of the angel slashing the infant
Christ with a knife, Wheelock clings to the Old English
phrase that describes the conversion of the child's flesh
and blood back into bread and wine shortly before com-
munion (ða wearð hit awend to hlafe and to wine) to declare triumphantly, Contra transubstantiationem, non ait,
in naturalem carnem Christi, et sanguinem; sed in panem
et vinum.[32]

By the end of the seventeenth century the textual tradition established by Parker and Foxe and embellished by
subsequent reformist editors had gained wide circulation.
On the Continent the Huguenot Jean Claude praised the
sermon for its sound doctrine during the period when

"l'ignorance et la superstition appliquerent leurs soins
à nourrir et à élever l'erreur de Paschase."[33]   Claude
observed that Ælfric's sermon was taken almost word for
word from Ratramnus, but was also the first scholar to
concede that Ælfric had made use of the miracle stories
found in the work of Paschasius:

> On y trouve ce ramas de nouveaux miracles de
> l'invention de Paschase et de ses sectateurs,
> ce qui marque manifestement l'une de ces
> deux choses, ou que ces bonnes gens ne pre-
> noient point ces miracles pour des preuves
> de la Transsubstanciation, mais seulement
> pour des confirmations de la presence
> mystique et efficace de Iesus-Christ au
> Sacrement . . . ou qu'ils ne savoient gueres
> bien ce qu'ils croyoient de ce mystère.[34]

Though far from developing a coherent interpretation of
Ælfric's eucharistic teaching, Claude does acknowledge
the sermon's textual integrity. And his suggestion that
the originators of the miracle stories did not regard the
stories as proof of transubstantiation may be technically
accurate. The term transubstantiation did not gain circulation until centuries after the stories had been recorded. Claude, however, did not intend for his words to
be taken in this way; he followed the Anglican editors,
indiscriminately equating the term transubstantiation
with any literalist interpretation of the eucharistic
presence. Nevertheless, Claude's analysis of the sermon
affirmed the integrity of Ælfric's text and recognized,
albeit grudgingly, the influence of Paschasius.

In the final decades of the seventeenth century,
Ælfric's sermon captured the attention of several scholars, most notably William Hopkins and William Cave. Interest in Ælfric's work was no doubt spurred, as suggested earlier, by the accession of a Catholic monarch
to the English throne. A new spirit of controversy, as
well as caution, entered the Protestant community as it
met the challenge of Catholics in positions of influence
both at court and in the universities. Under these un-
favorable circumstances William Hopkins, using a cipher
(LMQDDDCQ, VVHSAEPR) to guard his identity, published his
polemical treatise Bertram or Ratram Concerning the Body
and Blood of the Lord .[35] Hopkins contended that the
doctrine of Ratramnus was "contrary to that of Paschasius,
and the present Roman Church, but very agreeable to the
Doctrine of the Church of England." He invoked Ælfric's
sermon to counter charges that extant copies of Ratramnus's De Corpore were textually corrupt: "For Ælfrick,

Abbot of <u>Malmsbury</u>, in a Homily translated by him into
the <u>Saxon</u> tongue about the year 970, hath taken word for
word most of those passages which now sound harsh to
<u>Roman</u> Ears."36

Hopkins acknowledged the source studies made by Ussher,
and expanded upon Ussher's work. Printing sections from
some twenty chapters in Ratramnus parallel to corresponding passages in Ælfric, Hopkins offered substantial evidence for his claim that "after the Homilist comes to
treat of the Sacrament . . . there scapes hardly one Page
without somewhat out of <u>Bertram</u>." But Hopkins's religious
beliefs prevented him from fully acknowledging the influence of Paschasius:

> Nevertheless this carnal Doctrine of
> <u>Paschasius</u> did daily get ground in that
> obscure and ignorant Age next that he lived
> in, as may appear by some Passages in this
> Homily (which I have not recited, because
> they are not in <u>Bertram</u>) the absurd conse-
> quences of that <u>errour</u>. For instance . . .
> there are two Miracles inserted to prove
> the Carnal Presence contrary to the scope
> of the whole Discourse.37

Despite the troubling presence of these miracle stories, Ælfric's reputation as a proponent of reformist
thought prospered through the final years of the seventeenth century. William Cave praised Ælfric as an en-
lightened man of letters living in an otherwise uncul-
tured and barbaric age:

> Fuit Ælfricus Anglo-Saxonum suo tempore
> longe doctissimus, Grammaticae, Logicae,
> Poeticae, Historiae non infoeliciter peri-
> tus, in rebus Theologicis ad amussim eru-
> ditus, vir prudens, pius, et Religionis
> Christianae zelo fervidus, ad scientiam,
> fidem, et pietatem Christianam aevo rudi
> barbaroque, promovendam natus.38

Perhaps this is a fitting epitaph for Ælfric, but it is
largely based upon a single piece of prose. Tendentiously
edited, translated, and annotated, pressed into the ser-
vice of the Reformation in the sixteenth century by
Parker and Foxe, Ælfric's sermon had matured into a
profoundly Anglican document:

> In Homilia ista repens tunc sensim in
> Ecclesiam Transubstantiationis dogma

Ælfricus aggreditur, ac productis argumen-
tis quamplurimis, ex Ratramni libro maximam
partem desumptis, funditus convellit, adeo
ut quaenam Ecclesiae Anglicanae isto aevo
de Eucharistia fides fuerit, luculentissimis
exinde pateat indiciis.[39]

Cave and the other scholars and theologians of the sixteenth and seventeenth centuries misconceived the full
range of Ælfric's eucharistic thought, and only in this
century have Ælfric's contributions to medieval eucharistic theology begun to be properly appreciated.

Notes

1. Protestants favorably cited Ælfric's eucharistic
teaching throughout the eighteenth and nineteenth cen-
turies. Among the many works that could be cited, see
F. Warner, The History of England as it Relates to
Religion and the Church (London: Davis and Reymers,
1759), 1: 220-23; Henry Soames, The History of the
Reformation of the Church of England, 4 vols. (London:
Rivington, 1827) 3: 160-65; Soames, An Inquiry into
the Doctrines of the Anglo-Saxon Church (Oxford:
Rivington, 1830), pp. v-vii, 367-88, et passim; and
Soames, The Anglo-Saxon Church: Its History, Revenues,
and General Character (London: J. W. Parker, 1835),
pp. 218-48. For further references, consult the bib-
liography recently updated by Malcolm Godden in C. L.
White's Ælfric: A New Study of His Life and Writings,
Yale Studies in English, no. 2 (1898; reprinted
Hamden, Conn.: Archon Books, 1974). In the middle of
the nineteenth century Catholic opinion was divided;
John Lingard evidently considered Ælfric unorthodox
and unpatriotic: "one thing is certain, that the language in which he [Ælfric] expressed himself was novel,
and borrowed from Bertram, a foreign writer." See
John Lingard, History and Antiquities of the Anglo-
Saxon Church (London: C. Dolman, 1845), 2:314. On
the other hand, the Catholic author Daniel Rock defended Ælfric's orthodoxy; see The Church of Our
Fathers, 3 vols. (London: C. Dolman, 1849-53), 1:
22-24.
2. A Testimonie of Antiquitie (London: John Day,
1566). On the date of the London edition, see Eleanor
N. Adams, Old English Scholarship in England from 1566-
1800, Yale Studies in English, no. 55 (1917; reprinted
Hamden, Conn.: Archon Books, 1970), pp. 23-25; and
John Bromwich, "The First Book Printed in Anglo-Saxon

Types," <u>Transactions of the Cambridge Bibliographical
Society</u> 3 (1962): 271.
3. I have quoted from Article 28; see E. C. S. Gibson,
<u>The Thirty-Nine Articles of the Church of England</u>
(London: Methuen, 1915), p. 640.
4. <u>Testimonie</u>, fols. 76v and 7. References are to
the King's College, Cambridge, copy of the <u>Testimonie</u>
(shelfmark: C.66.46), an example of the so-called
second edition of the <u>Testimonie</u>, listed in the STC as
159(ii). The foliation of this copy is incomplete,
and in my references I have supplied folio numbers for
the remainder of the text. Further references to the
<u>Testimonie</u> are given parenthetically in the body of
the paper.
5. Because of the <u>Testimonie</u>'s irregularities in punctuation and word-division, I have generally followed
Benjamin Thorpe's Old English text of Ælfric's sermon
in <u>The Homilies of the Anglo-Saxon Church: The First
Part, Containing the Sermones Catholici or Homilies of
Ælfric</u> (1844-46; reprinted New York: Johnson Reprint, 1971), 2:262-82.
6. The fact that <u>ehtan</u> takes the genitive in this
example was doubtless a further source of confusion to
the editors of the <u>Testimonie</u>.
7. The first edition of the <u>Testimonie</u> lacks this
marginal note.
8. See C. L. Wrenn, "Some Aspects of Anglo-Saxon
Theology," <u>Studies in Language, Literature, and Culture of the Middle Ages and Later</u>, ed. E. Bagby
Atwood and Archibald A. Hill (Austin: University of
Texas Press, 1969), p. 185; and the critical edition
of Ratramnus's <u>De Corpore et Sanguine Domini</u>, ed.
J. N. Bakhuizen van den Brink, 2d ed., Verhandelingen
der Koninklijke Nederlandse Akademie van Wetenschap-
pen, Afd. Letterkunde, ms 87 (Amsterdam: North-
Holland, 1974), p. 128.
9. See chapters 6 through 33 of Ratramnus's <u>De
Corpore</u>. Reference should also be made to the recent
critical study by Jean-Paul Bouhot, <u>Ratramne de
Corbie: Histoire littéraire et controverses doctri-
nales</u> (Paris: Etudes Augustiniennes, 1976), though I
must disagree with Bouhot's poorly substantiated assertion that Ælfric had no direct knowledge of
Ratramnus.
10. Ratramnus, <u>The Boke of Barthram Priest Intreatynge
of the Bodye and Blode of Chryst</u>, trans. Sir W.
Hughe[?] (London: Raynalde and Kyngstone, 1548).
Other editions appeared in 1549, 1582, and 1623.
11. The material preceding the miracle stories is a
conflation of chapters 88, 60, and 25 from

Ratramnus's eucharistic treatise; the material following is excerpted from chapters 20, 27, and 28.
12. John Foxe, Ecclesiastical History containing the
Acts and Monuments (London: John Daye, 1570). This
is an expanded version of the 1563 edition, and the
first version to contain Ælfric's sermon. Two subsequent editions containing the sermon appeared in
Foxe's lifetime, in the years 1576 and 1583. Further
references to Foxe's 1570 edition are given in the
text.
13. Bromwich, "The First Book," p. 265.
14. E. Thomson states in Godcunde Lar 7 þeowdom:
Select Monuments of the Doctrine of the Catholic
Church in England before the Norman Conquest (London:
Lumley, 1849), that the translation has been corrected
by Foxe, but Eleanor Adams argues more convincingly
that "there is no evidence that Foxe had any knowledge
of Old English" (Adams, Old English Scholarship,
p. 31).
15. Quoted in E. Cardwell's A History of Conferences
and Other Proceedings Connected with the Revision of
the Book of Common Prayer from the Year 1558 to the
Year 1690 (Oxford: Oxford University Press, 1840),
p. 354. See also C. W. Dugmore, Eucharistic Doctrine
in England from Hooker to Waterland (London: SPCK,
1942), pp. 71-74. The "Black Rubric" explained that
no "adoration is done, or ought to be done . . . unto
the sacramental bread or wine" by kneeling at com-
munion.
16. William L'Isle, A Saxon Treatise concerning the Old
and New Testament (London: John Haviland, 1623).
17. William Guild, Three Rare Monuments of Antiquitie
(Aberdeen: Edward Raban, 1624), pp. 117-41.
18. Ibid., pp. 8, 11.
19. Ibid., p. 121.
20. Ibid., p. 125.
21. James Ussher, An Answer to a Challenge made by a
Jesuite in Ireland (Dublin: Societie of Stationers,
1624).
22. Ibid., p. 77.
23. Ibid., p. 68. I have omitted parentheses in the
quotation.
24. Ibid., p. 77.
25. Ibid., p. 69.
26. Ibid., p. 70.
27. Ibid., p. 45.
28. William L'Isle, Divers Ancient Monuments in the
Saxon Tongue (London: E. Griffin, 1638). Abraham
Wheelock, Historiae Ecclesiasticae Gentis Anglorum
(Cambridge: Roger Daniel, 1643). A second edition

of Wheelock's edition appeared in 1644; my references
are to this second edition.

29. Wheelock, Historiae, pp. 463, 464, 466. After
page 463, Wheelock's edition is misnumbered for several pages, and I have corrected the pagination in all
references to this work.

30. Ibid., pp. 466, 467.

31. Ibid., p. 468.

32. Ibid., p. 468.

33. Jean Claude, Réponse aux deux Traitez intitulez
la Perpétuité de la Foy de l'Eglise Catholique tou-
chant l'Eucharistie (The Hague: J. Rammazeyn, 1666),
p. 44. An earlier edition, printed at Charenton,
appeared in the previous year.

34. Ibid., p. 473.

35. William Hopkins, Bertram or Ratram Concerning the
Body and Blood of the Lord (London: H. Clark, 1688).
All references are to this edition, although earlier
versions appeared in 1686.

36. Ibid., pp. 23, 37-38.

37. Ibid., pp. 38, 53.

38. William Cave, Scriptorum Ecclesiasticorum Historia
Literaria, 2 vols. (London: Richard Chiswell, 1688-
98), 2:321.

39. Ibid., 1:589.

Byrhtferth of Ramsey
and the Renaissance Scholars

Peter S. Baker

The researcher who wished to learn something about
Byrhtferth of Ramsey might reasonably turn to the article
by Henry Bradley in the Dictionary of National Biography.
There he would read that Byrhtferth lived around the year
1000, studied at Ramsey under Abbo of Fleury, and wrote a
number of works on mathematics and astronomy, including
Latin commentaries on four of the scientific works of
Bede, two lost treatises entitled De Principiis Mathematicis and De Institutione Monachorum, and a scientific
work in Latin and Old English, unpublished when Bradley
wrote but preserved in a manuscript of the Bodleian
Library. He would also read that a life of St. Dunstan
had been dubiously ascribed to Byrhtferth. Unfortunately,
the researcher would come away from his reading of the
DNB sadly misinformed. As far as we know, Byrhtferth did
not write the commentaries that go under his name or a
life of Dunstan, and his two "lost" treatises probably
never existed. The unpublished manuscript described by
Bradley is Byrhtferth's Manual, or Encheiridion, to use
Byrhtferth's own title, one of the only two works he
signed; his other signed work, an Epilogus (Byrhtferth's
word for "preface") to an anthology of scientific texts,
was not known to Bradley. These two genuine works were
not printed in full until the late 1920s.[1] Up to that
time, Byrhtferth's reputation rested largely on works
that he did not write. The origin of this elaborate
false identity must be sought in Renaissance antiquarian
circles.

In 1563, the first printed edition of the complete
works of Bede was published at Basel by John Herwagen the
younger. Two of the works in this edition, De Natura
Rerum and De Temporum Ratione, were each accompanied by

several extensive commentaries, one of which was ascribed
without explanation to Byrhtferth of Ramsey. Two chapters of De Temporum Ratione, with commentaries, were
printed by Herwagen as separate works, hence the ascription to Byrhtferth of four commentaries on Bede.[2] For
this ascription, generations of scholars from the seventeenth to the twentieth century assumed that Herwagen had
the authority of a medieval manuscript,[3] but no such
manuscript has ever been found.

The first scholar to question Byrhtferth's authorship
of the commentaries was Karl Classen, who in 1896 argued
from internal evidence that they had been written for a
non-English audience by an author who himself had very
little interest in England.[4] Classen was followed by
George Forsey, who thought that the turgid, pedantic
Latin style of the Encheiridion and Epilogus, Byrhtferth's
signed works, had little in common with the more re-
strained and polished Latin of the commentaries.[5] But
those scholars who believed Herwagen's ascriptions to be
based on medieval authority treated these arguments with
contempt. For example, Robert Steele wrote in a review
of Samuel Crawford's edition of Byrhtferth's Encheiridion,
"A colleague of Professor Crawford has raised the question of the other works ascribed to Byrhtferth, apparently
because the notes on the De rerum natura of Bede are not
written in the turgid metaphorical style of his fine
writing. Why should we expect them to be? I must pro-
test against the superseded fashion of treating manuscript ascriptions as prima facie proof of their own
falsity."[6] But Steele's outburst, as it turned out, was
the last gasp of a dying opposition. Soon afterwards
Charles W. Jones found commentaries nearly identical to
portions of those ascribed to Byrhtferth in manuscripts
dated to the ninth century, many years before Byrhtferth's
birth. Further, Jones demonstrated that the commentaries
could not have been written by any one man, but were an
accumulation of notes by several authors who worked at
Auxerre in the late ninth and early tenth centuries.[7]

If Herwagen's manuscript contained an ascription to
Byrhtferth, it was surely mistaken. But Jones believed
that the manuscript contained no such ascription.
Rather, Herwagen had read in the Englishman John Bale's
Scriptorum Illustrium Maioris Brytanniae . . . Catalogus,
a literary history published in Basel only a few years
before Herwagen's edition appeared, that one Bridferthus
Ramesiensis was responsible for commentaries on De Natura
Rerum and De Temporibus. Finding similar commentaries in
his own manuscript of Bede, Herwagen rashly attached
Byrhtferth's name to them.[8] Such a lighthearted attitude

toward evidence of authorship was apparently typical of
this editor, of whose work Jones said, "I doubt whether
any other single edition of any author has ever foisted
upon the public more spurious or corrupt works without
substantiating evidence."[9] For his erroneous ascriptions, Herwagen relied on his own lively imagination and
on Bale's Scriptorum Illustrium. But Bale's work itself
is somewhat mysterious in its attributions, for it describes several works by Byrhtferth of which we have no
other knowledge. Bale lists four works, whose titles he
gives as De Principiis Mathematicis, In Bedam De Temporibus, In [Bedam] De Natura Rerum and De Institutione
Monachorum.[10] In fact In Bedam De Temporibus probably
refers to Byrhtferth's Epilogus, which is about De Temporibus, but is not a commentary at all, being instead an
encomium on the scientific genius of Bede. It is the
only one of the four works mentioned by Bale that we can
confirm as Byrhtferth's own.

Some of the mystery surrounding the three remaining
works can be cleared up by looking at Bale's sources.
The main source for his discussion of Byrhtferth was De
Scriptoribus Britannicis, a literary history by Bale's
contemporary and friend John Leland.[11] Most of Bale's
article on Byrhtferth was quoted directly from Leland,
who praised the monk of Ramsey's works at some length,
but specifically mentioned only one, namely a commentary
on Bede's De Natura Rerum. Leland's De Scriptoribus was
based largely on material that he had gathered in the
course of extensive travels throughout England and later
compiled in his De Rebus Britannicis Collectanea.[12] If
Bale had seen this work, he did not use it in his discussion of Byrhtferth. One of the antiquities Leland described in his Collectanea was a scientific anthology
then in the possession of the antiquary Robert Talbot and
now preserved as St. John's College, Oxford, MS 17.[13] It
contained Byrhtferth's Epilogus and his well-known diagram of the physical and physiological fours. It also
contained Bede's scientific works with marginal commentaries very different from those printed by Herwagen, and
a lavish calendar. About these works Leland said,
"Videtur (quamvis pro certo affirmare non ausim) hoc
calendarium à Bryghtferdo fuisse scriptum. Ita enim
illius commentario in librum Bedae de natura rerum ad-
haeret, sed sine authoris nomine. Quisquis scripsit non
indocte scripsit."[14] The text of De Natura Rerum in St.
John's 17 is in fragmentary condition, and of course so
is the marginal commentary. We cannot tell whether the
manuscript was mutilated before or after Leland saw it;[15]
but in its present condition it contains no evidence that
Byrhtferth was the author of the commentaries on Bede

that it contains. In fact, evidence of style and subject
matter suggests that Byrhtferth may have written some of
these glosses, but Leland, who knew only Byrhtferth's
Epilogus and diagram, could hardly have recognized such
indications of authorship.[16] Thus, unless there was an
attribution to Byrhtferth in the missing section of the
manuscript he examined, Leland's own attribution was little more than a guess. And while Leland noted Byrhtferth's signed Epilogus and diagram in his Collectanea,
he mentioned only the glosses in his De Scriptoribus,
which he based on the Collectanea. The distorted picture
of Byrhtferth's canon presented by Leland is reflected in
Bale's Scriptorum Illustrium.

We are fortunate in having a notebook that Bale kept
while he was preparing his Scriptorum Illustrium.[17] In
it we find that he used two works that he erroneously
ascribed to one "Boston of Bury." The first was a
Catalogus Scriptorum Ecclesiae actually written by Henry
of Kirkstede, a fourteenth-century monk of Bury St.
Edmunds,[18] and the second was a tract on the history of
monasticism whose title Bale reported as De Prima
Monachorum Institutione.[19] From Bale's notebook we
learn that it was from "Boston" that he got his reference
to Byrhtferth's Epilogus, which Herwagen mistakenly
thought to be a commentary on De Temporum Ratione.[20]
Also from "Boston" Bale took the information that Byrhtferth lived in the time of Abbo of Fleury, and accordingly assigned him a floruit date of about 980, which is
somewhat early. Abbo was at Ramsey for two years beginning in 986; Byrhtferth was his pupil, and so it is a
safe assumption that he did not begin to write until some
time later. His Encheiridion was written in the year
1011.[21] Nevertheless, the Cambridge History of English
Literature follows Bale in stating that Byrhtferth wrote
around the year 980, a date that would make him something
of a child prodigy.[22]

Perhaps the most interesting thing to be learned from
Bale's notebook is the origin of his reference to
Byrhtferth's "lost" treatise, De Institutione Monachorum.
At the very bottom of the entry on Byrhtferth in the
notebook are the words Ex Institutione Monachorum, an
acknowledgment of Bale's use of the work he attributed
to "Boston of Bury," De Prima Monachorum Institutione.
But when Bale compiled his literary history, he took this
reference to be the title of yet another work by Byrhtferth. Thus he ascribed to that author a work not only
that he did not write, but that never existed.

I have now mentioned three of the four works that Bale ascribed to Byrhtferth; we have seen that two of these three ascriptions were erroneous--a poor record by any standard--and that Herwagen misunderstood the third. The fourth text mentioned by Bale, De Principiis Mathematicis, is more difficult to explain as an error, for although we know of no such work by Byrhtferth, we also have no evidence to explain how Bale could have introduced the title in error. But I am hesitant to conclude that Bale saw such a work, simply because there is otherwise not the slightest indication that he ever examined at first hand any work by Byrhtferth. While we cannot state conclusively that no such work existed, it seems likely, since Bale's attributions are elsewhere reliably unreliable, that his reference to this work is due to some untraced confusion in his notes.

In this little saga of the commentaries on Bede, it is impossible to identify a single villain. John Leland was guilty of ignoring in his De Scriptoribus Byrhtferth's signed works that he earlier had taken careful note of. John Bale was guilty of relying wholly on secondary sources without examining the manuscripts themselves. He was also extremely careless in using the work of others and even his own notes. John Herwagen was guilty of rashly assuming Byrhtferth to be the author of the commentaries in his possession--an assumption based only on his impression that Byrhtferth was the author of similar commentaries. What is most surprising, however, is the way in which later, even modern, scholars accepted unquestioningly this network of error by Renaissance writers and trusted naively that Herwagen's attributions had been based on medieval authority. In this way, as Samuel Johnson once observed, "Many things which are false are transmitted from book to book, and gain credit in the world."[23]

Not much about the life of St. Dunstan needs to be said. It was ascribed to Byrhtferth by Jean Mabillon in his great collection of saints' lives, Acta Sanctorum Ordinis S. Benedicti, published 1668-1701.[24] The evidence for Mabillon's ascription was simply that the life was signed with the initial "B"--Byrhtferth had lived around Dunstan's time and had been acquainted with Abbo of Fleury, who in turn had been acquainted with Dunstan. Such slight evidence requires little exertion to disprove. The life was halfheartedly accepted as Byrhtferth's by various scholars until it was rejected by William Stubbs in 1874.[25] Paradoxically, however, Stubbs argued that the life was written in a far more flamboyant style than the commentaries on Bede, which he, like so many before

him, unquestioningly (and mistakenly) accepted as Byrhtferth's. But Mabillon's unhappy conjecture will not be
resurrected either by the fact that Byrhtferth did not
write the commentaries, or by the fact that the life of
Dunstan, like Byrhtferth's genuine works, is written in
the flamboyant and turgid "hermeneutic" style so popular
in the tenth and early eleventh centuries; for the
available evidence suggests that the life was written at
Canterbury, not at Ramsey.[26]

In view of the many profound contributions of the
Renaissance scholars to the study of Anglo-Saxon, digging
up and exposing the errors of the distant past may seem
invidious. But even after a mistake has been corrected,
it is often interesting and instructive to see how it
came about. Even as we honor these sixteenth- and
seventeenth-century scholars for their achievements, we
ought to remind ourselves that they were not infallible.
Just as modern scholars occasionally scramble their file
cards or mistake another scholar's idle conjecture for an
established fact, so too did our Renaissance precursors
commit occasional blunders. In view of the conditions
under which they worked, it is surprising that they did
not blunder more often. When these men made mistakes,
it was as often as not for want of the accumulation of
scholarly tools that we now take for granted; and yet
oddly enough, as the case of the Byrhtferth ascriptions
clearly shows, it is our very dependence on these tools,
the fruits of past scholarship, that makes us liable to
perpetuate the errors of our illustrious Renaissance
forebears.[27]

Notes

1.   Samuel J. Crawford, ed., Byrhtferth's Manual, Early
   English Text Society, vol. 177 (1929; reprinted
   London: Oxford University Press, 1966); George F.
   Forsey, ed., "Byrhtferth's Preface," Speculum 3 (1928):
   505-22. In his introductory remarks Forsey attempted,
   without much success, to determine the origin of the
   ascription of the commentaries on Bede to Byrhtferth.
2.   John Herwagen (d. 1564), ed., Opera Bedae Venera-
   bilis Presbyteri, Anglosaxonis: Viri in Divinis atque
   Humanis Literis Exercitatissimi: Omnia in Octo Tomos
   Distincta (Basel: Herwagen, 1563), 2:1-173. The two
   detached chapters (1:164-84) have the titles De Loquela
   per Gestum Digitorum, et Temporum Ratione and De
   Ratione Unciarum; see Charles W. Jones, "The Byrhtferth
   Glosses," Medium Ævum 7 (1938): 85-86. The glosses
   were reprinted in PL, 90:188-518.

3. For example, John Pits (1560-1616), Ioannis Pitsei . . . Relationum Historicarum de Rebus Anglicis Tomus Primus (Paris: Thierry and Cramoisy, 1619), pp. 177-78; Thomas Tanner (1674-1735), Bibliotheca Britannico-Hibernica: sive, de Scriptoribus, qui in Anglia, Scotia, et Hibernia ad Saeculi xvii Initium Floruerunt (London: G. Bowyer, 1748), p. 125; Max Manitius, Geschichte der lateinischen Literatur des Mittelalters (Munich: Beck, 1911-31), 2:699-706; Peter Hunter Blair, An Introduction to Anglo-Saxon England, 2d ed. (Cambridge: Cambridge University Press, 1977), p. 359.

4. Karl M. Classen, Über das Leben und die Schriften Byrhtferðs, eines angelsächsischen Gelehrten und Schriftstellers um das Jahr 1000 (Dresden: Teubner, 1896), pp. 9-18.

5. Forsey, "Byrhtferth's Preface," pp. 513-16.

6. Robert Steele, Modern Language Review 26 (1931): 351.

7. Jones, "The Byrhtferth Glosses," pp. 81-97; Jones, Bedae Pseudepigrapha (Ithaca, N.Y.: Cornell University Press, 1939), pp. 21-38.

8. Jones, "The Byrhtferth Glosses," pp. 94-97.

9. Jones, Bedae Pseudepigrapha, p. 14.

10. John Bale (1495-1563), Scriptorum Illustriū Maioris Brytanniae, quam nunc Angliam & Scotiam Vocant: Catalogus (Basel: Oporinum, 1557-59), 1:138. An earlier edition appeared under the title Illustrium Maioris Britanniae Scriptorum, hoc est, Angliae, Cambriae, ac Scotiae Summariū (Wesel: Plateanus, 1548), but this edition contained no discussion of Byrhtferth.

11. John Leland (ca. 1503-1552), Commentarii de Scriptoribus Britannicis, ed. Anthony Hall (Oxford: Oxford University Press, 1709), 1:171.

12. Joannis Lelandi Antiquarii de Rebus Britannicis Collectanea, ed. Thomas Hearne, 2d ed. (London: Richardson, 1770), 4:97.

13. For the identity of the two MSS, see N. R. Ker, "Membra Disiecta," British Museum Quarterly 12 (1937-38): 131-32.

14. Hearne, ed., Collectanea, 4:97.

15. The codex was for a time in the possession of Robert Cotton (1571-1631), mutilator of many manuscripts, who removed a part of the chronicle that formed a part of it (Ker, "Membra Disiecta," pp. 131-32). Perhaps it is to Cotton that we owe the loss of a portion of the text of De Natura Rerum.

16. I have discussed the possibility of Byrhtferth's authorship of the glosses in my "Byrhtferth's Encheiridion and the Computus in Oxford, St. John's College 17," Anglo-Saxon England 10 (1981), 126, n. 19.

17. Reginald Lane Poole, ed., Index Britanniae Scriptorum quos ex Variis Bibliothecis non Parvo Labore Collegit Ioannes Baleus, cum aliis. John Bale's Index of British and other Writers, Anecdota Oxoniensia, Medieval and Modern Series, no. 9 (Oxford: Clarendon Press, 1902), pp. 49-50.

18. See Richard H. Rouse, "Bostonus Buriensis and the Author of the Catalogus Scriptorum Ecclesiae," Speculum 41 (1966): 471-99. The Catalogus was printed in the preface of Tanner's Bibliotheca Britannico-Hibernica, pp. xvii-xliii. "Bostonus" was actually the name of a scribe who supplied a colophon at some stage in the textual history of the Catalogus.

19. This is the same tract as "Joannis Bostoni Speculum Coenobitarum," a version of which was printed by Anthony Hall in Nicolai Triveti Annalium Continuatio (Oxford: Oxford University Press, 1722), pp. 157-92. See Rouse, "Bostonus Buriensis," p. 473 and n. 7.

20. The Catalogus entry reads as follows (Tanner, Bibliotheca Britannico-Hibernica, p. xxx): "Birdferthus monachus Ramesiae floruit A.C. . . . et scripsit Super librum Bedae de temporibus, lib. 1. Pr. Spiraculo. 82." Spiraculo is the first word of Byrhtferth's Epilogus; the number 82 indicates that the MS was at Bury St. Edmunds. St. John's College 17 was apparently at Thorney or at Oxford in the late Middle Ages (Ker, "Membra Disiecta," 131-32), so the MS here described has presumably been lost.

21. For the date of the Encheiridion, see Classen, Über das Leben, pp. 18-19.

22. John S. Westlake, "From Alfred to the Conquest," in The Cambridge History of English Literature, ed. A. W. Ward and A. R. Waller (New York: Putnam, 1907-33), 1:145.

23. G. B. Hill and L. F. Powell, eds., Boswell's Life of Johnson (Oxford: Oxford University Press, 1934-50), 3:55.

24. Luc d'Achery (1609-85) and Jean Mabillon (1632-1707), eds., Acta Sanctorum Ordinis S. Benedicti in Saeculorum Classes Distributa, 2d ed., 9 vols. (Venice: Coleti and Bettinelli, 1733-38), 7 (saec. 5): 639-40. The first edition had been published in Paris. Luc d'Achery collected the lives and Jean Mabillon supplied the editorial matter, including the discussion of the "B" life of Dunstan, which was not, however, printed in the collection.

25. Memorials of St. Dunstan, Archbishop of Canterbury, Rolls Series (London: Longman, 1874), pp. xviii-xxii. Stubbs printed the life on pp. 3-52.

26. See Michael Lapidge, "The Hermeneutic Style in Tenth-Century Anglo-Latin Literature," Anglo-Saxon England 4 (1975): 82.
27. Twentieth-century scholars have carried on the task of determining the extent of the Byrhtferth canon. Samuel J. Crawford attributed the Vita S. Oswaldi in MS Cotton Nero E. i. to Byrhtferth; see his "Byrhtferth of Ramsey and the Anonymous Life of St. Oswald," in Speculum Religionis, ed. F. C. Burkitt (Oxford: Clarendon Press, 1929), pp. 99-111. Michael Lapidge, in two articles, "The Hermeneutic Style," pp. 90-94, and "Byrhtferth and the Vita S. Ecgwini," Mediaeval Studies 41 (1979): 331-53, confirms Crawford's discovery and adds to the canon the Vita S. Ecgwini found in the same MS with the Vita S. Oswaldi. Lapidge also has shown that Byrhtferth was a historian as well as a hagiographer; see his "Byrhtferth of Ramsey and the Early Sections of the Historia Regum Attributed to Symeon of Durham," forthcoming in Anglo-Saxon England 10 (1981). In The Old English Illustrated Hexateuch, ed. C. R. Dodwell and P. A. M. Clemoes, Early English Manuscripts in Facsimile, vol. 18 (Copenhagen: Rosenkilde and Bagger, 1974), pp. 42-53, Clemoes suggests that Byrhtferth was probably responsible for portions of the Old English Hexateuch and for the Old English version of the Penitential of Halitgar of Cambrai. I have disputed Clemoes's attributions and suggested the addition of several minor Old English texts to the Byrhtferth canon; see my article, "The Old English Canon of Byrhtferth of Ramsey," Speculum 55 (1980): 22-37.

The Recovery of the Anglo-Saxon Lexicon

M. Sue Hetherington

During the reigns of Elizabeth I, James I, and
Charles I, titled Englishmen patronized the early schol-
ars of Old English and encouraged the first lexicograph-
ers to compile dictionaries of that language. William
Cecil, Elizabeth's chief secretary of state, assisted
Laurence Nowell, the first known lexicographer of Old
English, for the benefit of the realm; Archbishop Matthew
Parker assigned his Latin secretary, John Joscelyn, to
work with Anglo-Saxon for the sake of the Anglican church;
Sir Robert Bruce Cotton and Sir Henry Spelman enlarged
their spheres of influence through the Society of Antiquaries and assisted a number of students of Old English,
among them Sir William Dugdale and Sir Simonds d'Ewes.
Yet it was William Somner, whose work had to be financed
by subscription and by the heirs of Cotton and Spelman,
who finally brought his work to publication.

The connections among these lexicographers and their
patrons make the early history of Old English lexicography a continuous chain whose links, neither identical nor
equal, reveal the individual strengths and weaknesses of
their makers. The dictionaries that these men produced
reveal the continuity of their work and the readiness of
each scholar to make available to successors the results
of his labors.

The first patron of Old English lexicography, William
Cecil, became master of the court of wards for Elizabeth
in 1561, and he employed Laurence Nowell as tutor of one
of his wards a year or two later. Nowell spent much time
at Cecil's home in London not only tutoring a young earl
but also studying and transcribing Cecil's Anglo-Saxon
manuscripts, which include a copy of Bede's History, an
Anglo-Saxon chronicle, homilies, a psalter, and laws.

Nowell, as well as Cecil, was particularly interested in the old laws. He may have been a cousin of Robert Nowell of Gray's Inn, attorney for the court of wards, and he taught William Lambarde Old English when Lambarde was studying law at Lincoln's Inn.[1] As the great English jurist John Selden remarked a generation or so later, "To refer the original of our English laws to the Conquest is a huge Mistake, for they are of far more distant Date."[2] Cecil was wise to represent Elizabeth's legal system as rooted firmly in the tradition and law of centuries long before the coming of William the Conqueror.

In order to read the old manuscripts, Nowell needed a dictionary of Old English. There was none. As he studied, therefore, he began to compile his own as an aid to his work and later as an aid to his student, Lambarde, to whom he eventually left his "Vocabularium Saxonicum." Nowell found help in such works as the Anglo-Saxon psalter, with its Old English glosses to the Latin text. He also found manuscript glossaries, compilations of Latin and Old English glosses taken from whatever manuscripts the early monastic compilers had in their libraries. Another significant aid was Ælfric's Grammar, written near the end of the tenth century to teach Latin to young Anglo-Saxons. (Of the extant manuscripts of that grammar, Nowell's entry-words attributed to Ælfric seem most closely derived from MS 154 at St. John's College, Oxford.[3]) At length he compiled his "Vocabularium," although it remained unpublished for almost four hundred years.[4] When Nowell went abroad in 1567 to continue his study of languages on the Continent, it was unique, the only vocabulary of Old English and Modern English in existence and an indispensable tool to William Lambarde, who at Nowell's urging was preparing an edition of Anglo-Saxon laws. Lambarde published the laws under the title of Archaionomia the following year. Shortly thereafter he probably lent either the "Vocabularium" or some of Nowell's word-lists, or both, to John Joscelyn.

While William Cecil was the man to whom Elizabeth entrusted the affairs of state, Matthew Parker was her choice for the spiritual leadership of England. The archbishop of Canterbury, seeking support for the tenets of the Anglican Church, gathered as many Anglo-Saxon manuscripts as he could--more manuscripts, in fact, than Cecil owned. He established a scriptorium at Lambeth Palace and directed Joscelyn and others of his staff in preparing some of the texts, with Modern English translations, for publication. Joscelyn eventually found it necessary, as Nowell had, to compile his own dictionary of Old English. He further prepared an Old English grammar (which has since been lost, although its index, written by Parker's son John, survives).[5]

Joscelyn had three advantages over Nowell. First, he had Nowell as a predecessor, whereas Nowell had none. Second, Joscelyn had his employer's son, John Parker, to help him as a scribe in copying entries from Joscelyn's word-lists into the dictionary itself. Third, he had more Old English manuscripts to work with than did Nowell or Lambarde. As a result, Joscelyn's dictionary is considerably larger than Nowell's, with 612 folios in its two volumes, in contrast to Nowell's 179 folios. Under the letter A, for example, Joscelyn has about six times as many entries as Nowell. We can positively identify some 35 to 40 manuscripts that Joscelyn used, and we know that Parker's collection contained a number of others that he may have used as well. The Appendix below indicates some of the sources that he read: Ælfric, Lambarde's A Perambulation of Kent, the Benedictine Rule, and Nowell's "Vocabularium." He collected from these and his other sources as many definitions of a word as he could find. In his entry for dædbote, for instance, he provides a different gloss from each of three sources. The dictionary gives far more information than Nowell's does about the sources used, and the definitions are on the whole less anecdotal. (See, however, John Parker's comment on cycenan.)

Yet the treatment of entries is not consistent throughout the dictionary, a fact that can hardly be due to ignorance of technique on Joscelyn's part. As a classical scholar he must have known good examples of lexicographical method, such as Calepine's great Latin Dictionarium, which dealt systematically with grammatical information and citations. Joscelyn's contemporaries included the Estiennes in France and Bishop Thomas Cooper in England, who were developing the techniques of lexicography in their Latin-French and Latin-English dictionaries. On the other hand, Joscelyn was working, as Nowell had been, with an almost unknown language. He could not attempt phonology, and he did not take chances with etymology. The earlier sections of his "Dictionarium" show that he knew the value of source-citations and examples; the later sections, entered by John Parker, show that the younger Parker did not record information as faithfully as Joscelyn himself did, thus accounting for at least some of the inconsistencies.

Nevertheless, the "Dictionarium" was a great contribution to scholarship in its considerable enlargement of the recorded and defined vocabulary of Old English. Later

lexicographers consulted the work; Continental scholars
came to England to transcribe it; and Sir Simonds D'Ewes
in the next century prepared to publish the "Dictionarium"
in toto with some additions of his own. Archbishop Parker
had planned to publish both Joscelyn's dictionary and his
grammar, "that ingenious men might be the more willing to
engage in the study of this language,"[6] but the idea
perished with Parker's death in 1575. Joscelyn nevertheless continued to study old English manuscripts, probably
until the time of his own death in 1603.

During the last quarter of the sixteenth century, the
older generation of English antiquaries, such as Lambarde
and Joscelyn, encountered and cooperated with the younger
generation who were preparing for active careers in politics, law, or scholarship. The young Robert Cotton, for
instance, studied at Westminster School with William
Camden, who nourished in him a deep interest in English
history. About the time that Schoolmaster Camden published his Britannia, a group of friends began to meet
regularly to discuss their common interests, and from
these meetings emerged the Society of Antiquaries.[7]
Cotton's home and library became the regular meeting
place of the society. Cotton was a man who would readily
make the resources of his library available to others of
like interests and scholarly pursuits. At the age of
seventeen he had already acquired a notable collection
of literary and historical treasures; and it was to the
young Cotton, not to the university (where the study of
Old English had not yet begun), that Joscelyn left his
"Dictionarium" and his own Anglo-Saxon manuscripts.[8]

By 1612, Sir Henry Spelman had become so devoted to the
study of antiquities that he moved to London to be near
the library of his friend Cotton, and resided in the same
neighborhood for some twenty years. Spelman also visited
Cambridge to study Anglo-Saxon manuscripts. There he met
and encouraged Abraham Wheelock. When Spelman decided to
sponsor a lectureship in Anglo-Saxon at Cambridge, he
chose Wheelock for the post. He urged the poverty-
stricken scholar to become proficient in Old English and
to prepare an edition of Bede. Wheelock also compiled an
Old English glossary.

It was to Spelman that a friend introduced another future lexicographer, a young Warwickshire gentleman named
William Dugdale. Spelman took the promising Dugdale to
others who were at that time in London. One of them in
turn led Dugdale to Sir Christopher Hatton, who became
Dugdale's first patron. Spelman also recommended Dugdale
to Thomas Howard, the Earl of Arundel and earl marshall

of England; through this connection Dugdale was soon
appointed a herald. Spelman advised Dugdale to study
Anglo-Saxon in order to further his historical researches
and sent him a copy of the Anglo-Saxon psalter edited and
published by Spelman's son. During the Civil War, Dugdale
accompanied Charles I to Oxford; and there he compiled
the "Dictionarium Saxonicum," which he dedicated to
Hatton. Dugdale made his entries in a small, neat hand,
listing them in three columns on each side of a total of
328 large folios. His work as a herald made him probably
the first seventeenth-century Englishman to use many of
the old Anglo-Saxon charters, wills, and records of property transactions. The "Dictionarium" also contains a
few words from some Old English poetic works, which were
for the most part still impossibly difficult for contemporary Englishmen to translate. Dugdale's work contains
some errors, as do all of these early attempts, but it
also exhibits his meticulous care in transcribing and re-
cording variant forms of the same word from different
manuscripts. Dugdale's recognition of variants and the
emphasis he gives them probably constitute his major contribution to Old English lexicography.[9]

Sir Simonds D'Ewes entered both Cotton's and Spelman's
circles of Anglo-Saxon studies, although he was not entirely at home in either. He also knew Dugdale and
William Somner, and later he was acquainted with Francis
Junius. D'Ewes had a prickly, Puritanical temperament;
yet it was he who introduced modern methods to Old English lexicography.[10] He was likewise a born antiquary,
so fortunate in his inheritance that, although he studied
law after leaving Cambridge, he never had to practice for
a living. In the 1620s he began to study manuscripts in
Cotton's library, and in 1630 he met Spelman. The next
year he began to "transcribe and enlarge" what he called
a "manuscript Saxon dictionary."[11] He continued to work
intermittently on the project for a few years without
revealing his intentions to his friends. When D'Ewes
heard that the Dutch scholar Jan De Laet was working with
Old English lexicography, he then divulged his own work,
and a brisk rivalry arose between the two. Having earlier
encouraged De Laet, Spelman tried to play the peacemaker,
until De Laet died suddenly in December 1649, leaving the
field to D'Ewes.[12]

D'Ewes gave more thought to the technique of writing
entry-articles than had any other lexicographer of Old
English since Joscelyn; he also added words from new
sources to the body of collected Old English vocabulary--
as had the other lexicographers; most important, he knew
the value of combining the products of his predecessors

and the knowledge of his contemporaries in one work. He
decided that Joscelyn's dictionary, not the vocabulary
which he himself had begun years earlier, should supply
the bulk of his dictionary. Yet he faced the problem of
borrowing the manuscripts of Joscelyn's work. Sir Thomas
Cotton was less hospitable toward D'Ewes than his father
Sir Robert had been; and the Cottonian librarian who
compiled two Old English glossaries, Richard James, was
almost belligerent toward him. D'Ewes finally had to
obtain a copy of Joscelyn's dictionary by subterfuge.
After scribes made the copy, he began to add Modern
English glosses to Joscelyn's Latin ones, to supply
cross-references, and to make separate entries for a
number of variant forms. He also had a scribe copy the
manuscript of Ælfric's Grammar in the Cambridge University Library and included it in his first volume preceding the main part of the dictionary.

D'Ewes originally wanted for himself all the glory of
publishing an Old English dictionary; but as time passed
and he became aware of the unexpected competition of De
Laet, he realized the magnitude of the task and the un-
likelihood of accomplishing it by himself. He finally
enlisted the aid of the two most able Old English students in his day, Somner and Junius. Earlier Junius had
been keeper of the library of Thomas Howard and tutor to
Howard's son. Now pursuing his own interests, Junius
visited D'Ewes's home in 1648 and again in 1649 to glean
words for his philological collections from the Anglo-
Saxon manuscripts that D'Ewes owned. In return Junius
helped D'Ewes collate his copy of Ælfric's Grammar with
other manuscripts. Junius also collected for his own
glossaries Old English words and their meanings from a
Royal Library manuscript of the Liber Scintillarum. He
apparently let D'Ewes use some of these words, for they
were added to the manuscript of D'Ewes's dictionary in
the hand of Somner.

D'Ewes's "Dictionarium" contains entries that cite
seventeen sources beyond those used by Joscelyn. The
percentage of new entry-words added to Joscelyn's dictionary from Anglo-Saxon manuscripts, however, is small
compared to the total number of words added. The reason
is that most of the "new" words came from earlier Old
English dictionaries--those of Nowell, Dugdale, and
Richard James. Dugdale had lent D'Ewes his own dictionary; Nowell's "Vocabularium" and the James glossaries
were lent by their current owner, John Selden.[13] D'Ewes
was thus using the method employed for centuries by lexicographers of other languages, incorporating into his own
dictionary all of the previous work that was available

and useful. D'Ewes had begun negotiations for publication when death prevented the completion of his work, as
it had that of his rival De Laet. With D'Ewes's death,
the hope of students of Old English for the publication
of a dictionary fell upon the willing and capable William
Somner.

Somner was not a university man, but he was nevertheless a scholar with practical experience in the preparation of glossaries for publication before he undertook
his Dictionarium Saxonico-Latino-Anglicum (Oxford, 1659).
His diligence as a clerk and later as registrar in the
ecclesiastical court of Canterbury won the approval of
Archbishop William Laud, who encouraged his study of
church law and legal tradition. In his early thirties
Somner became a friend of Meric Casaubon, son of the
European scholar Isaac Casaubon. He also met Junius at
least by the time that he and Junius had stayed in
D'Ewes's home while helping with D'Ewes's dictionary.
Laud, Casaubon, and Junius possibly account for Somner's
broader approach to language studies; perhaps the changing times also had their influence. Somner was much more
aware of continental scholarship than any of his predecessors, save Spelman; and he applied his knowledge
wisely. He set himself to work on an Old High German
glossary for a small volume which Casaubon published in
1650. Moreover, he prepared a more extensive glossary
for Roger Twysden's anthology of ten medieval historians.
After D'Ewes's death, Somner began work on his own dictionary of Old English.

Somner had no idea of the number of hapax legomena in
surviving Old English texts; he thought that the several
manuscripts that he examined probably contained the whole
of the Old English lexicon. If he had not been so de-
ceived, he might never have published. His preface tells
us that his work with a manuscript of medical material
and with the so-called Caedmon manuscript was particularly difficult. Junius, who had just published the latter (now Bodleian Library, MS Junius 11) probably helped
Somner with it in the last year or two before the Dictionarium went to press. Like D'Ewes, Somner took many
entries from his predecessors, but he also tried to improve them. Like Nowell, he used contemporary Latin-
English dictionaries for English definitions. Like
Dugdale, he treated dialectal variants with respect.
Unfortunately, he did not as a rule identify his source
manuscripts unless to blame them for what he considered
questionable entry-words or definitions.

Somner relied heavily on the observations of contemporary grammarians in matters of pronunciation and spelling which he cited frequently. He also provided for his reader the rules of grammar from Wheelock's edition of Bede. At the end of his dictionary he appended a copy of Ælfric's Grammar and a reproduction of Ælfric's Glossary extant in the Netherlands.[14] The transcript of that glossary had come to Somner by way of Junius; it was only one of many gifts that made Somner's dictionary possible. The university press at Oxford had Anglo-Saxon type cast of the proper size for printing the work. Friends, of whom Dugdale seems to have been the chief promoter, sought public and private subscriptions to help pay the cost of publication. Part of the benefits that Spelman had established for the Anglo-Saxon lectureship at Cambridge were diverted, after Wheelock's death, to help support Somner while he worked on his dictionary. Sir Thomas Cotton entertained Somner for months in his house and, of course, opened his library to him.

Somner's is not a scholar's or a theorist's dictionary, but a practical, student's dictionary. It is the product of his years of experience and scholarship--but not of his alone. Rather, it is the accumulation of generations of scholarship, of men who toiled patiently with remarkably difficult manuscripts and who generously transmitted their own work, one to another, in order to recover the literary and historical treasures of their ancient countrymen.

Appendix

Excerpts from some of the manuscript dictionaries show how the early lexicographers of Old English used the entries of their predecessors. Somner, the last cited below, shortened the entry for maðu written by Nowell approximately a century earlier but retained Nowell's wording. D'Ewes picked up entries from both Joscelyn's and Dugdale's work, expanding Dugdale's. Somner picked up D'Ewes's entry beowyrt to expand it with material from a Cottonian glossary and from contemporary Latin and English dictionaries.

MS Selden Supra 63, Laurence Nowell's "Vocabularium Saxonicum"

"Maðu. Cymex. A kinde of stinking woorme that biteth men in their beddes as fleas doo. We have presently none of them in Englonde & therfore they have none Englisshe name. The French calleth them punais, the Italians cimci . . ."

MSS Cotton Titus A. xv and xvi, John Joscelyn's "Dictio-
narium Saxonico-Latinum"
    "beddige. sterno ælf. 54." [I lie down. Ælfric's
    Grammar, folio 54]
    "Cycenan, a kitchin if ye believe Lambert, in his
    peramb. p. 300" [Lambarde, "A Perambulation of Kent,"
    manuscript copy]
    "Dædbote. Foem. gen. Patientia. Ælf. Satisfactio.
    Reg. Ben. [Benedictine Rule] Poenitentia. Laur."
    [Laurence Nowell]
MS Dugdale 29, Sir William Dugdale's "Dictionarium
Saxonicum"
    "bedda a wife"
MSS Harley 8 and 9, Sir Simonds D'Ewes' "Dictionarium
Citeriorum Saeculorum Anglo-Saxonico-Latinum . . ."
    "bedda. uxor. a wife."
    "beddige. sterno. ælf. 54. to lie downe on a bedd."
    "Beowyrt, apiastrum, an hearb wherwith bees are
    greatlie delighted."
    "Dædbote. Foem. gen. Patientia. Ælf. Satisfactio.
    Reg. Ben. Poenitentia. Laur."
MS Cotton Cleopatra A. iii (published in Thomas Wright
and Richard Paul Wülcker, Anglo-Saxon and Old English
Vocabularies, 2d ed. (1884: reprinted Darmstadt:
Wissenschaftliche Buchgesellschaft, 1968)
    "Apiastrum, beowyrt" (I, col. 267)
    "Marubium hune, oððe beowyrt" (I, col. 443)
Cooper, Thomas. Thesaurus Linguae Romanae & Britannicae
(London, 1584)
    "Apiastrum, apiastri, Herba. Plin. Dicitur & Melisso-
    phylum. An hearbe wherein bees are greatly delite
    [sic]: Baulme or Baulme gentle . . ."
[John] Rider's Dictionarie . . . Whereunto is joyned a
Dictionarie Etymologicall . . . (London: Kingston, 1648)
    "Apiastrum, ri, n. Plin. ab apes, ut . . . herba qua
    apes delectantur. An hearbe which Bees delight in,
    Balme-gentle, or Mint."
Somner, William. Dictionarium Saxonico-Latino-Anglicum
(Oxford: William Hall, 1659)
    "Beo-wyrt. Apiastrum. balme-gentle, balme-mint: an
    herb wherewith Bees are wonderfully delighted. Mar-
    rubium. MS al. Acanthion, Achillea, Venerea."
    "Maðu. Cimex. a kind of stinking worme that biteth
    men in their beds, as fleas do: a punie, a wall-
    louse."

Notes

1. For some important refinements of what we know of
   the identity and activity of Nowell, see the recent

studies by Retha M. Warnicke, "Note on a Court of Requests Case of 1571," English Language Notes 11 (1974): 250-56, and Pamela M. Black, "Laurence Nowell's 'Disappearance' in Germany and Its Bearing on the Whereabouts of His Collectanea, 1568-1572," English Historical Review 92 (1977): 345-53.

2. David C. Douglas, English Scholars 1660-1730, 2d ed. (London: Eyre and Spottiswoode, 1951), p. 35.

3. Julius Zupitza collates several manuscripts in his edition, Ælfrics Grammatik und Glossar, Text und Varianten (1880; reprinted. Berlin: Max Niehan, 1966). For Nowell's source, however, see the study by Ronald E. Buckalew in this volume.

4. Albert H. Marckwardt, ed., Laurence Nowell's "Vocabularium Saxonicum," University of Michigan Publications in Language and Literature, vol. 25 (Ann Arbor: University of Michigan Press, 1952).

5. For a detailed analysis of the sources used by Joscelyn and the other early lexicographers, see James L. Rosier, "The Sources of John Joscelyn's Old English-Latin Dictionary," Anglia 78 (1960): 28-39; "Lexicographical Genealogy in Old English," Journal of English and Germanic Philology 65 (1966): 295-302; Albert H. Marckwardt, "The Sources of Laurence Nowell's Vocabularium Saxonicum," Studies in Philology 45 (1948): 21-36; and "Nowell's Vocabularium Saxonicum and Somner's Dictionarium," Philological Quarterly 26 (1947): 345-51.

6. John Strype, The Life and Acts of Matthew Parker (Oxford: Clarendon Press, 1821), 2:514.

7. See Joan Evans, History of the Society of Antiquaries (Oxford: Oxford University Press, 1956), pp. 6-8.

8. See C. E. Wright, "The Dispersal of the Monastic Libraries and the Beginnings of Anglo-Saxon Studies. Matthew Parker and His Circle: A Preliminary Study," Transactions of the Cambridge Bibliographical Society 1 (1949-53): 208-37.

9. My own examination of the "Dictionarium" supports this conclusion by J. A. W. Bennett, "The History of Old English and Old Norse Studies in England from the Time of Francis Junius till the End of the Eighteenth Century" (Ph.D. diss., Merton College, Oxford, 1938), p. 360. See also David Yerkes, "Dugdale's Dictionary and Somner's Dictionarium," English Language Notes 14 (1976): 110-12.

10. See M. S. Hetherington, "Sir Simonds D'Ewes and Method in Old English Lexicography," Texas Studies in Literature and Language 17 (1975): 75-92.

11. James O. Halliwell, The Autobiography and Corre-
     spondence of Sir Simonds D'Ewes, Bart., during the
     Reigns of James I and Charles I (London: Richard
     Bentley, 1845), 2:4.
12. See B. J. Timmer, "De Laet's Anglo-Saxon Dictio-
     nary," Neophilologus 41 (1957): 199-202.
13. Bennett, "The History," p. 359.
14. The Grammar is now British Library MS Royal 15 B
     XXII, and Junius's transcript of the Glossary is
     Bodleian Library MS Junius 71. The original, now
     Plantin-Moretus Museum MS 47 and British Library MS
     Add. 32246, is not the glossary that is included in
     some of the manuscripts of Ælfric's Grammar.
15. A more extensive discussion of the Old English dic-
     tionaries and glossaries mentioned herein, of their
     sources and relationships, as well as a discussion of
     two continental Old English dictionaries, appears in
     my monograph, The Beginnings of Old English Lexicog-
     raphy (Austin, Texas: By the Author, 1980).

The Saxonists' Influence on Seventeenth-Century English Literature

Sandra A. Glass

Saxonists in the early seventeenth century generally knew of the historical, ecclesiastical, and antiquarian explorations of their sixteenth-century predecessors. They understood the political and religious impetus to Saxon studies that the Tudor scholars had provided, and they increasingly realized the bounty of manuscript sources which these scholars had preserved and made accessible. The Tudors, however, had transmitted no especial pride in their country's Anglo-Saxon heritage. Admiration of their British or other non-Saxon forebears persisted, and as late as 1597 Richard Harvey even wrote of the Saxons, "Let them lye in dead forgetfulnesse like stones."[1] It was left to the scholars and authors of the Stuart era to generate the true literary impact of the Anglo-Saxon revival--to favor Saxon themes or characters in their writings, to assert the propriety of the native language, and to alter critical assessments of earlier English authors.

Two works in particular, both published in 1605, profoundly affected the scholarly and popular attitudes of seventeenth-century Englishmen toward the Anglo-Saxons. These were the first editions of William Camden's Remaines of a Greater Worke[2] and Richard Verstegan's A Restitution of Decayed Intelligence.[3] Presenting "remaines" of the country's entire past, Camden paid unprecedented tribute to the Saxons in his spirited description of their era. In his account of the conversion to Christianity, for example, the Saxons are almost seraphic:

> This warlike, victorious, stiffe, stowt,
> and rigorous nation, after it had as it
> were taken roote heere about one hundred
> and sixtie yeares, and spread his branches

91

> farre and wide, being mellowed and mollified
> by the mildenes of the soyle and sweete aire,
> was prepared in fulness of time for the
> first spirituall blessing of God. . . .
>
> (<u>Remaines</u>, p. 9)

There is no mention of the Saxons' entry into England as
barbarian conquerors. Rather, they are commended for
erecting monuments "to the glory of God" and for carrying
the Christian faith to the Continent in the eighth century.

Richard Verstegan, also known as Richard Rowlands, a
Dutch Catholic who had studied at Oxford in the mid-
sixteenth century, focused more specifically on the task
of restoring the Anglo-Saxons to their rightful role as
noble English progenitors. Verstegan asserted that
Englishmen had no need to claim an ancient heritage from
the Britons, for their Saxon ancestors had been even more
valiant. Using Bede as his chief source, Verstegan described the migration of the Saxons from Germany, their
establishment of organized kingdoms, and their acceptance
of Christianity. He minimized aggression and internal
strife and portrayed civilized, pious, literate Saxons,
who "buylded colleges and schooles for the encrease of
learning" (<u>Restitution</u>, p. 146). After the publication
of Verstegan's popular work, which went through eight
editions by 1673, few references appeared in prose or
poetry to brutish, war-loving, pagan Saxons. Moreover,
the Stuart kings became eager to acknowledge their Saxon
ancestors. Verstegan dedicated <u>Restitution</u> to King
James, "considering that your Majestie is descended of
the chiefest blood royall of our ancient English-Saxon
kings." Such praise continued into the reign of Charles
I and culminated in 1634 with a small volume by Robert
Powell containing brief biographies of King Alfred and
King Charles, "a paire of Peerelesse Princes, who
[possessed] religion, piety, devotion, institution and
renovation of good lawes, government, justice, mercy,
truth, meeknesse, temperance, patience, abstinence, con-
jugall castimony. . . ."[4] Powell's encomium to Charles I
is no landmark of Saxon scholarship. Indeed, he seemed
barely aware that Alfred was an Anglo-Saxon ruler. Yet
the impact of the Saxon revival is attested in Powell's
selection of Alfred as a model ancestor and not, for
example, King Arthur, William the Conqueror, or Edward
III.

The broad scope of the seventeenth-century authors'
appreciation of their Saxon heritage may stem in part
from the awareness of Royalists and Parliamentarians,

Anglicans and Puritans alike, that political and religious appeals to the Saxon past continued to be important. Moreover, up to and during the Civil Wars, scholars continued to correspond and exchange materials across
ideological lines. Archbishop Ussher, for example, maintained his correspondence with Sir Robert Cotton and John
Selden; Cotton himself opened his magnificent collections
to the scholarly public and liberally sent materials to
politicians, lawyers, and clergymen.[5] Pride in one's
Saxon ancestry was important and useful for urging one's
fellows either to discover the origins of the true
church or to cast off the Norman Yoke.

The consummate literary expression of this pride appears in Michael Drayton's Poly-Olbion.[6] Drayton has in
fact been called a poetical Camden, since the descriptive
plan of his work, as well as its content, was greatly
influenced by the Britannia. He also knew Stow and
Lambarde personally. Realizing that his complex weaving
of sources might require explication, Drayton invited
John Selden to add annotations explaining historical
allusions to the reader. The notes reveal not only
Selden's immense knowledge of early English history but
also the difference between Drayton's acceptance and use
of Geoffrey of Monmouth's accounts of British lore and
Selden's rejection of these early legends. Selden con-
cedes, however, that these stories are appropriate for
poetry. He tolerantly observes that Drayton is only part
historian and part "chorographicall poet." Therefore,
says Selden in his preface, he must "insert oft, out of
the British story, what I importune you not to credit."[7]
As for descriptions of the Saxons, both the poet and the
historian agree that their complimentary sources (chiefly
Camden) are reliable. Hardy heroism predominates in
Poly-Olbion:

> These noble Saxons were a Nation hard and
>   strong,
> On sundry Lands and Seas, in warfare nuzzled
>   long;
> Affliction throughly knew; and in proud
>   Fortunes spight,
> Even in the jawes of Death had dar'd her
>   utmost might:
> Who under Hengist first, and Horsa, theer
>   brave Chiefes,
> From Germany arriv'd, and with the strong
>   reliefes
> Of th'Angles and the Jutes. . . .
>   (11.179-85)

Drayton goes on to trace the coming of Christianity during the reign of "Good Ethelbert of Kent," and then describes the establishment of the heptarchy and the eventual unification of the isle. He even includes an apology
for the pagan Saxons who despite some wicked, barbarous
deeds should be forgiven:

> A people from their first bent naturally to
>   spoyle,
> That crueltie with them from their beginning
>   brought.
> Yet when the Christian fayth in them had
>   thoroughly wrought,
> Of any in the world no story shall us tell,
> Which did the Saxon race in pious deeds
>   excell.
>
> (11.388-92)

Drayton also stresses the value of a unified nation. In
the fourth song:

> England and Wales strive, in this Song,
> To whether, Lundy doth belong . . .
> The Britaines, with the Harpe and Crowd:
> The English, both with still and loud.
> The Britaines chaunt King Arthurs glory:
> The English sing their Saxons storie.
>
> (4.Argument)

After both the British and the English nymphs present
their cases for superiority, which include hereditary
right to rule and testimony of national prowess, the wise
Severn River pronounces the judgment that Lundy is "like
ally'd to Wales and England," for under King James
"three sever'd Realmes in one shall firmlie stand"
(5.39-80). There is no longer a national imperative to
stress Tudor-British superiority; and, since Anglo-Saxons
have been granted national recognition, there is no reason that they should continue their ancient struggle with
the Britons. Drayton can take pride in all elements of
England's past.

Although no other poet of the early seventeenth century described the Anglo-Saxons in as much detail as
Drayton, other authors included Saxon rulers and events
in historical poems or alluded to Saxon matters, which
their readers presumably understood. In 1621 William
Slatyer devoted one of the ten odes in his History of
Great Britanie to the Saxons, describing each kingdom of
the heptarchy and including a two-page genealogical
chart.[8] Slatyer acknowledged that the Saxons had come

as conquerors, forcing the Britons to retreat, but he
considered the invasion salutary:

> Brave warriours hither came.
>   Whose mightie stocke,
>   Like Hydra bud,
>   So hugh a flocke
>   Of Saxon Brood;
>   That Brytanie bends
>   To th'Pagan force . . .
>   When Welshmen faene,
>   Fly into Wales
>   Leave Albion's faere
>   The best parts free
>   To th'Foe, to reare
>   The Heptarchye;
>   Which flourisht long with fame
> Till Egberts warre-like force
> Brought all to one; and England names,
> Faere speede to th'honoured Saxon Horse.
>
> (Ode 7)

Thomas Deloney also included an account of Anglo-Saxon
valor in one of his ballad collections entitled "The
Valiant Courage and Policie of the Kentishmen with Long
Tayles, whereby They Kept Their Ancient Lawes and Cus-
tomes, Which William the Conquerer Sought to Take from
Them."[9] The Saxons rally and attack William's troops
with the cry:

> Let vs not liue like bondmen poore
>   to Frenchmen in their pride,
> But keepe our ancient liberties,
>   what chance so ear betide:
> And rather die in bloudie field
>   in manlike courage prest:
> Then to endure the seruile yoake,
>   which we so much detest.

Poetically depicting the theory of the Norman Yoke,
Deloney added that after the conquest William granted the
Kentishmen the right to keep King Edward's laws.[10]

John Milton, of course, is the most famous seventeenth-
century author to write about the Anglo-Saxons. He did
not, however, immortalize the Saxons in his poetry. Sig-
nificantly, Milton never wrote his proposed Arthurian
epic. He did make notes of possible subjects for thirty-
three tragedies drawn from early English history, and he
suggested that King Alfred might be an appropriate

subject for an heroic poem, especially in his attacks on
the Danes, for his "actions are wel like those of
Ulysses."[11]

Milton's interest in the Saxons may have originated
during his school days. The classical curriculum at St.
Paul's School made no formal provisions for the study
of English history; but when Milton was in school
(ca. 1617-24) the high master was Alexander Gil, whose
many interests included English history, topography, and
the development of the English language.[12] In 1619 Gil
published his Logonomia Anglica, which analyzed the history, changes, and present condition of the English language.[13] Although this work may never have been used as
a school text, the students would certainly have seen it
and may have read portions of the preface, which traced
the history of the English race and language and included
an account of the dignity and respectability of the
Saxons. After Milton left Cambridge in 1632, he read
widely in ancient and modern history. When he returned
from Italy in 1639, he concentrated on learning as much
as possible about early English history. In his Common-
place Book he included numerous entries from Bede,
Gildas, William of Malmesbury, Henry of Huntingdon,
Holinshed, Stow, Speed, Lambarde, and Sir Thomas Smith.
He also became especially familiar with such seventeenth-
century historians as Camden, Selden, Spelman, and Ussher,
whose works he used in preparing the History of Britain.[14]

Major sources of Milton's information about the Saxons
were the publications of Abraham Wheelock, the oriental-
ist and lecturer in Arabic at Cambridge and the first
incumbent of the university lectureship in Anglo-Saxon.
In 1643 Wheelock published an edition of Bede's Ecclesiastical History--the first edition of the Latin text
printed in England and the first edition of the Anglo-
Saxon version; the volume also contained the first edition of the Anglo-Saxon Chronicle.[15] Although more than
half of Milton's History of Britain concerns the Anglo-
Saxon period, Milton did not consider himself a Saxon
specialist. He had not studied Old English as a pre-
requisite for writing the History, and he relied on
Wheelock's Latin texts. Milton even disparaged antiquaries "who take pleasure to be all thir life time, rakeing
in the Foundations of old Abbies and Cathedrals."[16] Yet
he freely drew upon their findings. His literary fascination with dramatic, tragic, or romantic events in Saxon
history is also evident in the History. For example, the
account of the conversion of King Edwin is packed with
circumstantial details and includes a description of
Paulinus's miraculous revelation, though Milton admits

that the account is "savouring much of Legend."[17] Even
when Milton doubted the historicity of an event, he included it in the History for its narrative interest.
Among such passages are a mention of King Osbert's rav-
ishing of the nobleman Bruern's wife and descriptions of
the amorous adventures of King Edgar--which Milton admits
are "fitter for a Novel then a History."[18]

In 1655 Francis Junius published in Amsterdam and sent
to England copies of his edition of Cædmon's paraphrase
(as he called it) of Genesis.[19] Junius had received the
manuscript from Archbishop Ussher about 1651. If it
could be shown conclusively that the Cædmonian poems had
influenced Milton's composition of Paradise Lost, either
directly or indirectly, the impact of the Anglo-Saxon revival upon seventeenth-century letters would be far more
conspicuous. Scholars in the late nineteenth and early
twentieth centuries felt that Milton and Junius might
have met or might even have become friends in London during the 1640s; in 1947 Julius W. Lever printed portions
of letters written by Junius's nephew Isaac Vossius which
indicate that Junius was indeed acquainted with Milton.
In a letter of 1651 to Nicholas Neinsius in Leiden,
Vossius states, "De Miltono iam certior factus sum ab
avunculo meo Junio, qui cum eo familiaritatem colit." On
the strength of this remark Lever concludes that Junius
and Milton were close acquaintances and that the Cædmonian Genesis certainly influenced Paradise Lost[20]--a conclusion which others might regard as overconfident. It
is more reasonable to maintain that Milton probably knew
Junius and that the two may have discussed the Cædmonian
poems. It is also possible that Milton learned something
about the contents of the poems from other English scholars after they were published. At any rate, information
about Old English poems of the Creation and the Fall was
certainly circulating in England when Milton was writing
Paradise Lost; such information may well have been a part
of Milton's great store of knowledge.

Saxon themes appealed also to a number of seventeenth-
century dramatists. There survive approximately a dozen
plays written between 1550 and 1755 that treat themes of
Saxon history or involve Saxon characters. The plays,
generally based on material found in the chronicles, include tragedies, comedies, and romances. None of the
playwrights was a Saxonist, though several of them apparently studied British and Saxon history closely. A
few representative examples are of especial interest for
our survey.

Thomas Middleton, writing at the time of Drayton, completed Hengist, King of Kent between 1616 and 1620.21 He based the play on the alliance between Hengist and Vortigern and described the downfall of both. The play ends with the defeat and execution of Hengist by Aurelius and Uther, who stress the evils of Saxon paganism. It is important to note, however, that Middleton and his audience, who might have been familiar with the work of Verstegan, could view the downfall of Vortigern as the first stage in the rise of the Saxons in England. As Hengist exhorts when preparing to attack Vortigern, "Deere Saxons fasten we now, and our unshaken firmnesse will assure after ages."

In 1617 Anthony Brewer wrote a drama of a much different kind, The Love-sick King, an English Tragical History: with the Life and Death of Cartesmunda, the Fair Nun of Winchester.22 The "love-sick king" is Canute, who is struggling with Edmund Ironside for the English throne in the early eleventh century. Brewer anachronistically included King Alfred in the play as one of Canute's opponents.

Among several other plays featuring prominent Saxon figures is Thomas Rymer's Edgar, or The English Monarch: an Heroick Tragedy, written in 1677 and published the following year.23 The play is a classical tragedy whose primary purpose is to exalt the virtues of monarchy. It is dedicated to Charles II, who is compared with the noble Edgar, especially as a peacemaker. At the end of the play a nobleman addresses Edgar, just as Rymer might have spoken to Charles, "Kings their Just Rights to know from you shall gain, / And those Just Rights, a courage to maintain." Rymer was thirty-six years old when he wrote these lines in his only drama, and his years of medieval scholarship still lay ahead of him. Of all the dramatists of his era who used Saxon themes or subjects, he surely had the most comprehensive knowledge of medieval history and law; yet his play had the least dramatic success.

In deference to other essays in this collection on early grammarians and lexicographers of Old English, I shall refrain here from discussing in detail the impact that their work had on the use of language and on Restoration and eighteenth-century literature. It should be stressed, however, that the makers of lexicons and grammars established the view that the Saxons' language was worthy of study along with the classical languages. Likewise, historians and critics reaffirmed the sixteenth-century acceptance of Modern English as "an excellent

language" and believed that this excellence of the language derived in great part from its Saxon origins. As
Camden said in the <u>Remaines</u>, "Great verily was the glory
of our tongues before the Norman Conquest, in this, that
the old English could expresse most aptly, all the conceits of the minde in their own tongue without borrowing
from any" (p. 18). And Verstegan, whose <u>Restitution</u> included a 32-page Saxon glossary, added this vocabulary to
indicate not merely the Anglo-Saxons' contribution to
modern English, but the Saxons' extensive, sophisticated
language.

In his preface to <u>A Saxon Treatise Concerning the Old</u>
<u>and New Testament</u> by Ælfric, the Anglican scholar William
L'Isle expressed the highest praise for the English language. Although much of L'Isle's hostility toward borrowed words or inkhorn terms came from his antipathy
toward Catholic translators of the Bible, his desire to
revive the study of Old English and to exalt the modern
tongue extended beyond his wish to preserve religious
documents. He asserted that the English language, which
had grown out of the Anglo-Saxon, had become a language
excellent for every kind of communication--"for what
tongue is able more shortly and with lesse doubtfulnesse,
to give utterance and make way for the cumbersome conceits
of our minde than ours?"[24] Echoing Verstegan, L'Isle continued, "Thankes be to God that he that conquered the
Land could not so conquer the Language. . . ."[25] L'Isle
thus applied the historians' feelings of anti-Normanism
to his assessment of the language and even asserted that
his contemporaries had a moral obligation to study Old
English: "I conclude then with the point of honour, what
more concerneth us in honour, then to avoid disgrace?
but sure to neglect the beginnings of such an excellent
tongue, will bring upon us the foule disgrace not onely
of ignorance . . . but of extreme ingratitude toward our
famous ancestors."[26]

When sixteenth-century writers honored "ancient"
English poets, they usually meant Chaucer, Gower, or
Langland; but after Verstegan had distinguished between
the language of "our Saxon ancestors" and that of the
Norman conquerors, critics became aware of the stages in
historical linguistic development and began to favor elements in prose and poetry which they felt more closely
resembled Anglo-Saxon.

One of the first elements to achieve a new respectability in literature was the often-disdained English
monosyllable. Verstegan pointed out that the Saxons had
used monosyllables to great poetic effect, often combining

them--two or three together--into new words of more di-
versity of sense and signification.[27] Alexander Gil accepted this theory and applied it to contemporary usage;
he asserted that modern English could be enriched not
only by using words of Saxon origin, but also by employing the techniques of word combination first practiced by
erudite ancestors.[28] Other critics also began to urge
the acceptance of the monosyllable in poetry, although
some poets still maintained that it was not adaptable to
classical metrical feet. Thomas Campion, for example,
claimed that monosyllables were "so loaded with consonants, as that they will hardly keepe company with swift
notes, or give the vowell convenient liberty."[29] Taking
the other side of the issue in his Defence of Ryme,
Samuel Daniel argued eloquently for the use of rhyming
monosyllables.[30] Though he erred in his perception of
Anglo-Saxon rhymed verse, Daniel knew the importance of
citing Saxon precedent to justify contemporary usage.
George Chapman, in his preface to the works of Homer,
also encouraged the use of monosyllabic rhyme: "Our
Monosyllables, so kindly fall / And meete, opposed in
rime, as they did kisse. . . .[31] Sir John Beaumont,
brother of the dramatist, had equal esteem for the sound
of the simple word:

> The relish of the Muse consists in rime,
> One verse must meete another like a chime.
> Our Saxon shortnesse hath peculiar grace
> In choise of words, fit for the ending
>   place,
> Which leaue impression in the mind as well
> As closing sounds, or some delightful
>   bell.[32]

To my knowledge the ultimate possibility in the use of
monosyllables--sustained verse of one-syllable words only
--was achieved only once during this period: in 1620
William Loe, pastor of the English Church in Hamburg,
published a small volume of biblical paraphrases to be
used by the English-speaking community as prayers, songs,
and meditations.[33] Loe attempted in his simple expression to emulate what he felt were the pure forms of wor-
ship of his early English ancestors. So should men pray
who "seeke, and serve God in sincerity without hipocrisie
or faction." Contrast, for example, a passage in the
Authorized Version of the Song of Solomon (7.1),

> How beautiful are thy feet with shoes, O
>   princes daughter!
> The joints of thy thighs are like jewels,
> The work of the hands of a cunning workman,

with Loe's rendering:

> Her feet are sweet, her gate a grace
>> All shod with Peace and Truth,
> Of gods own spell to runne the race
>> From bane, and woe, and ruth.
>
> Her loynes are girt fast with the fame,
>> The price of it is rare.
> The skill is framd with hand of might
>> And full of cost, and care.
>> > (Songs of Sion, p. 151)

No contemporary reactions to Loe's volume have survived. We should perhaps be grateful that he remained well removed from the literary mainstream of seventeenth-century England.

Many historians and critics proposed a compromise between using the original Saxon vocabulary and terms from other languages, especially if they were intended to enrich the English language. Camden and L'Isle fell into this more liberal group. Yet other critics, siding with Verstegan and Gil, remained steadfast against borrowing and now found themselves censuring the poet who had formerly been revered for his synthesis of the best features of Saxon, French, Italian, and classical languages into superior English poetry--Chaucer. The best Verstegan could say was that he respected Chaucer "as an excellent poet for his tyme."[34] Alexander Gil was the harshest of all in his condemnation of Chaucer and those who admired him: "Tandem circa annum 1400, Galfridus Chaucerus, infausto omine, vocabulis Gallicis, & Latinis poesin suam famosam reddidit. Hic enim vulgi indocti stupor est, ut illa maximè quae non intelligit admiretur."[35] Some of this antipathy persisted into the Restoration; authors such as Stephen Skinner continued to censure both Chaucer and the borrowing.[36] The critical climate had indeed changed since Spenser had described Chaucer as the "well of English undefyled, On Fames eternall beadroll worthie to be fyled." And it was the Saxonists who accomplished this change of taste.

One could perhaps conclude that the impact of Saxon studies upon language awareness and language usage was greater than its impact as a source of themes for poets and dramatists. In either case, seventeenth-century authors did not yet have the poetic texts of Hickes and Wanley, and few of those who were not Saxonists knew the works of Junius or Somner. Certainly, that such a spirit of confidence in Saxon ancestry could develop and prevail is noteworthy. This spirit emerged in part from the wide circulation of Camden and Verstegan and confidence in their accuracy; it also came from the fact that authors were at least acquainted with the Saxonists, even if they did not read their writings. Samuel Pepys, for example, consulted Wanley about sources of early works.[37] Wanley tried to date and identify more than thirty manuscript fragments belonging to Pepys and pointed out for him some specimens of Anglo-Saxon handwriting. Sir Thomas Browne, another non-Saxonist, revealed his scientific and historical interest in England's past in his correspondence with Dugdale, seeking information on burial mounds and drainage, checking references in Leland to Saxon burials, and forwarding to Dugdale skeletons of fish he had unearthed.[38] That Browne--a man of such diverse interests in antiquities, language, and the influence of the past on his own time--was knowledgeable about the work of the Saxonists illustrates the influence these scholars had upon the educated populace of England in the seventeenth century. Although there was no Miltonian epic of Alfred, no Jonsonian drama about the evils of Penda of Mercia, a sense of indebtedness to the Anglo-Saxon heritage pervaded many aspects of literary culture, because the Saxonists were influential in the mainstream of seventeenth-century political, religious, and literary thought in which they flourished.

Notes

1. Richard Harvey, Philadelphus, or a Defence of Brutes, and the Brutans History (London: J. Wolfe, 1593), p. 97.
2. William Camden, Remaines of a Greater Worke, Concerning Britaine, the Inhabitants Thereof, Their Languages, Names, Surnames, Empreses, Wise Speeches, Poësies, and Epitaphes (London: Waterson, 1605).
3. Richard Verstegan, A Restitution of Decayed Intelligence: In Antiquities Concerning the Most Noble and Renowmed English Nation (Antwerp: Bruney, 1605).
4. Robert Powell, The Life of Alfred, or Alured: the First Institutor of Subordinate Government in This Kingdome, and Refounder of the University of Oxford, Together with a Parallel of Our Soveraigne Lord, K. Charles untill This Yeare (London: Badger, 1634), pp. 151-52.
5. See Henry Ellis, ed., Original Letters of Eminent Literary Men of the Sixteenth, Seventeenth, and Eighteenth Centuries, Camden Society Publications, vol. 23 (London: Nichols and Son, 1843), pp. 131-34, 138-39. On Cotton's library and its use by contemporary

scholars, see C. E. Wright, "The Elizabethan Society of Antiquaries and the Formation of the Cottonian Library," The English Library before 1700, ed. Francis Wormald and C. E. Wright (London: Athlone Press, 1958), pp. 191-208. Loan lists in Cotton's hand survive in several MSS of ca. 1606-1621; see esp. MS Harley 6018.

6. London, 1612 and 1622; Michael Drayton, The Works of Michael Drayton, ed. J. William Hebel (Oxford: Blackwell, 1931-41), vol. 4.
7. John Selden, "From the Author of the Illustrations," prefaced to Poly-Olbion, p. x.
8. William Slatyer, The History of Great Britanie from the First Peopling of This Iland to This Presant Raigne of Our Happy and Peacefull Monarke K. James; or Palae-Albion (London: Stansby, 1621).
9. This is the first poem in Thomas Deloney's Strange Histories, of Kings, Princes, Dukes, Earles, Lords, Ladies, Knights, and Gentlemen (1602) in The Works of Thomas Deloney, ed. Francis Oscar Mann (Oxford: Clarendon Press, 1912), pp. 381-416.
10. Deloney also included the tale of one Saxon ruler in his Garland of Good Will (ca. 1593) in The Works, pp. 295-380; but in this tale, "How King Edgar Was Deceiued of His Love," it was irrelevant that Edgar was an Anglo-Saxon.
11. The notes in Milton's hand are found on pp. 35-41 of his Notebook in MS Cambridge, Trinity College, R.3.4 (583) in The Works of John Milton, ed. Frank Allen Patterson et al. (New York: Columbia University Press, 1931-38), 18:228-45.
12. See Donald Lemen Clark, John Milton at St. Paul's School (New York: Columbia University Press, 1948), pp. 69-77; "Milton's Schoolmasters: Alexander Gil and His Son Alexander," Huntington Library Quarterly 9 (1946): 129-33; Harris F. Fletcher, The Intellectual Development of John Milton (Urbana: University of Illinois Press, 1956-61), 1:169-76, 185-87; and Thomas A. Carnicelli, "Milton's Knowledge of the Anglo-Saxon Period," A Milton Encyclopedia, ed. William B. Hunter, Jr., et al. (Lewisburg, Penna.: Bucknell University Press, 1978-), 1:51-53.
13. Alexander Gil, Logonomia Anglica (London: J. Beale, 1619).
14. See James Holly Hanford, "The Chronology of Milton's Private Studies," PMLA 36 (1921): 251-314.
15. Historiae Ecclesiasticae Gentis Anglorum Libri V a Venerabili Beda Presbytero Scripti Tribus Praecipue MSS. Latinis, à Mendis Haud Paucis Repurgati, ed. Abraham Wheelock (Cambridge: Roger Daniel, 1643).

16. Milton, History of Britain in The Works, 10:180.
17. Ibid., p. 155. In like manner Milton recounted the
    legendary tales of early Britain in the first book of
    the History. He drew much of his material from
    Geoffrey of Monmouth, whom he nevertheless considered
    untrustworthy. Milton concluded, "I have therefore
    determin'd to bestow the telling over ev'n of these
    reputed Tales; be it for nothing else but in favour of
    our English Poets, and Rhetoricians, who by thir Art
    will know, how to use them judiciously" (p. 3).
18. Ibid., pp. 207, 245-48.
19. Caedmonis Monachi Paraphrasis Poetica Genesios ac
    Praecipuarum Sacrae Paginae Historiarum, abhinc Annos
    MLXX, ed. Francis Junius (Amsterdam: Cunrod, 1655).
20. "Paradise Lost and the Anglo-Saxon Tradition,"
    Review of English Studies 23 (1947): 97-106.
21. First printed in 1661; Thomas Middleton, Hengist,
    King of Kent, ed. R. C. Bald (New York: Scribner's,
    1938). Bald believes that this play may be based on
    an earlier work, now lost, called Hengist or
    Vortigern. See also Richard H. Barker, Thomas
    Middleton (New York: Columbia University Press,
    1958), pp. 116-21, and Irving Ribner, The English
    History Play in the Age of Shakespeare, rev. ed.
    (New York: Barnes and Noble, 1965), pp. 259-61.
22. First printed in 1655, in Materialien zur Kunde
    des älteren englischen Dramas, vol. 18, ed. A. E. H.
    Swaen (1907; reprinted Vaduz: Kraus, 1963). See
    also M. Hope Dodds, "Edmond Ironside and the Love-Sick
    King," Modern Language Review 19 (1924): 158-68.
23. Printed in London in 1678, 1691, and 1693. Rymer
    was never able to arrange a stage production of his
    tragedy. See David Douglas, English Scholars 1660-
    1730 (London: Eyre and Spottiswoode, 1951), p. 223,
    and Roberta F. Brinkley, Arthurian Legend in the
    Seventeenth Century (Baltimore: Johns Hopkins Univer-
    sity Press, 1932), p. 116.
24. William L'Isle, ed., A Saxon Treatise Concerning
    the Old and New Testament (London: Haviland, 1623),
    sig. e3v.
25. Ibid., sig. fv.
26. Ibid., sig. f3.
27. Verstegan, Restitution, p. 189. Verstegan repeated
    this idea of combining syllables in his chapter on
    Anglo-Saxon proper names, pp. 242-43, saying that
    names were made up of "composed woords."
28. Yet Gil, like Camden, did not find monosyllables
    suitable for poetry, for he believed that they tended
    to clog metrical movement.

29. Thomas Campion, "Two Bookes of Ayres," The Works of
     Thomas Campion, ed. Walter R. Davis (New York:
     Doublday, 1967), pp. 55-56.
30. Samuel Daniel, A Defence of Ryme, against a Pam-
     phlet Entituled: Observations in the Art of English
     Poesie in The Complete Works in Verse and Prose, ed.
     Alexander B. Grosart (1885-96; reprinted New York,
     1963), 4:29-67. Observations was written by Campion
     in 1602 (Works, pp. 291-317). To Campion, classical
     civilization, as well as classical poetry, represented
     perfection. Saxons were merely a barbarian tribe.
31. George Chapman, "Preface," The Whole Works of Homer
     (London: N. Butler, 1616).
32. Sir John Beaumont, "To His Late Majesty, Concerning
     the True Forme of English Poetry," in The Poems of Sir
     John Beaumont, ed. Alexander B. Grosart (Blackburn:
     Tiplady, 1869).
33. William Loe, Songs of Sion (Hamburg: privately
     printed, 1620).
34. Verstegan, Restitution, pp. 203-04.
35. Gil, Logonomia Anglica, sig. Bv.
36. Stephen Skinner, Etymologicon Linguae Anglicanae,
     2d ed. (London: Brome, 1671).
37. See the letter from Wanley to Pepys, dated 25 June
     1699, in Ellis, ed., Original Letters, pp. 272-82.
38. Sir Thomas Browne, The Works of Sir Thomas Browne,
     ed. Geoffrey Keynes. rev. ed. (Chicago: University
     of Chicago Press, 1964), 4:299-327.

The Elstobs and the End of the Saxon Revival

Sarah H. Collins

Historians have for some time pointed to the development of knowledge about Anglo-Saxon literature in the
sixteenth and seventeenth centuries, to the mixed motives
for the growth of scholarship on the native past, and to
the solid accomplishment of the major scholars. Even
more notable achievements were part of the eighteenth
century, but much less is known about them. In the first
two decades of that century twelve books containing
Anglo-Saxon were printed in England--twelve books, that
is, which made more than sporadic use of Old English
words. This seemingly modest total, it must first be
noted, is more than twice the number of such books published in the last two decades of the seventeenth century.[1] But the number of published works alone does
little more than suggest the quality of the careful and
extensive efforts at this time. In addition to published
works, several significant manuscripts were prepared during the period 1700-1720; though never published, they
are crucial to an evaluation of the accomplishment of
early eighteenth-century scholarship on Anglo-Saxon
England. The quality of preparation of some of these
manuscripts exceeds that of most of the printed books
and indicates a maturity of Anglo-Saxon scholarship which
was unequaled until the nineteenth century. I wish to
underline the achievement of early eighteenth-century
Saxon scholarship by discussion some unpublished manuscripts of two important scholars of the period, Elizabeth
and William Elstob, sister and brother. The circumstances
in which they produced three particularly important manuscripts, their futile efforts to get them published, and
some of the implications of their failure are all significant for an understanding of this important period of
scholarship.

William Elstob (b. 1673), a member of Queen's College, was granted the Oxford baccalaureate in 1694 and two years later became a fellow of University College, where he remained until early in 1703. During this time, Queen's College and University College were the principal centers of Old English studies, and William became a regular contributor to projects undertaken or sponsored there. Many of his jobs were piece work for larger efforts, such as his Latin translation of Sermo Lupi or his contribution to Andrew Fountaine's essay on Anglo-Saxon coins, both published in Hickes's Thesaurus.[2] But he also prepared an edition of the Alfredian translation of Orosius with the encouragement of George Hickes and Edward Thwaites. An edition of Orosius had been desired for some time. Thomas Marshall, rector of Lincoln College, Oxford, had collated the Junius transcript of the Cotton Orosius (MS Cotton Tiberius B. I.) with the British Library Add. MS 47967 between 1668 and 1685. To this transcript Marshall had later added copious notes. For a time in 1698, the Orosius project was considered by Thwaites, then dean of Queen's College, probably at the instigation of Hickes, a friend and pupil of Marshall and a teacher of Thwaites. In the press of other studies, Thwaites dropped the project and William Elstob took it up. The easy sharing and collaboration was more the rule than not among these scholars. Proposals for the Elstob Orosius were issued, and a title page and two leaves were printed in 1699.[3] It was not to be published, however, until 1773 when Daines Barrington had it printed at his own expense.[4] The text, with variant readings and notes, remained in William's possession until his death in 1715. He did not have the money to bear the expense of publication himself and, as a newly appointed fellow of University College, he lacked the powerful backing of patron or institution for his work. Nevertheless, when support for the publication failed to materialize, William continued to perfect the edition from time to time between work on other projects.

In 1703 William moved to London as minister of St. Swithin's and St. Mary Bothaw. His sister Elizabeth (b. 1683) joined him here as his housekeeper. As he taught her Greek, Latin, Old English, and other Germanic languages, she became first his assistant and then his colleague in Septentrional endeavors. She described the Orosius edition and their other projects to Ralph Thoresby in March, 1709:

> He [William] has many things to do, if he
> had leisure and encouragement; King Alfred's
> Orosius, he had ready for the press, and a

great many materials towards the Saxon Laws,
and a promise of more. He would be glad to
publish Gregory's Pastoral, after the
Homily, and being a University College Man,
would willingly publish all that King
Alfred did. I continue my resolution concerning the Saxon Psalms, which I set about
as soon as possible after the Homily is
done.[5]

These two scholars were constantly at work: transcribing, translating, editing manuscripts. Whether completed work was published or not, the next project was at
hand. William set to a splendid edition of the laws
while Elizabeth was planning a major edition of Ælfrician
homilies as soon as her edition of Ælfric's Homily on the
Birthday of St. Gregory was sent to subscribers. When
William's carefully constructed manuscript for the
Orosius edition was published, seventy-four years later,
Barrington, the final editor, placed sufficient trust in
Elstob's work that he managed only a casual comparison of
Elstob's manuscript with the Junius transcript and virtually no check against the Cotton Orosius. Barrington's
confidence was not ill-placed, as it turns out, but his
cavalier announcements of his own editorial practice
serve only to underline the impressive scholarly virtues
of his predecessor. William Elstob's manuscript edition
of Orosius, later bought by John Ames, still later sold
to Samuel Pegge and lent by him to Barrington for publication, was mute witness, at least for many decades, to
Elstob's careful but unrewarded research.[6]

Elstob's edition of laws that Elizabeth refers to in
the Thoresby letter of 1709 is the second of these three
important manuscripts. William proposed to reedit the
Old English laws first published by Lambarde in 1568 and
revised by Wheelock in 1644.[7] He planned to add the
previously unpublished laws in the "Textus Roffensis" and
to translate Somner's Gavelkind into Latin; to add annotations to laws scattered in Spelman, Selden, Junius,
D'Ewes, and Hickes; to prepare a general introduction
dealing with the Norman Conquest and Magna Carta; to
write brief prefaces to the laws of each king; and to
conclude with glossaries and an index.[8] Nothing so
ambitious had yet been attempted on this subject. Certainly it was needed, for Wheelock's edition, published
more than sixty years earlier, was not widely available.
And William's edition proposed to go well beyond
Wheelock's Archaionomia.

By August 1712 William Elstob's ambitious collection
of laws was ready for the press. But encouragement was
not forthcoming.[9] William and Elizabeth lived on his
modest income as a London clergyman, and expenses of preparing an edition were necessarily great. The scholar
had to travel to Canterbury, Cambridge, and Oxford to
examine and transcribe manuscripts, or occasionally to
pay for a copyist when he was unable to go to the manuscript itself. In addition, the press often expected
the author to bear part or all of the expense of printing. That expense might be offset by advances of subscribers' pledges, but in the absence of numerous subscribers, patrons, or royal favor, the scholar of modest
means was helpless. With only £140 a year in addition to
a small stipend as the chaplain to William Nicholson,
bishop of Carlisle, Elstob could not advance large sums
of money on his publications.[10] From 1712 to 1715, he
tried repeatedly but unsuccessfully to interest printers
in his edition. He also tried to secure a better living.
Appeals to the earl of Oxford and Lord Chief Justice
Parker, both notable patrons of Anglo-Saxon learning,
brought no preferment.[11] But the work went on. When
William collated his copy of the "Textus Roffensis" with
the original when it was in London in 1712, he and his
sister also made fair copies, as did their ten-year-old
serving boy, James Smith.[12] Elizabeth made a fair copy
on vellum which she presented to the Harley library, and
it was judged by Humfrey Wanley as a fine imitation of
the distinctive Rochester hand[13]--but still no prefer-
ments came to William. The manuscript of the laws was
still unpublished at his death in March 1715. Elizabeth
continued to look for a publisher for the laws and for
some of William's other manuscripts. When she offered
his "Essay Concerning the Latin Tongue" to the book-
sellers, she recalled many years later, they "were very
willing to print it, but wou'd give nothing for the Copy,
but a few Books printed, which I think is hard . . . that
they shou'd reap the profit of other Men's Labours."[14]

Spurred by the need for a new edition of the Old English laws, David Wilkins, a protégé of the bishop of
Carlisle, was preparing his own edition of laws based on
Wheelock's Archaionomia. After William's death, Wilkins
sought to examine Elstob's manuscript. Elizabeth repeatedly put him off, encouraged by John Fortescue-Aland, who
had used William's edition while preparing a revised edition of his grandfather's Difference Between an Absolute
and Limited Monarchy. Wilkins's entreaties were seconded
at last by Bishop Nicholson. Wilkins maintained to the
bishop that he merely wanted to see some of Somner's
notes, "which I or any body else that can read Latin may

copy at Canterbury. I would fain save my eyes in such a
transcription."[15] Elizabeth finally let him see the
manuscript in 1719, but it was probably too late to help
him. The prospectus for his edition was published early
in the same year, although his edition did not appear
until 1721. Even this fully subscribed edition sponsored
by Bishop Nicholson, Wilkins later said, cost him over
£100 in expenses.[16] Thus, the financial plight of the
Elstobs must have played a large part in their inability
to publish major works which had a limited audience.
While fellow antiquaries were generous with time and en-
couragement--recall that Bishop Nicholson had made Elstob
his chaplain to enhance his income--few of them had the
means to subsidize a major work.

William Elstob's manuscript edition of Anglo-Saxon
laws, an ambitious, admired, and mature work, never saw
print even as a prospectus. His work did influence
Fortescue-Aland and perhaps also Wilkins. Indeed,
Wilkins's work could well have gained detail and accuracy
from Elstob's manuscript. Beyond Fortescue-Aland and
Wilkins, Elstob's achievement remains a vivid reminder of
what could have been, for the manuscript has been lost
since the 1720s.

An even more significant work, at least to twentieth-
century students of literature, was Elizabeth Elstob's
edition of both series of Ælfric's Catholic Homilies.
When William was first contemplating an edition of laws,
Elizabeth had determined to undertake this major work,
shortly after her edition of Ælfric's Homily on the
Birthday of St. Gregory was published in 1709. She announced to Ralph Thoresby in October, "Having nothing
else to do, I have some thought of publishing a set of
Saxon homilies, if I can get encouragement, which I believe will be very useful; the doctrine being for the
most part very orthodox."[17]

Her edition was to be the first complete edition of
Ælfric's greatest work and the first time that many of
the homilies had been edited at all. Although it was
never printed, Elizabeth's manuscript represented the
only edition of the Catholic Homilies until 1844 when
Benjamin Thorpe published his edition; and, by good for-
tune, most of her work survives as MSS Lansdowne 370-374
and Egerton 838.

By February 1710 she had borrowed "two very ancient
manuscripts from the Cottonian Library" and was transcribing homilies.[18] One of these manuscripts, British
Library Cotton Vitellius C. V (Ker 220), contained all of

111

the first series of homilies except the prefaces, and
seven items of the second series. Elizabeth's practice
was, when possible, to transcribe more than one manuscript of a text and to work toward selecting the best
readings. Between 1709 and 1714 she spent most of her
time transcribing manuscripts for this edition; at the
same time William, we must remember, was working on his
edition of the laws. Their methods were similar; frequently they used Junius's transcripts as well as original Anglo-Saxon manuscripts of the same text, a curious
practice but one which seems to have encouraged accuracy.
For example, the Creation homily in the first series was
copied by Elizabeth from a Junius transcription and then
collated with one of the three original manuscripts in
the library of Corpus Christi College, Cambridge.[19] Her
final draft was written in her characteristically clear,
fine hand on a quarto sheet with wide-ruled margins.[20]
The Old English text for the whole edition was copied on
the verso of each leaf with space in the outer margin for
reference to manuscript and page source and with space in
the lower margin for additional notes. The translation
was written on the facing recto, with space in the outer
margin for biblical references. This format represents
the final version of the proposed edition of the First
Series of homilies. It is elegantly written in imitation
of the original manuscripts, establishing a clear form
for a printed edition. The titles are done in red and
the first line and capitals are often decorated in red.
The manuscript as a whole looks like a fine copy of an
Anglo-Saxon codex.

It is possible to trace Elizabeth's progress on her
edition as she prepared the final copy for the press, for
near the end of the first series she began to date each
homily; beginning with the homily for the seventeenth
Sunday after Pentecost, she wrote the date December 12th,
1711.[21] On the basis of the intervals indicated in the
first series and those of the more hastily prepared second series which I shall discuss shortly, I estimate that
she may have begun this final copy around March 1711. It
appears that she thus spent a little over a year transcribing and collating manuscripts for this edition as
well as helping William complete his work on the laws and
transcribing miscellaneous texts, several of which survive. The press of time can also be discerned from the
manuscripts themselves. She abandoned the practice of
adding her translations on the facing rectos halfway
through the homily for Epiphany;[22] the facing rectos are
blank through the rest of the manuscript, which is now
bound in five volumes.[23] Although the translations were
no longer copied in, many had been drafted earlier on

smaller paper; and some of those are bound in Lansdowne 373.[24] The date on the last homily of the first series is Feb. 5, 1711/12.[25]

Written in the top right-hand corner of the page where the Old English preface to the second series begins is the date Feb. 12, 1711/12, but the format of the edition is now changed.[26] The second series is copied on folio sheets without space for translations. One homily begins immediately after the end of the previous one. The handwriting is still careful and beautiful; titles, first lines, and capitals are still decorated in red. This page size and the spacing may have represented Elizabeth's intention for the printed edition. Directions in a different hand are pasted onto Egerton 838, one of the quarto volumes of the first series, which read: "The spaces of the breadth of the Margents . . . though they be different in the Quarto manuscript, yet let the same spaces be observed throughout . . . as it is in the Fair Copy in folio."[27]

Although she began her final copy of the second series on February 12, she had copied in only five homilies by August 19. This first half of 1712 was largely spent seeking support for her project, including a prospectus printed in London by William Bowyer some time before the middle of March.[28] Since William's edition of the laws was ready for the press in August, much of Elizabeth's time may also have gone toward his final preparations. During this time, she and William also made fair copies of the "Textus Roffensis" as well as of several miscellaneous manuscripts in the Bodleian. Beginning on August 19, however, she moved quickly to make a fair copy of the second series of the homilies for the press, and she completed the series by November 28, 1712.[29] She must have taken her manuscript almost immediately to the Oxford press, for in December George Hickes wrote to Dr. Charlett, Master of University College:

> I suppose you have seen Mrs. Elstob . . .
> and the manuscript she hath brought to be
> printed at your press. . . . the publica-
> tion of the Manuscript she hath brought
> (the most correct I ever saw or read) will
> be of great advantage to the Church of
> England against the Papists. . . . I de-
> sire you to recommend her, and her great
> undertaking to others, for she and it are
> both very worthy to be encouraged. . . .[30]

But the hoped-for response did not materialize. William and Elizabeth returned to Oxford in February 1713, preceded by letters from Hickes to Charlett and Hearne, to stir up support for some better post for William.[31] In July Bowyer published her essay, Some Testimonies of Learned Men in Favor of the Intended Edition of the Saxon Homilies.[32] In the form of a letter to her uncle, Charles Elstob, canon of Canterbury Cathedral, Testimonies consists of quotations from Hickes, Wanley, L'Isle, Leland, Ussher, Wheelock, and Henry Wharton that demonstrate the need for an edition of Ælfric's homilies. She also defends the propriety of a woman's doing such an edition, a defense which suggests to the modern reader that the reluctance of heads of colleges in Oxford and Cambridge to subscribe was due in part to the sex of the editor.

The great patrons of Saxon learning gave little more help. Elizabeth applied to Harley to secure the Queen's bounty for her project, but with no success. She gave a fine copy on thin vellum of the "Textus Roffensis" to the Harleian Library but, with excessive modesty, failed to bring the handsome gift to Harley's attention. Hickes arranged that Harley be tactfully informed of the gift, and Elizabeth reapplied for the bounty through his offices. At Elizabeth's suggestion, Hickes sought the assistance of George Smallwood, the Queen's Almoner and bishop of Bristol. By June 1713 the queen agreed to grant the bounty with the consent of the Lord High Treasurer Harley. By the end of July, however, Harley was turned out of office, accused of corruption. Then, on August 1, Queen Anne died before she executed her intention for bounty. Weeks later there was a threat of renewed persecutions of the non-juring bishops, those who had earlier refused to recognize the legitimacy of King William. The most prominent of the non-jurors was George Hickes. Elizabeth persisted, however, in her efforts to publish the Catholic Homilies. Early in 1715 the Oxford press issued a new set of proposals and a two-page specimen of the edition. However, the final blow to the edition and to Elizabeth's career as a scholar came with the death of William in March. William had been consumptive since youth, and his death was probably expected. In December 1715 George Hickes died after a long illness. Elizabeth had announced in the 1715 proposals that the book would be in the press by Michaelmas (September 29), but only thirty-two pages of proof were actually produced, ending in mid-sentence in the fifth homily.[33]

Elizabeth, without any regular income, was now responsible for both her own debts and William's. With the

collapse of the publishing project, she was also responsible for the advance payments brought in by the 1712 and
1715 subscriptions. In a letter to Hearne in 1716,
Thomas Baker, who sold subscriptions in Cambridge, voiced
his concern that he would have to make up the unfulfilled
subscriptions out of his own pocket.[34] Baker wrote
Humfrey Wanley in 1718 that he understood Elizabeth
could pay her debts. Wanley notes on the letter, "only
a few small scores."[35] In a letter dated November 30,
1718, Baker wrote that Elizabeth "is lately gone off for
debt, for whose Saxon Homilies I was above ten pounds
deep."[36] Elizabeth left suddenly and secretly, leaving
most of her books and manuscripts with a neighbor. When
she returned later to retrieve her possessions, the
neighbor had moved, and Elizabeth never again saw the
books and manuscripts which had meant so much to her.[37]
Many of those manuscripts, including some of the letters
written by and to William and Elizabeth, may have turned
up in the sale of her Uncle Charles's library after his
death in 1721.[38] During this time William's manuscript
edition of the laws was probably lost and the manuscript
of the Catholic Homilies was jumbled and partly lost.
John Ames bought the quarto manuscripts that now comprise
Egerton 838, of which the history after 1718 is unknown
until its acquisition by the British Library.[39] The
order of the manuscript volumes is also confused. A pen-
ciled reordering of unknown date in Lansdowne 370 does
not represent a plausible Ælfrician order. What Ames
failed to get of the original manuscript were the second
through the sixth and the nineteenth through the twenty-
fifth homilies. Homilies three through six comprise
Egerton 838. The second homily and the nineteenth
through the twenty-fifth homilies were lost. Ames did
get, however, the Modern English translations of the
second through the eighth homilies on small paper, which
he bound with the prefaces and first homily to make up
Lansdowne 373.

Ames's prize was never to be published, although
Hickes's judgment that the edition was "the most correct
I ever saw or read" has been curiously borne out by the
twentieth-century editor of Ælfric, Peter Clemoes. He
has examined Elizabeth Elstob's manuscript edition of the
homilies and has told me that he found her text remarkably accurate and at least potentially helpful in determining some now difficult readings for any new edition of
the Catholic Homilies.

Elizabeth's whereabouts remained unknown until 1735,
when George Ballard, a ladies' stay maker and an inde-
fatigable antiquary, discovered her running a small

school in Evesham, Worcestershire. She ended her days as governess to the children of the Duchess of Portland, the daughter of William Harley, in whose house she died in 1756 at the age of seventy-three.

Thus, the decline of the Saxon revival was not altogether a decline in the quality or quantity of scholarship and interest; two of the chief scholars, William and Elizabeth Elstob, simply lacked financial support. Without a secure place in the university or a wealthy patron, no scholar could publish the fruits of his labor. The three manuscripts discussed here--William Elstob's edition of the Old English Orosius, his edition of the Anglo-Saxon laws, and Elizabeth's massive edition of Ælfric's homilies--represent scholarly work of a very high order which was never published. The Orosius did become the basis of Barrington's edition, but the other two remarkable works remained silent testimony to the dedication, imagination, and pioneering achievement of two of the most learned scholars of the early eighteenth century. The two seem to be harbingers of a decline of Saxon scholarship, but their frustration by poverty, ill health, and sexual prejudice cannot eclipse a proper modern appreciation of their work and its worth.

Notes

1. Eleanor N. Adams, Old English Scholarship in England from 1566-1800, Yale Studies in English, no. 55 (1917; reprinted Hamden, Conn.: Archon Books, 1970), pp. 178-80.
2. George Hickes, Linguarum Vett. Septentrionalium Grammatico-Criticus et Archaeologicus (Oxford: Oxford University Press, 1703-05).
3. Hormesta Pauli Orosii quam olim Patrio Sermone Donavit Ælfredus Magnus (Oxford: Oxford University Press, 1696); British Library MS Lansdowne 373, fols. 86-87.
4. The Anglo-Saxon Version, from the Historian Orosius by Alfred the Great, together with an English Translation from the Anglo-Saxon (London: Bowyer and Nichols, 1773).
5. Ralph Thoresby, Letters of Eminent Men (London: Colburn and Bentley, 1832), 2:163-64.
6. Samuel Pegge, note to text, Archaeologia 1 (1770): xxvii.
7. William Lambarde, Archaionomia sive de Priscis Anglorum Legibus Libri (London: John Day, 1568); Abraham Wheelock, Archaionomia sive de Priscis (Cambridge: University Press, 1644).

8. Pegge, "An Historical Account . . . of the Textus Roffensis," Bibliotheca Topographica Britannica, no. 25 (1784), D2 (p. 19); John Nichols, Literary Anecdotes of the Eighteenth Century (London: Nichols and Bentley, 1812), 4:120-21.
9. Thoresby, The Diary, ed. Joseph Hunter (London: Colburn and Bentley, 1830), 2:158.
10. Sarah H. Collins, "Elizabeth Elstob: a Biography" (Ph.D. diss., Indiana University, 1970), pp. 71-74.
11. B. L. MS Harley 3778, fol. 230; B. L. MS Stowe 985, fol. 3.
12. B. L. MS Stowe 940.
13. B. L. MS Harley 1866.
14. Oxford, Bodleian Library, MS Ballard 43, fol. 17.
15. William Nicholson, Letters on Various Subjects (London, 1809), 2:462.
16. Adams, Old English Scholarship, p. 100.
17. Thoresby, Letters of Eminent Men, 2:198-99.
18. Ibid., 2:226-27.
19. Marginal notations throughout MS Stowe 985.
20. B. L. MS Lansdowne 373 consists of the Latin and Old English prefaces and the first eight homilies of the first series.
21. B. L. MS Lansdowne 372, vol. 111v.
22. B. L. MS Egerton 838, fol. 19.
23. The correct order of the manuscripts for the first series is Lansdowne 373, Egerton 838, Lansdowne 370, Lansdowne 371, Lansdowne 372. The second series was completed in folio, without space for translations, in Lansdowne 374.
24. B. L. MS Lansdowne 373, fols. 26-50.
25. B. L. MS Lansdowne 372, fol. 243v.
26. B. L. MS Lansdowne 374, fol. 3.
27. B. L. MS Egerton 838, fol. 70.
28. It is noted in a list of books printed by Bowyer in 1712; see Nichols, Literary Anecdotes, 1:50. No copy of the proposals is extant, but William Brome reported having subscribed fifteen shillings for the homilies on March 13, 1712 (Caroline White, "Elizabeth Elstob, the Saxonist," Sharpe's London Magazine 51 [1869-70], 150).
29. B. L. MS Lansdowne 374, fol. 109v.
30. Bodleian Library MS Ballard 12, fol. 129.
31. Ibid., fol. 130; Thomas Hearne, Remarks and Collections, Oxford Historical Society Publications (Oxford: Clarendon Press, 1885-1921), 4:87.
32. B. L. Dept. of Printed Books 695.18.
33. Collins, "Elizabeth Elstob," pp. 149-52.
34. Hearne, Remarks and Collections, 5:337.
35. Notes and Queries 9 (1854), 7.
36. Hearne, Remarks and Collections, 6:255.

37. Bodleian Library MS Ballard 43, item 38.
38. Pegge, "An Historical Account . . . of the Textus
   Roffensis," C2. Pegge says that his copy of the
   Elstob transcript of the "Textus Roffensis" was bought
      from Joseph Ames, who had bought it "with the rest
      of Mr. Elstob's Saxon transcripts" from the Charles
      Elstob estate.
39. Ballard and Ames corresponded about the Elstob papers over several years. In 1747 Ballard refused as
   too expensive Ames's offer to sell the entire set of
   homilies for five guineas (MS Ballard 40, fol. 137).

The Anglo-Saxon Grammars of
George Hickes and Elizabeth Elstob

Shaun F. D. Hughes

In the introduction to his Anglo-Saxon grammar, the
Reverend Joseph Bosworth included a survey of earlier
such grammars. There he says of the fourth of these
works:

> The next Grammar, compiled from the works of
> Dr. Hickes and Mr. Thwaites, was published
> with the following title: The Rudiments of
> Grammar for the English-Saxon Tongue; first
> given in English, with an Apology for the
> Study of Northern Antiquities, being very
> useful towards the understanding our Ancient
> English Poets, and other Writers. by
> ELIZABETH ELSTOB. Small 4to. London, 1715.
> This was the first Saxon Grammar that was
> published in English.[1]

With this little statement he apparently dispatched Mrs.
Elstob's effort from his mind--which was indeed a pity.
Had Bosworth looked at her work a little more closely and
profited from its clarity of expression and arrangement,
he might have made his own grammar more useful. Despite
his claim that his grammar "is an attempt to divest the
Saxon Grammar of the useless Latin incumbrances, put upon
it by preceding writers, and to offer one formed on the
true genius and structure of the original Saxon"
(p. xxxi), it is nothing of the sort. Bosworth's
arrangement is still on a model that is clearly Latin;
although he may have stripped away some of the Latin
encumbrances of the earlier grammars--an achievement to
his work's disadvantage--he overloaded his volume with
much other extraneous material, thus warranting Thomas
Jefferson's well-known despair over the inaccessibility

of the Anglo-Saxon language.[2] Bosworth claimed (p. xxxii)
to have been influenced by the 1817 grammar of Rasmus
Kristian Rask,[3] the first Anglo-Saxon grammar recogniz-
able to a modern audience. But even the most cursory
comparison of the two works reveals that this was hardly
so. Like the grammar of Mrs. Elstob, Bosworth's is in
fact "compiled from the works of Dr. Hickes."

   Jefferson had access to the grammar of Elizabeth
Elstob (1683-1756). Had he paid more attention to it,
rather than the more "modern" grammar of Bosworth, he
would have found the prospect of Anglo-Saxon studies
anything but daunting. Her grammar cannot be lightly
dismissed as another work extracted from Hickes and
Thwaites, even though it drew heavily on them. Hickes,
after all, had written reference grammars. The first,
the Institutiones Grammaticae Anglo-Saxonicae, et Moeso-
Gothicae (Oxford: Oxford University Press, 1689), had
been followed in 1703 by an expanded and revised "Institutiones" incorporated in his encyclopedic Linguarum
Vett. Septentrionalium Thesaurus Grammatico-Criticus et
Archaeologicus, published by Oxford University Press two
years later. In 1711 Thwaites published his slim Grammatica Anglo-Saxonica ex Hickesiano Linguarum Septentrionalium Thesauro excerpta (Oxford University Press),
of whose 48 pages only about half are devoted to grammar;
much of the rest is given to dialect studies, metrics,
and other arcana. Mrs. Elstob's grammar, on the other
hand, is not only the first grammar of Anglo-Saxon in
English, but also the first grammar to be mindful of the
reader. Otherwise, not until the appearance of Henry
Sweet's An Anglo-Saxon Reader (Oxford: Clarendon Press,
1876) were such matters as inflections and syntax clearly
explained.

   Mrs. Elstob's grammar is arranged in two parts. The
first is a preface of 35 pages containing a spirited defense of the study of Germanic languages, and Anglo-Saxon
in particular, against the attacks of Charles Gildon and
John Brightland in 1712, Jonathan Swift in the same year,
and Henry Felton in 1713.[4] In her preface she also ex-
plains the approach of her 70-page grammar that follows.

> The Method I have used, is neither entirely
> new, out of a Fondness and Affection of
> Novelty: nor exactly the same with what
> has been in use, in teaching the learned
> Languages. I have retain's the old Division
> of the Parts of Speech, nor have I rejected
> the other common Terms of Grammar; I have
> only endeavour'd to explain them in such a

manner, as to hope they may be competently
understood, by those whose Education, hath
not allow'd them an Acquaintance with the
Grammars of other Languages. There is one
Addition to what your self [Dr. Hickes] and
Mr. Thwaites have done on this Subject, for
which you will, I imagine, readily pardon
me: I have given most, if not all the
Grammatical terms in true Old Saxon, from
Ælfrick's Translation of Priscian, to shew
the polite Men of our Age, that the Language of their Forefathers is neither so
barren nor barbarous as they affirm, with
equal Ignorance and Boldness.

(The Rudiments, p. iii)

Before discussing the relation of Mrs. Elstob's work
to the grammatical thought of her time and to other
Anglo-Saxon grammars, I must consider the formats of the
works from which her grammar most immediately springs.
Hickes was the first scholar to describe any of the older
Germanic dialects. But he was also an antiquary, and
thus in his 1689 grammar he included much additional material. This included a catalog of books on the northern
languages, an "Etymologicon Britannicum" compiled by
Edward Bernard, and Runólfur Jónsson's "Grammaticae
Islandicae Rudimenta," which was first published in
Copenhagen in 1651.[5] In his presentation of his grammar,
Hickes obviously had no precedents except the Latin
school grammars whose traditional approach had its roots
in the works of Donatus and Priscian.[6] Hickes depended
heavily on this approach, and he laid out his paradigms
in the traditional order with chapters for articles,
nouns, adjectives, pronouns, numerals, verbs, adverbs,
conjunctions, prepositions, and interjections. In his
grammar each section contained considerable learned commentary and the corresponding portion of the grammar of
Gothic--in addition to a mass of supplemental material.
The Anglo-Saxon paradigms are reasonably easy to follow,
although Hickes, true to his Latin model and the dictates
of contemporary thought, insisted that Anglo-Saxon have a
vocative and an ablative case like modern English in
addition to nominative, accusative, genitive, and dative.
Likewise, he presented the verbs with the full range of
tenses, moods, and voices that are a feature of Latin
grammar. Each paradigm is clearly displayed and is supported by numerous examples.

Hickes's traditional Latin-based approach proved a
problem to him in the organization of the systems of the
adjectives and the verbs, where the Germanic is radically

121

different. In Latin it presents no particular problem to
take the nouns and the adjectives together as a single
word class consisting of nouns substantive and nouns adjective. But the adjectival system of the Germanic languages, with its distinction between strong and weak (or
definite and indefinite) declensions, must be handled
differently. Hickes devised his own explanation, but he
failed to reconcile the differences; even though he was
well aware that there were other approaches to be employed, he refused to abandon familiar organizing principles. Likewise, his handling of the verbs, though
based upon latest analytical opinion, was seriously in-
adequate. His analysis of the weak or regular verbs did
not sufficiently distinguish the three subclasses; he
despaired of the strong verbs and simply considered them
all irregular. For the adjectives Hickes adopted a position similar to Bosworth's approach in 1823 when he faced
the innovations of Rask's recent grammar. The different
analysis corroborated by several authorities, including
the Icelandic grammar of Jónsson in both his Anglo-Saxon
grammars, was far too radical, far too new.[7] Hickes was
prepared to discuss Jónsson's insights, just as he was
prepared to question the applicability of the Latin mood
and voice systems, but he was not ready to reject the
traditional principles of grammatical organization. Such
a conservative approach was to have tremendous consequences for the subsequent history of Anglo-Saxon grammatical studies. Hickes's incorrect analysis of the
adjective declensions could perhaps be disregarded, for
there were other authorities whose opinions could be
drawn upon. But in view of the authority his work assumed with the grammar of 1703, his wrong analysis of the
verbs probably delayed eventual understanding of the true
character of the Germanic verb system.

The 1703 edition of the grammar is organized according
to the same principles, except that the supplemental material includes several new chapters on Anglo-Saxon dialects and poetry. In all, the 1703 grammar covers 247
folio pages, including the preface. Clearly this was not
yet a teaching grammar, a lacuna which Thwaites met with
his simplified edition in 1711. This work follows the
same grammatical principles of Hickes, with all the examples taken from the grammar of 1703. But the paradigms
are laid out in a space-saving linear fashion and thus
they forfeit the clear presentation that is a remarkably
modern feature of Hickes's own grammars.

Such is the pedigree to which Mrs. Elstob's grammar
belongs. But hers is not a slavish imitation of these
earlier works. Rather, it is an entirely new compilation

drawing on the best features of her predecessors and re-
working them in accordance with her own ideas of presentation and arrangement. In a very important sense, as
will be seen, the principal influence on Mrs. Elstob was
not Hickes, but the Anglo-Saxon churchman and scholar,
Ælfric.

In his pedagogical program, Ælfric had assembled a
Latin-Anglo-Saxon grammar based on the Institutiones
Grammaticae of Priscian and the Ars Grammatica of
Donatus,8 although he was inclined to follow the former
more closely. If Ælfric was not always consistent in the
exact form of his terms, he still provided Anglo-Saxon
with a complete technical vocabulary for grammatical
treatises in the vernacular, something not even found in
present-day English. Ælfric's grammar, together with his
Latin-Anglo-Saxon glossary, was published a half a century before Mrs. Elstob began her grammar. It had appeared as Ælfrici, abbatis sui temporis dignissimi,
grammatici vulgo dicti, Grammatica Latino-Saxonica: una
cum ejusden, Ælfrici, Glossario Latino-Saxonica in William
Somner's Dictionarium Saxonico-Latino-Anglicum (Oxford:
William Hall, 1659), the first printed dictionary of
Anglo-Saxon. Mrs. Elstob relied heavily on this edition,
not only for the Anglo-Saxon grammatical terminology, but
also for much of her presentation. This is clearly seen
in large sections of her commentary. Where there is a
difference of interpretation between Ælfric, whose out-
look is heavily influenced by Priscian, and Hickes, whose
own grammars reflect the humanist interpretation of the
grammars of Priscian and Donatus, Mrs. Elstob tends to
favor Ælfric, although she is often ambivalent.9 Her
most conspicuous debt to Hickes and Thwaites is the selection of examples in her paradigms and commentaries.
Even though she draws heavily upon the lists given in
Thwaites, she is not bound by them. Repeatedly, she re-
turns to Ælfric's grammar or Hickes's Thesaurus. Moreover, the paradigm words she uses have a long history,
some of them going back to Ælfric; Bosworth still used
them, contrary to his apparent rejection of the traditional approach.10

Mrs. Elstob opens her grammar with a brief introduction. This is entirely conventional and parallels the
opening section of Ælfric's grammar--itself based on
Donatus, or more precisely on Sergius's Explanationum in
Artem Donati (Keil, ed., Grammatici Latini, 4:486-87).
Her first section, "Of Letters," obviously follows Ælfric
very closely at times:

A Letter in Saxon stæf, is the least part of
any Book or Writing, and cannot be divided.
A Book or Writing may be divided into Words,
S. cwydas, those Words into Parts, S. dælas,
those Parts into Syllables, S. stæf gefegas,
and afterwards Syllables into stafas Letters:
Beyond this there is no farther Division.

(The Rudiments, p. 2)

This is a fairly close translation of a passage in
Ælfric's grammar:

Litera is stæf on englisc. & is se læsta dæl
on bocum. & untodæledlic: we todælað þa boc
to cwydum & siððan þa cwydas to dælum. eft
þa dælas to staf gefegum. & siððan þa stæf
gefegum [recte gefegu] to stafum. þon beoð
þa stafas untodæledlice. forþon þe nan stæf
ne bið naht. gis [recte gif] he gæð on twa.

(Somner, ed., p. 2)[11]

Mrs. Elstob then briefly introduces the alphabet and the
phonetic system. (In the system there are five vowels,
clypigendlice or sylf swegende; consonants, samod
swegende, are either semivowels or mutes.) A brief note
on the syllable, stæf gefeg, leads her to outline the
eight parts of speech: noun, nama; pronoun, naman
speliend; verb, word; participle, dælnimend; adverb,
wordes gefera; conjunction, geðeodnys or gefegincg;
preposition, foresetnys; interjection, betwux aworpennys.
In her ensuing discussion, she gives a résumé of the
various kinds of nouns according to a traditional analysis; in keeping with Ælfric, Hickes, and other grammarians of her time, she posits six cases, nominative,
nemnigendlic; genitive, gestrinendlic or geagniendlic;
dative, forgifendlic; accusative, wregendlic; vocative,
clypigendlic oððe gecygendlic; ablative, ætbredendlic.
This section is then followed by brief accounts of gender
and number.

Like Hickes, she begins her paradigms with a part of
speech she had neglected to list earlier, the article.
To those writing vernacular grammars based on a Latin
model, the article had posed a problem. Latin, of course,
has no article, a fact which both Priscian and Donatus
had noted in their outlines of the parts of speech.
Nevertheless, in his section on the pronoun, Priscian
discussed the role of the article in Greek. His conclusions in fact determined the handling of the article in
some of the early grammars of English, particularly his

conclusions about the important connection between the
Latin demonstrative pronouns hic, haec, hoc, and the
Greek articles 'ό, 'ή, 'όϛ.

The whole difficult problem of the nature and position
of the article in the vernacular grammars had resulted in
various solutions adopted by the English grammarians.[12]
Some had considered the article a distinct part of speech.
Ben Jonson tentatively admitted the article as a ninth
part of speech, although he limited his discussion to his
section on pronouns.[13] In maintaining the article as a
form of the pronoun, Jōnson followed William Lily, whose
Latin grammar had become the standard text in English
schools.[14] On the Continent, however, grammarians had
been bolder. The so-called Port-Royal Grammar, the
Grammaire générale et raisonnée (1660), records the
article as one of the parts of speech.[15] Hickes regarded
this work highly.[16] Nevertheless, Hickes's attitude
toward the article, as well as a number of other grammatical matters, was crucially influenced by Ausführliche
Arbeit von der Teutschen Haubtsprache (1663) of Justus
Georg Schottelius.[17] Observing a tradition begun a century and a half earlier by Philip Melancthon,[18] Schottelius regarded the article as a separate part of speech
in the vernacular grammar: "Das Geschlechtwort (Articulus) ist ein Wörtlein, welches in Teutscher Sprache muss
vorn gefüget, und daraus das Geschlecht des Nennwortes,
oder Mittelwortes erkant werden: Solches ist zweyerley:
Benennend, und unbennend."[19] Hickes was not so bold; he
never listed the parts of speech as Mrs. Elstob was to
do. In "De Articula," chapter 4 of his 1689 grammar, he
states "Linguae Anglosaxonica, & Gothica, vel Moeso-
Gothica ejus mater, pro genio suo, haud secus, ad Graeca,
Articulo praepositivo delectantur, qui variatus per casu
in utroque numero nominibus praefigitur. Articulus
Anglosax. se, seo, þat, ό, ή, τό significat" (Institutiones,
p. 7). But in the grammar of 1703, Hickes was not
actually prepared to recognize the article as a separate
part of speech: "De Articulo, sive pronomine demonstra-
tivo, quod grammaticorum vulgus articulum vocant defini-
tum" (p. 6).[20] Hickes in fact achieved an effective compromise between the demands of the Latinate tradition and
the realities of the vernacular grammar. He gave the
article de facto recognition as a part of speech, yet the
chapter title shows that he knew where it belonged.[21]
Mrs. Elstob was content to follow Hickes and made no comment on the methodological inconsistency that resulted
from her naming the traditional parts of speech and then
singling out the article for special treatment. She
briefly summed up the issue before giving her paradigms

for the article and listing the Greek equivalents with the nominative singular and plural of the Anglo-Saxon: "As the Greeks and other Nations have had their Articles placed before their Nouns, so the Saxon Tongue hath used hers, both with Skill and Beauty. These are naturally to be consider'd according to their Cases or Endings, before we treat of the Nouns" (The Rudiments, p. 9).

On nouns, Mrs. Elstob follows Hickes by outlining six declensions, which in modern terminology may be listed as follows: masculine a-stems; masculine weak nouns, neuter a-stems with short preceding syllables; neuter a-stems with long preceding syllables; feminine ō-stems; masculine and feminine u-stems. She follows Thwaites by adding a seventh declension, masculine and feminine a-stems in -h. This paradigm Hickes also gives in his discussion of the irregular nouns in chapter 3 of his 1703 edition. All nouns which do not fit into these seven declensions are classified as irregulars, and even in a concise grammar such as Mrs. Elstob's they make quite a list. This unsatisfactory arrangement of the nouns seems to have been developed by Hickes. Schottelius had recognized only four declensions in German: masculine, feminine, neuter, and adjective. He treated strong and weak forms as declensional variations--though not a perfect solution, this was nevertheless a far more satisfactory arrangement than the one adopted by Hickes.

Mrs. Elstob's section on the nouns ends with a discussion of compounds, especially poetic compounds. There she considers Anglo-Saxon word-formation and nominal terminations, and uses examples from the latter part of Hickes's chapter 3, "De Nomine." Poetic vocabulary suggests another opportunity to defend the northern languages from the charges of "men who talk at random, and who are altogether ignorant of the Matter" (The Rudiments, p. 13).

The next section, on adjectives, is one of the weak areas of Mrs. Elstob's grammar. Yet the treatment of adjectives had not been better in the grammar of her mentor. Even as late as 1823 Bosworth did not represent an advance over Hickes, for he failed to notice what Rask had said about the form several years earlier.[22] In the old grammar, nouns were said to be of two kinds: nouns substantive, spediglice, and nouns adjective, names gefera. As a result, the adjective in Anglo-Saxon is restricted to only one form, a misunderstanding compounded by Hickes because of the declension system he had worked out for the nouns. But Mrs. Elstob noticed that certain adjectives appeared to have an unusual form: "Several

Adjectives, besides their common Termination, receive a
final a, which generally gives somewhat of a particular
Emphasis, as, Godcund, Divine, Godcunda, very Divine, or
very Holy" (The Rudiments, p. 18). Except for the concluding translation of godcunda, this is a close translation of a passage in Thwaites: "Complura adjectiva
assumunt A prostheticum, quod utplurimum emphasin
designat; ut, godcund divinus, godcunda:" (Grammatica,
p. 6).

Both these statements attempt to reduce Hickes's preliminary remarks in the Thesaurus on this matter (chapter 4, "De Adjectivis") to a concise form; and in the
process they err in interpretation. Hickes had said,

> notandum insuper, quod adjectiva, pronomina,
> & participia cujusvis generis non rarò
> terminentur in a prostheticum, aut finalem
> suam vocalem in a mutent, & tum declinentur
> ut substantiva secundae declinationis
> exeuntia in a . . . sic à godcunde divi-
> nus, fit godcunda, ut, miò þy godcundan
> fultume forlæten wæs, divino auxilio
> destitutus erat. . . . Maximè obtinet haec
> regula in adjectivis demonstrativè,
> emphaticè, & vocandi casu positis: ut in
> sequentibus. Oswald se Cristenesta cyning
> Norþan-hymbra-rice, Oswaldus Christianissi-
> mus rex Northanhymbrorum.
>   (Thesaurus: Anglo-Saxonica, p. 17)[23]

True, Hickes himself ignored the force of maximè in a
general statement a few lines later: "Supra dixi in
reg. I. adjectiva emphatice, & demonstrative usurpata
plerumque terminare nom. sing. in a, & tum declinari, ut
substantiva II. declinationis" (Thesaurus: Anglo-
Saxonica, p. 17). Even so, Mrs. Elstob and Thwaites gave
another coloring to these remarks. Nowhere does Hickes
offer any justification for Mrs. Elstob's translation of
godcunda as "very Divine, or very Holy." Actually,
Hickes was caught in his own compromise over the role of
the article. He had followed Schottelius in treating the
article separately, but he was no longer inclined to follow Schottelius in the handling of the adjective. In
this instance Hickes refused to budge from his classical
prejudices. Thwaites and Mrs. Elstob followed suit, and
it was a long time before their misconceptions were laid
aside.

Yet had Hickes paid closer attention to Runólfur
Jónsson's Icelandic grammar, the solution would have been

clear, especially since Jónsson's observations were confirmed by Schottelius. In his chapter, "De motione
Nominum Adjectivorum," Jónsson had observed, "Haec
Adjectivorum in omni genere duplex terminatio, duplicem
cujusvis generis producit Declinationem" (Thesaurus:
Grammatica Islandica, p. 30). His arrangement of the
adjective paradigms closely followed his system set up
for the nouns in chapter 2, "De Declinationibus Nominum
Simplicum." But every adjective paradigm in chapter 4
was given both strong and weak forms. It is unfortunate
that Jónsson had no section on syntax, where he might
have explained the difference in usage between these two
forms.[24] Nor did Hickes pay any attention to Schottelius
in the matter. The latter's division of the nouns into
four declensions, which originated in Clajus's Grammatica
Germanicae Linguae of 1578, prevented him from making the
kind of taxonomical error in Hickes. He also had a far
clearer concept of the relationship between the article
and the adjective, giving paradigms of adjectives with
both forms of the article. But in his section, "Von der
Enderung des Nennwortes," he gave paradigms without
either term of the article (Opus partim, pp. 235-43). He
could hardly have made the distinction between the two
forms of the adjective any clearer:

> Was die eintzele Zahl betrift, ist es
> damit, wie mit dem vorhergehenden in allem
> bewant: Die mehrere Zahl ist überal
> gleich, wird mit dem Zusatze en gemacht,
> nemlich so oft das Geschlechtwort davorn
> stehet: Uber ohn das Geschlechtwort, wird
> es wie alhie vorgestellet, anders geändert.
> Also sagt man: gute Worte verkauffen böse
> Waare, oder: die guten Worte verkauffen
> böse Waare. Ich habe böse Tage erlebet,
> oder: ich habe die bösen Tage erlebet.
> (Ausführliche Arbeit, p. 241)

None of these other ways of regarding the adjectives interested Mrs. Elstob. She adhered to Hickes's principles
and accompanied her remarks on "emphatic adjectives" with
a section containing a long list of formative suffixes.
She concluded this part of the grammar with comments on
the comparative (wiðmetendlice) and superlative (ofer-
stigendlice) forms. Her examples are taken from chapter 4 of Hickes.

Her next section, "Of Pronouns," is straightforward,
with examples once again taken from Hickes (chapter 5,
"De Pronominibus"). Her simple, unadorned presentation
and her decision to set forth all the paradigms in full

is much clearer than Hickes's. The section on the cardinal numbers, heafod getel, and the ordinals, endebyrdlice naman (The Rudiments, pp. 29-30), is a brief summary of Hickes's chapter 4, "De Nominibus Numerorum."

With the vernacular verbal system, grammarians following the Latin tradition of verbal conjugation found themselves in a frightful muddle. They insisted on analyzing a Germanic language such as English--with its two tenses and, historically at least, its two moods--as if it had the full range of tense, mood, and voice in the classical exemplar. In England, Lily's grammar established how this was to be done, although there was much disagreement among later grammarians over the details in applying the system.[25] But when Mrs. Elstob came to the Anglo-Saxon verbal system, two difficulties arose, one minor, the other major, and both involved a departure from the strict norms of the Latin tradition.

The minor difficulty resulted from Mrs. Elstob's two conflicting sources, Ælfric and Hickes. They agreed on the definition of the verb and matters of tense, but Ælfric considered only five moods,[26] while Hickes followed the humanist tradition of Latin grammar and insisted on six: indicative, imperative, optative, potential, subjunctive, and infinitive. Mrs. Elstob dutifully followed Hickes, giving the Anglo-Saxon equivalents for all six moods: gebicnigendlice, bebeodendlic, gewiscendlic, mægenlic, underþeodendlic, and unge-endigendlic. (The term mægenlic is a nonce word.) Describing the features of each, she borrowed from Ælfric five moods and simply omitted a definition of the potential, or mægenlic, mood.

This six-fold division of the moods actually originated with the school grammars of Thomas Linacre.[27] The earliest of these was his Progymnasmata Grammatices Vulgaria (London: Rastell, 1512?/1515?), later revised as Rudimenta Grammatices (London: Pynson, 1525?).[28] The third work is the best known: De Emendata Structura Latini Sermonis Libri Sex (London: Pynson, 1524). In his earliest grammar Linacre listed only five moods among his paradigms (sig. A4v), but in his section, "Generally of Construction," he added a sixth:

> The Potential mode sygnifieth a dede as
> wisshyd. sumtyme with an aduerb of wysshyng.
> and sum tyme with out. as Vtinam amer god
> graunt I be louyd. The potential mode
> signyfyeth a thyng. as mayyng or owyng to
> be doone. And his sygnes in englysshe be

these. may might. wold. or shuld. and hit
hath v. tens in euery verbe of lyke voyce
to the subiunctyue mode. as amem I may
loue. . . .

(<u>Progymnasmata</u>, sig. C3)

In his 1524 grammar, Linacre intended the potential to
capture the sense of the Greek construction which uses
the adverb 'άν with either an indicative or an optative
in order to express a future dependent action.[29] Nevertheless, in his earliest grammar, as well as in its subsequent revision, Linacre discussed the potential only in
the section on construction, where the complexities of
the grammar were further expounded in English. Just as
Melancthon found that the Greek article, though absent
from Latin, could still be found in German, so Linacre
identified this "mood" in Greek, a refinement that he
could clearly articulate through the use of the English
modal verbs. Although this distinction of potentiality
could not be specifically indicated in Latin, it could be
identified through the necessary English translation, and
the understanding of Latin thereby made that much more
precise. This potential mood was eventually introduced
into the authorized versions of Lily's grammar (which is
in fact heavily influenced throughout by Linacre). As a
result it became an accepted part of the grammatical description of the verb used by English writers of both
English and Latin grammars.

In chapter 8, "De Verbo Activo Regulari," of his 1703
grammar, Hickes provided separate paradigms for the optative, subjunctive, and potential forms, with a long description of the last.[30] Thwaites combined the paradigms
for the optative and the subjunctive under one heading
and then followed this with the potential. Mrs. Elstob
copied Hickes and gave separate paradigms for each form,
although in her description of the potential she relied
heavily upon Thwaites's paraphrase of Hickes's account.
According to Elstob,

> The <u>Potential</u> Mood is two-fold, either
> Simple, or Compound: Simple, when it is
> exprest by the Verb alone; for example:
> Astige nu of rode, þ[æt] we Geseon &
> Gelyfon. Come down from the Cross, that
> we may see and believe. The Compound does
> express the Power, Liberty, Inclination,
> or Necessity, of doing any thing, by the
> Aid or Addition of some other word, such

as Mæg, Miht, Wold, Nold, Sceold, Mot, Most,
exprest by our May, Might, &c. . . .
(The Rudiments, pp. 40-41)

In Hickes, Thwaites, and Elstob the discussion of the potential is followed by one on the infinitive mood, but
here Mrs. Elstob sidesteps the others and sets forth her
own arrangement of the examples. She illustrates the
derivative infinitive mood in a fashion unabashedly mod-
eled on the Latin: gerunds in [Latin] di,[31] do, dum;
first and latter supines; future participles in [Latin]
rus, dus (The Rudiments, p. 42). She then inserts a very
brief discussion of the participle, reducing even further
Thwaites's short summary of Hickes.

The resolution of this conflict over grammatical moods
shows Mrs. Elstob true to both Ælfric and Hickes, as she
was in dealing with the article. Even though she set out
rules as she found them in Ælfric's grammar, she accepted
the modifications of them in Hickes without demur or concern about the methodological inconsistencies that might
result. In this respect she was not alone; Hickes himself had handled the verbal system of Anglo-Saxon very
differently from the way he treated the verb in his grammar of Franco-Theotisca, where the influence of Schottelius is much more apparent. Hickes made no attempt to
reconcile the two different systems of presentation, nor
did he comment on the different handling of the verbs in
Runólfur Jónsson's Icelandic grammar. Thus terminological consistency in Mrs. Elstob's grammar cannot be expected when such consistency is so lacking in Hickes's
own work.

The major difficulty posed by description of the verbs
in Mrs. Elstob's grammar is not of her own making. The
problem goes back to Hickes and to some extent results
from his admiration and partial adoption of the principles in Schottelius's chapter, "Von dem Zeitworte."
Moreover, he had been reluctant to abandon altogether
the traditional description of the verb in Lily's school
grammar, even though Schottelius shared in that same
tradition but from a continental perspective.

It is no surprise that the classification of verbs in
the early English grammars is extremely confused.[32]
Hickes's description of the Anglo-Saxon verb is especially tricky, because in it he coalesces several discrete traditions without ever quite admitting it. With
verbs he further rearranges his technique in his grammar
of Franco-Theotisca. In fact, in the latter grammar,

131

"De verbo, & iis, quae verbo accidunt" (chapter 9), includes comments on his view of verbal classification:

    I. Verbum est pars orationis attributum
      de subjecto affirmans.
    II. Convenit haec definitio primariò
       verbo substantivo, ac proinde aliis
       verbis, quatenus verbum substantivum
       in se implicitè continent; sic <u>lego</u>
       idem valet, ac <u>ego sum legens</u>. . . .
    VIII. Verbum, secundum receptam partitionem,
        dividitur in <u>Activum</u>, <u>Passivum</u>, &
        <u>Neutrum</u>. . . . Neutrum autem duplex
        est, vel quod actionem significat,
        vel quod rem aliquam sine actione
        significat. . . .
                (<u>Thesaurus: Franco-Theotisca</u>, p. 62)

    These statements do not adequately describe the way
Hickes actually treats the verbs; there is more to his
treatment than he indicates here. To perceive the modifications he was prepared to make of his own professed
system, we must look more closely at the background of
the terminology employed here and elsewhere in Hickes's
grammars.

    Describing the signification of the verb, Priscian had
made a distinction between active and passive, further
dividing the former into active and neuter.[33] These
divisions and their implications greatly exercised the
grammarians in the following centuries. When Melancthon
wrote his <u>Grammatica Latina</u> in 1526, he still accepted
the tradition established by Priscian, and made the primary division of the verb the distinction between active
and passive. He followed with a discussion of the verb
neuter.

    During the Middle Ages, however, another kind of divi-
sion had developed. Parallel to the distinction between
<u>nomen substantivum</u> and <u>nomen adjectivum</u>, there emerged a
distinction between the <u>verbum substantivum</u> and the
<u>verbum adjectivum</u>.[34] Linacre recognized this distinction
in his first grammar, but in his revision of 1525? he
abandoned it. Here the verb is divided into verbs substantive, verbs absolute (intransitives), and transitives
(which in turn were divided into active, passive, common,
neuter, and deponent). Even so, Linacre retained some
terminological inconsistency. At one point the verb substantive and the verb absolute are also called verbs
neuter (<u>Rudimenta</u>, sig. H3v), and in the supplement he
terms such "transitive neuters" as <u>placere</u> "third person

neuter verbs." Admittedly, the definition of the "verb neuter" was another controversial distinction. Even though Priscian had meant the intransitive verbs, a distinction such as "third person neuter" shows that by the sixteenth century the term was also likely to include impersonal forms.[35]

The primary meaning of the verbum substantivum is the verb "to be." The term originated in Priscian's discussion of the perception of tense (Keil, ed., Grammatici Latini, 2:414). Far from being the first to do so, Hickes combined the two sets of distinctions--verbs substantive/verbs adjective and verbs active/verbs passive-- separating the verb substantive (wesan in his 1689 grammar, wesan and weorþan in 1703) from the verbs active and passive. Thwaites, however, admitted only the distinction between the verba substantiva and the verba adjectiva (Grammatica, pp. 12, 14).

Still another major means of distinction between the verbs was to divide them into personal and impersonal forms. It was this kind of primary distinction that Melancthon chose in his Integrae Graecae Grammatices Institutiones (Dresden, 1520). Although he did not make the same primary division in his Latin grammar, he provided a separate section on the Latin impersonal verbs that was to prove crucial in making the distinction between personal and impersonal verbs a feature of the German and English grammatical traditions:

> Impersonalia dicuntur, quae personam certam
> nominativo casu in indicativo non recipiunt,
> sed mutatur nominativus personae in obliquos,
> ut quod Germanice personaliter dicimus, Ich
> mus Virgilium aussen lernen, Latine imper-
> sonaliter effertur, Oportet me ediscere
> Virgilium. . . .
> Et Germani habent hoc genus impersonalia,
> Sic enim efferunt, Legitur, man list,
> Dicitur, man sagt. Ex his figuris Germanici
> sermonis, facile intelligent pueri naturam
> horum verborum, sentientque nullam certam
> personam impersonalibus praeponi.
>
> (Opera 20:323)

Just as Melancthon had declared an article a part of speech in German and bequeathed it as such to the German grammatical tradition, so his distinction between personal and impersonal verbs became the primary verbal division for German grammarians. In his Grammatica Germanicae Linguae (Leipzig: Rhamba, 1578), Johannes Clajus was unequivocal about it: "Verbum aliud est personale, aliud impersonale" (p. 93). In this manner, Melancthon directly influenced both the German and the English tradition. When Lily's grammar reached its final form in the 1550s, the Latin version, the Brevissima Institutio (London: R. Wolf, 1567), defined the verb, "Verbum, est pars orationis quae modis & temporibus inflexa, esse aliquid, agereue, aut pati significat. . . . Verbum diuiditur in primis in Personale, vt Doceo: & Impersonale, vt Oportet" (sig. C3v). This echoes the opening sections on the verbs from both the Latin and the Greek grammars of Melancthon, though they are not a direct transmission of his statements into English. But Melancthon probably provided a starting point. Lily's debt to Melancthon's Latin grammar becomes even more apparent in his special chapter, "De Verbis Impersonalibus":

> Et de personalibus quidem hactenus dictum esto, deinceps verò de Impersonalibus dicendum, quae nominatiuum certe personae non recipiunt, sed mutatur nominatiuus personae in obliquos: vt quod Anglicè personaliter dicimus, I must reade Vergil. Latinè Impersonaliter effertur, Oportet me legere Vergilivm.
>
> (Brevissima, sig. D3v)

In this instance Lily's grammar differs quite markedly from Linacre's grammar. Not only does Lily make the distinction between personal and impersonal verbs--the Vergil example appears to come from Melancthon--but he also abandons those distinctions found in Linacre. Verbs are of five kinds: active, passive, neuter, deponent, and common. The verb substantive is recorded among the forms of the verbs neuter (Brevissima, sigs. C3v-C4).

If Hickes had drawn only upon this background for his analysis of the Anglo-Saxon verb, the unraveling of the various strands of the tradition would have been complicated enough. But there was yet another important influence, that of Schottelius's handling of the verb in his German grammar of 1663. Even though Schottelius organized his grammar on principles in the Latin tradition, he did not always interpret that tradition as Hickes does. But the latter credited Schottelius with being the first person to reduce the unruly grammatical structure of German to scientific principles, and consequently, whatever Schottelius said was important.

Schottelius's treatment of the verb begins with a distinction between active and passive:

> Das Zeitwort ist ein solches Wort, <u>Particul</u>
> oder Teihl in der Rede, welches ein <u>Tuhn</u>
> oder ein Leiden, samt seiner Zeit, bedeu-
> tet. . . . Und in diesen allen vernimt man
> zugleich ein Tuhn oder Werk, und darum ist
> solches Zeitwort wirkender Art, oder wir-
> kendes Geschlechts, <u>Generis Activi</u> . . .
> vernimt man auch allegemahl eine Zeit, ob
> es nemlich jetzo geschehe, oder kurtz,
> oder lang vorher geschehen sey, und zu-
> glich dabey ein Leiden, und darum wird
> das Zeitwort leidender Andeutung, oder
> leidender Art, leidendes Geschlechts
> <u>Generis Passivi</u>.
>
> (<u>Ausführliche Arbeit</u>, p. 547)

He proceeds with a distinction between personal and impersonal verbs, and then makes still another distinction when he comes to the auxiliary verbs:

> Alldieweil aber kein Zeitwort kan völlig
> verwandelt, noch in Teutscher Sprache er-
> kant und verstanden werden, ohn gewisse
> Kündigkeit der Hülfwörter, als müssen zur
> nohtwendigen Vorbereitung dieselbige Hülf-
> wörter zu erst in ihrer Zeitwandelung vor-
> gestellet werden. Es sind bey uns solcher
> genanten Hülfwörter drey, ich bin, ich
> werde, ich habe.
>
> (<u>Ausführliche Arbeit</u>, p. 550)[36]

Schottelius next gives his conjugations--first the auxiliaries, then the active and passive verbs, and finally the impersonal verbs.

What Hickes did was to bring this arrangement into line with the terminology of his own grammatical tradition. He renamed the auxiliary the <u>verbum substantivum</u>, restricting it to <u>wesan</u> in the grammar of 1689 but adding <u>weorþan</u> in 1703. In his grammar of Franco-Theotisca he had two chapters of <u>verba auxiliaria sive instrumentalia</u> (<u>Thesaurus: Franco-Theotisca</u>, pp. 49-61), in which he included not only <u>habban</u>, <u>wesan</u>, and <u>werthan</u>, but also <u>willan</u>, <u>sculan</u>, <u>maghan</u>, and <u>mussen</u>. These chapters preceded his discussion of the verb. There is of course no separate potential mood in Franco-Theotisca, and in all conjugations it was included with the optative and subjunctive in a single paradigm. Hickes maintained

135

Schottelius's division into active and passive, for it
did not contradict his own tradition. Moreover, that
tradition demanded such a distinction, even though Hickes
recognized that there was no formal passive in Franco-
Theotisca and thus, by implication, none in Anglo-Saxon:

> Haec est communis verborum divisio, quam
> admittendam & à nobis esse duximus, tametsi
> lingua Francica non agnoscat verbum passi-
> vum, utpote in quâ vox passiva non peculiari
> inflexione formatur, ut apud Graecos, &
> Latinos; sed circumscribitur in modis omni-
> bus & modorum temporibus per participium
> praeteriti temporis, & auxiliaria wesen &
> werthen, ut infra docetur.
> (Thesaurus: Franco-Theotisca, p. 62)

Hickes also began his section on the Anglo-Saxon verb
with a distinction between the personal and impersonal
(Thesaurus: Anglo-Saxonica, p. 39), and included a further brief chapter entitled "De Verbo Impersonali"
(Thesaurus: Anglo-Saxonica, pp. 52-53). Yet in his
definitions of the verb quoted above, he did not recognize this distinction. Nevertheless, since a similar
distinction was a familiar feature of the school grammars, and since Schottelius chose to emphasize it, it
created no particular problems for Hickes to introduce it
into his grammars.

The distinctions considered up to now are not remarkable. They were all in Hickes's own school books; he did
not have to consult foreign language grammars. But
Hickes depended on Schottelius for more than just his description of the verbal system. He also took from the
German scholar the method of conjugating the verbs and so
made that method a fixture of Anglo-Saxon grammar for
nearly a century and a half. It was this aspect of
Schottelius's work that made all the rest fall into place.
His discussion of the conjugational system began with the
following distinction:

> Der Zeitwandelungen (Conjugationes ver-
> borum,) seynd bey den Teutschen zwo: Die
> gleichfliessende (Regularis,) und ungleich-
> fliessende (Irregularis,) oder die ordent-
> liche un[d] unordentliche.
> Zu der ersten oder zu der gleichfliessen-
> den Zeitwandelung gehören alle die Zeitwörter,
> welche einerley Stambuchstaben behalten in
> ihren abfliessenden Zeiten. . . .

> Zu der anderen oder ungleichfliessenden
> Zeitwandelung gehören alle andere Zeit-
> wörter, welche nicht einerley Stammbuch-
> staben in ihren abfliessenden Zeiten
> behalten.
>
> (Ausführliche Arbeit, p. 549)

This division of the German verb into just two conjugations appears to go back to Johannes Becherer, Synopsis
Grammaticae tam Germanicae quam Latinae et Graecae (Jena:
Steinmann, 1596).37 Hickes followed this arrangement
closely. Not only are verbs "personale vel impersonale,"
but "personale autem est regulare, vel irregulare"
(Thesaurus: Anglo-Saxonica, p. 39). Under such a system, all the weak verbs are regular and all the strong
verbs irregular, as in Schottelius:

> Aller ungleichfliessenden Teutschen Zeit-
> wörter, dahin gehören alle die, welche in
> ihren Zeiten, Weisen, Zahlen und Personen
> nicht einerley gleiche Stammletteren be-
> halten, sondern die Wurtzel oder den Stamm,
> ungleichfliessender Weise, in der Zeit-
> wandelung gebrauchen. Es ist aber allhie
> keine geringe Ungleichkeit, sonderen eine
> oftmalige Veränderung bald in dem einen,
> bald in dem anderen.
>
> (Ausführliche Arbeit, p. 569)

Schottelius spent considerable time discussing the various
forms of the irregular verb (Opus partim, pp. 569-78) before giving a long list of such verbs with their present
and preterite forms (Thesaurus: Anglo-Saxonica, pp. 578-
603). Handling these verbs in chapter 9, "De verbis
anomalis, sive irregularibus," Hickes gave no paradigms
but he did follow Schottelius's example in a long list of
verbs with present and preterite forms.

What Hickes found in Schottelius was not any single
innovation, for Schottelius was also a man of tradition.
Hickes was, however, taken by the arrangement of the conjugations; it was a system which obviously worked, one
which, with a few minor adjustments, would not do vio-
lence to the traditional sensibilities of Hickes's English colleagues. This arrangement was attractive for
its reduction of the conjugations to two, an arrangement
which was clearly better than the clumsy classification
that had been attempted by Runólfur Jónsson.38 Even in
1823, Bosworth was able to state cavalierly, "In Anglo-
Saxon, all the inflections of the verb may be arranged

under one form: there is, therefore, only one conjugation" (The Elements, p. 132). Bosworth even criticized
Rask for setting up "a second conjugation"; "as the personal inflections are similar to other verbs, it is not
necessary to make a separate conjugation of them" (The
Elements, p. 156).[39] But where Bosworth's handling of
the verb is full of more than his usual obfuscation,
Rask's two conjugations, a first (weak) conjugation of
three classes, and a second (strong) one of six classes,
are exemplary in their clear presentation.

While Mrs. Elstob's discussion of the verb is not as
accurate as Rask's, she shares with him a remarkably
clear presentation. Although she followed Thwaites
closely in her selection of examples, she looked to
Hickes for her arrangement. Her treatment begins with
the verb substantive (both wesan and weorþan), followed
by the verb active regular, the passive voice, and the
irregular verbs. Neither she nor Thwaites recognized the
impersonal verb. In their attempts to fit Anglo-Saxon
into the verb system of traditional grammar, neither of
these early grammarians recognized that Anglo-Saxon had
one form of a true passive surviving in hātte.

The remainder of Mrs. Elstob's grammar is straightforward. The section on adverbs, wordes gefera (The
Rudiments, pp. 49-52), treats them as a part of speech
having two kinds (primitive and derivative), two figures
(single and compound), and twenty-four varieties of signification, all based on Hickes's "De Adverbiis" in his
1703 edition. Of the eleven kinds of conjunctions in
Hickes, Thwaites excluded the completive and the diminu-
tive, as did Mrs. Elstob, who also excluded the condi-
tional. In the sections on adverbs and conjunctions,
Mrs. Elstob displayed a spectacular technical vocabulary
in Anglo-Saxon taken from Ælfric's grammar without even
exhausting Ælfric's category of subdivisions. Her section on prepositions presented examples from Thwaites,
while her section on interjections (now betwux alegednyss,
after Ælfric's change of terminology) observed Hickes's
distinctions. For the last five subdivisions of the
interjection--none with equivalents in Ælfric--Mrs.
Elstob used the terms gewiscendlice and tihtendlice for
two of them (wishing and exhorting) borrowed from the
adverbial subdivisions, and she invented the terms
wundrigende, æteowigende, and lofigende for the other
three subdivisions (admiring, shewing, and praising).

Her grammar then turns to syntax, by which she means
rules of concord and governance (The Rudiments, pp. 57-
64). She teaches the three concords--agreement between

subject and verb, between noun and adjective, and between antecedent noun and relative pronoun. This section of the grammar is her own doing---there is no equivalent section in Thwaites or Hickes--and she marks it strongly with her own distinctive style:

> For the Adjective being a proper Attendant
> upon the Substantive, it hath been thought
> decent that it should not only be of the
> same Sex, that is, a Male to wait upon a
> Male, and a Female upon a Female, but like-
> wise to appear in a Dress, or Habit, by
> which it may easily be discern'd to which
> Sex they belong.
>
> (The Rudiments, p. 58)

The first part on governance, "Of the Construction of Adjectives" (i.e., adjectives which govern the genitive, dative, and ablative), is likewise hers while the second part, "Of the Construction of Verbs," takes its examples from Thwaites's summary of Hickes. She did, however, present these examples in a clear and systematic form, in contrast to the cramped jumble in both Hickes and Thwaites.

The last three sections of her grammar, "Of the Dia- lects" (The Rudiments, p. 65),[40] "Of the Saxon Poetry" (pp. 66-69), and "Of Accent" (p. 69), are all loosely based on Thwaites. He had culled the first two from the massive concluding sections of Hickes's Thesaurus and apparently devised his own section on accents.

Mrs. Elstob concluded her grammar praising the efforts of Hickes and Thwaites. The simple eloquence has not faded:

> I could not think of finishing this Treatise,
> without acknowledging how much I am obliged,
> both for Method and Materials, to the
> learned Mr. Thwaites's most useful and in-
> genious Epitome of Dr. Hickes's great The-
> saurus, and to the Thesaurus itself: Of
> which learned Work too great Encomiums
> cannot be given, either for the amplitude
> of the Subject, or justness of the Perfor-
> mance. . . . As to the Thesaurus itself,
> which can produce as many Testimonies of
> learned Men in its Praise, as perhaps any
> Book has receiv'd that has ever been
> printed; yet it hath not indeed escaped the
> undeserved Censure of some Men, as being

> defective in some things: but I, who have
> had occasion strictly to peruse it, believe
> upon due Reflection, and a nearer Inspection
> into the Work, its most severe Censurers,
> will find reason rather to complain of their
> own, than of the Author's Mistakes. However
> in a Work of so great bulk, illustrating so
> many Languages, it cannot be conceived, but
> that some things, might well escape the
> greatest Care, and exactest Judgement: The
> Author would be glad could she promise her-
> self to have given as few occasions of
> blame in this little Book.
>
> (The Rudiments, pp. 69-70)

These words are a fitting comment on Hickes's achievement,
and it is probably fair to say that Mrs. Elstob's own
book has given few occasions for blame. It cannot be
dismissed as a mere summary of Hickes and Thwaites. She
contributes to Anglo-Saxon grammar clarity, concision,
and flair. If better known, her work would have speeded
the prosperity of Anglo-Saxon studies. It is impossible
to say if wider distribution of her work would have meant
earlier resolution of the unsatisfactory sections of the
grammar (and of Anglo-Saxon grammars in general). But
her grammar does improve upon Hickes's Thesaurus and presents Anglo-Saxon in an easily assimilable fashion. Remarkable and impressive as Hickes's Thesaurus was, it
proved a liability to the progress of Anglo-Saxon studies.
The breakthrough came only in 1817 at the hands of a
Dane. Nearly a decade later, despite all his claims in
innovation, Joseph Bosworth remained in the shadow of the
great book. The development of Anglo-Saxon grammar for
the remainder of the eighteenth century was the barrenest
of wastelands.

Mrs. Elstob's grammar had one other remarkable feature.
In her resurrection of Ælfric's grammatical terminology,
she had tried single-handedly to revise linguistic history, and at the same time answer the critics of Anglo-
Saxon studies. The English language since Anglo-Saxon
times had been in the grip of a Latin grammatical tradition; even its entire grammatical lexicon had been taken
over by Latin. History was inexorably against the sur-
vival of Anglo-Saxon vocabulary, and along with the
poetic terms, the scientific words had been among the
first to disappear. Mrs. Elstob, for all her enthusiasm,
was seven centuries too late. As Father Shook has reminded us, "It is possible that if English had been per-
mitted to develop in its own way, there would have resulted a technological vocabulary comparable in ingenuity

with that of modern Icelandic where the device of seman-
tic and translation loan has infinitely enriched the
native vocabulary."[41] Anglo-Saxon was able to deal with
learned concepts, a scientific language reflecting the
concerns of an educated and cultured people. Mrs. Elstob
would surely have agreed, for she did her best to compose
a humane and cultured Anglo-Saxon grammar to restore some
dignity, in the face of her sneering, self-satisfied contemporaries, to an otherwise belittled language and time.

Notes

1. Joseph Bosworth, The Elements of Anglo-Saxon Grammar (London: Harding, Mavor, and Lepard, 1823),
pp. xxviii-xxix. Bosworth seemed to think that the
study of Anglo-Saxon was an appropriate pursuit for
women: "It is to the liberal spirit of our Gothic
ancestors that the female sex owe their present important and independent rank in society. . . . Perhaps,
therefore, the present work will not be quite uninter-
esting to the female sex. Some ladies, who are an
ornament to their sex, and who are most successfully
exerting their talents in the diffusion of useful
knowledge, have studied Saxon with evident advantage.
Were it not for the retiring modesty of an amiable female, whose highest pleasure is derived from confer-
ring a benefit unobserved, the author would be gratified to record the name of the accomplished lady to
whom we have been recently indebted for the first English translation of the Saxon Chronicle. . . . Let it
be remembered to the honour of her sex, that the first
Anglo-Saxon Grammar written in English was by the
learned Mrs. Elstob, who is also celebrated as the
translator of the Anglo-Saxon Homily on the birth-day
of St. Gregory" (pp. xxxiii-xxxiv).
2. See Hans Aarsleff, The Study of Language in England
1780-1876 (Princeton: Princeton University Press,
1967), p. 183. Jefferson owned a copy of Mrs.
Elstob's grammar; see Catalogue of the Library of
Thomas Jefferson, ed. E. Millicent Sowerby, 5 vols.
(Washington, D.C.: Library of Congress, 1952-59),
5:p. 26, item 128.
3. Rasmus Kristian Rask, Angelsaksisk Sproglære
tilligemed en kort Læsebog (Stockholm: Wiborg,
(1817).
4. See my article, "Mrs. Elstob's Defense of Antiquarian Learning in her Rudiments of Grammar for the
English-Saxon Tongue (1715)," Harvard University
Bulletin 27 (1979):172-91.

5.   Runólfur Jónsson, Recentissima Antiquissimae Linguae Septentrionalis Incunabula, id est Grammaticae Islandicae Rudimenta, nunc primum adornari caepta & edita per Runolphum Jonam Islandum (Copenhagen: P. Hakins, 1651).

6.   On the tradition of Latin grammar in the sixteenth and seventeenth centuries, see G. A. Padley, Grammatical Theory in Western Europe, 1500-1700: The Latin Tradition (Cambridge: Cambridge University Press, 1976).

7.   See Ann Royal Arthur, "The Icelandic Language as Described by Runólfur Jónsson in his Grammaticae Islandicae Rudimenta (1651)" (Ph.D. diss., University of North Carolina at Chapel Hill, 1965).

8.   Priscian's Institutiones are edited in vols. 2 and 3 of H. Keil, ed., Grammatici Latini, 7 vols. (Leipzig: Teubner, 1855-80); the Ars Grammatica of Donatus is edited in vol. 4. All citations of these authors are from Keil's edition. Ælfric's technical vocabulary has been thoroughly investigated by Lawrence K. Shook, "Ælfric's Latin Grammar: a Study in Old English Grammatical Terminology" (Ph.D. diss., Harvard University, 1939).

9.   On the entire question of the grammatical traditions in the vernaculars during the sixteenth and seventeenth centuries, see Max Hermann Jellinek, Geschichte der neuhochdeutschen Grammatik von den Anfängen bis auf Adelung, 2 vols. (Heidelberg: Winter, 1913-14); Ian Michael, English Grammatical Categories and the Tradition to 1800 (Cambridge: Cambridge University Press, 1970); and Emma Vorlat, The Development of English Grammatical Theory, 1586-1737 (Louvain: University Press, 1975).

10. The seven declension words used for the nouns are 1) smið (Ælfric, 2d decl.); 2) witega; 3) andgit (Ælfric, 4th decl.); 4) word (Ælfric, 2d decl.); 5) wiln (Ælfric, 1st decl.); 6) sunu; and 7) freo, -eoh.

11. This passage is based on Sergius, De Littera de Syllaba de Pedibus de Accentibus de Distinctione Commentatius, in Keil, ed. Grammatici Latini, 4:475: "Littera dicta est quasi legitera, eo quod quasi legentibus iter ad legendum ostendat vel quod scripta deleri possit. Ideo dixit partem minimam esse litteram vocis articulatae, quod, cum omnis oratio solvatur in verba, verba denuo solvantur in syllabas, rursum syllabae solvantur in litteras, littera sola non habet quo solvatur. Ideo a philosophis atomos dicitur."

12. See Michael, English Grammatical Categories, pp. 350-62, and Vorlat, The Development, pp. 241-55.

13. Ben Jonson, The English Grammar (London, 1640),
p. 56: "In our English speech, we number the same
parts with the Latines. . . . Only, we adde a ninth,
which is the Article: And that is two-fold, Finite.
as The. Infinite. as A." Jonson discusses the articles in chapter 15, "Of Pronounes" (p. 61).
14. William Lily, A Shorte Introdvction of Grammar
generally to be vsed . . . (London: R. Wolf, 1567),
sig. A5v: "Articles are borowed of the Pronoune, and
be thus declined. Nominatiuo hic, haec, hoc." For
this text I have used the facsimile edition, A Shorte
Introduction of Grammar by William Lily, ed. Vincent J.
Flynn (New York: Scholar's Facsimiles and Reprints,
1945); this volume also includes a facsimile of Lily's
Latin companion text, Brevissima Institutio seu Ratio
Grammatices . . . (London: R. Wolf, 1567).
15. [Antoine Arnaud and Claude Lancelot], Grammaire
générale et raisonnée (Paris: Pierre le Petit, 1660),
p. 30: "Les mots de la premiere sorte [l'objet de
nostre pensée] sont ceux que l'on a appellez noms,
articles, pronoms, participes, prepositions, &
aduerbes. Ceux de la second [la forme ou la manière
de nôtre pensée], sont les verbes, les conjonctions,
& les interjections." See also pp. 52-58.
16. "Et ut à Veteribus ad recentiores transeam, quantam
sibi gloriam comparavit nobilis ille Gallus, qui de
arte Grammatica rationis principiis stabilita scripsit
libellum Grammaire générale & raisonnée inscriptum
. . . optime addisci possunt?" (Institutiones Grammaticae, sig. B2).
17. "Quantam quoque nominis existimationem consecutus
est Nobilis & Amplissimus ille Vir Georgius Schottelius . . . qui opus ex quinque libris constans de
Germanica lingua condidit, in quo Theotiscum sermonem
longe lateque diffusum, & a regularum impatientem
antea creditum, praeceptis Grammaticis subjecit, & ad
justae artis formam redigit?" (Hickes, Institutiones
Grammaticae, sig. B2).
18. The credit for recognizing the article as a part of
speech in a vernacular language appears to belong to
Melancthon. In his Integrae Graecae Grammatices
Institutiones (Dresden: n.p., 1520), he states in his
section on the article, "Ignorat articulum omnino
Latinus sermo, quare Latinis vocibus reddi aut exponi
nequit. Nam quod grammatici nominum declinandorum
casibus addiderunt, hic, haec, hoc, docendi gratia
fecere, non quod sermo Latinus hos haberet articulos.
Germanicus sermo habet articulum, nec Graeci articuli
vim exacte cognoveris, nisi ex Germanico idiomate"
(Philippi Melancthonis Opera [1834-60; reprinted.
New York: Johnson, 1963], 20:29). This passage is

not in the earlier version of this grammar, Institutiones Graecae Grammaticae (Tübingen: Academia
Anshelmiana, 1518). In his Grammatica Latina
(Dresden: Secerius, 1526), Melancthon is even more
specific: "Nam Latinus sermo in universum caret
articulis, Germani habent articulos, quemadmodum et
Graeci, ἄναρθρον est, cum particula ein utuntur: Es
ist ein man da. Articulatum est: Ich hab dem man das
gelt geben, ἔδωκα τῷ ἀνδρὶ τὸ ἀργύριον. Id Latine non
recte vertas: Dedi huic viro hanc pecuniam" (Opera,
20:298). This view became standard in German vernacular grammars, as for example in Johannes Clajus, Grammatica Germanicae Linguae (Leipzig: Rhomba, 1578),
and Schottelius, Ausführliche Arbeit (see n. 19). See
also Jellinek, Geschichte, 2:193-96.

19. Justus Georg Schottelius, Opus partim renovatum et
auctum partim plane novum de Lingua Germanica quinque
libris constans. Ausführliche Arbeit von der Teutschen Haubtsprache . . . (Braunschweig: Zilligern,
1663), p. 224.

20. The first use of the terms "definite" and "indefinite" for the articles in English appears to be in
James Howell's A New English Grammar, Prescribing as
certain Rules as the Language will bear, for Forreners
to learn English (London: Williams, Brome, and Marsh,
1662), p. 42: "Ther be Eight Parts of Speech in the
English Toung, as in other Languages . . . whereunto,
we adde the prepositive articles The and A, which the
Latin only lacks; whereof the first is definit . . .
the other is indefinite." It is possible that Howell
borrowed his terminology here from the Grammaire
générale, p. 52: "Les Langues, nouuelles en ont deux
[articles]; l'vn qu'on appelle défini; comme le, la,
en françois: & l'autre indéfini, vn, vne." Even so,
this terminology harks back to Priscian's "articuli
finiti" and "articuli infiniti" (Keil, ed., Grammatici
Latini, 2:54). Schottelius also refers to the articulus definitivus (Ausführliche Arbeit, p. 225).

21. Michael Maittaire, The English Grammar: or An
Essay on the Art of Grammar Applied to and Exemplified
in the English Tongue (London: W. B. for H. Clements,
1712), marks the first occasion when a grammarian
makes the article an indisputable part of speech in
the English language.

22. Bosworth, The Elements, pp. 92-94, gives the form
only of the strong adjective. Cf. Rask, Angelsaksisk
Sproglære, pp. 32-33: "De angelsaksiske Till[ægsor-
dene]. ere ligesom de islandske meget simplere og
lettere end Navneordene, efterdi de böjes alle næsten
paa samme Maade. Vel inddeles de rettelig i to Klasse,
men disse ere dog blot i Smaating forskjellige. De

adskille i övrigt som i andre gotiske Sprog en bestemt
og en ubestemt Böjningsart, og i hver af disse tre
Kjön svarende til Navneordenes simple og kunstige
Hovedart og trende Böjningsmaader i hver."
23. Bosworth, The Elements, p. 100, compounds the
error: "Adjectives, in all cases and degrees of comparison, besides the common termination, sometimes
admit of an emphatic a, which increases the force of
the expression. The last vowel is often changed into
a, which has still the same emphatic effect: as
Godcund or godcunde divine or holy; godcunda very
divine or holy. . . . The emphatic a is most frequently added to adjectives used demonstratively, or
in addressing a person, as in the Greek and Roman
vocative cases. Oswald se Cristenesta cyning Norþan-
hymbra-rice, Oswald the most Christian king of
Northumbria. . . . All words terminating with the
emphatic a are declined like the second declension."
24. Hickes dismissed Jónsson's presentation in his 1703
edition, Thesaurus: Anglo-Saxonica, p. 82:
"Runolphus in cap. iv. docet apud Islandos omnia
adjectiva in omni genere bifariam terminari, vel
secundum certas quasdam regulas, quas ibi tradit; vel
in e, & a, si articulus praeponatur. . . . His non
absimile quid notavimus in regula x, capitis IV.
nostrae grammaticae, ubi observavimus adjectiva &
participia Gothica emphaticè, demonstrativè, & vocandi
casu posita, terminari, si sint masculini generis, in
a; si foeminini vel neutrius in o; quod etiam in idem
ferè redit cum regulâ Runolphi, quum neque demonstre-
tur, neque emphaticè quid dicatur sine praemissis
articulis, neque quis quem vocare vel invocare potest
in Anglo-Saxonicâ non praeposito pronomine ðu, quod
inter articulos numerat Auctor noster." This last
statement is something of a quibble, for Jónsson makes
it quite clear that he regards the article as a pronoun, although he and Hickes disagree on exactly what
kind of pronoun it is.
25. See Michael, English Grammatical Categories,
pp. 395-439, and Vorlat, The Development, pp. 302-49.
26. After Priscian (Keil, ed., Grammatici Latini,
2:421): "Modi sunt diversae inclinationes animi. . . .
sunt autem quinque: indicativus sive definitivus,
imperativus, optativus, subiunctivus, infinitus."
27. For a survey of these works see D. F. S. Thomson,
"Linacre's Latin Grammars," in Francis Maddison et al.,
ed., Linacre Studies: Essays on the Life and Works of
Thomas Linacre (Oxford: Clarendon Press, 1977),
pp. 24-35.
28 The dating of these works involves considerable
controversy. See Giles Barber, "Thomas Linacre: A

Bibliographical Survey of His Works," in Maddison et
al., eds., Linacre Studies, pp. 290-336. My references to the Rudimenta Grammatices are to the final
revision of 1525? (STC 15636). I have expanded ab-
breviations.
29. "Hec uero nostra sententia cui placebit, potest, si
uolet, hunc, quem nouamus modum, potentialem appellare.
Cui diuersa sententia erit, siue optatiuum esse con-
tendat, (nam subiunctiuum esse (ut Priscianus non
recte censet) nulla ratio efficit), siue uoces quinque
temporum, que publice subiunctiuo tribuuntur, triplici
significato donet, optandi, potentiae, subiunctiui
(hoc autem est indicandi, caeterum sub altero uerbo
subiecti, ut post dicetur) dummodo significationis
ipsius et usus admonitus, latinius loqui incipiat, me
certe non offendet" (De Emendata, sig. D1v).
30. Despite all this attention, Hickes did not think
much of the potential; except in his consideration of
the Anglo-Saxon active and passive verbs, he merged it
with the optative and subjunctive.
31. Apparently out of a sense of propriety, both
Thwaites and Mrs. Elstob change Hickes's example, from
"hit is tima to lufienne, tempus est amandi," to "hit
is tima to rædanne, tempus est legendi."
32. See Michael, English Grammatical Categories,
pp. 363-94, and Vorlat, The Development, pp. 258-76.
33. "Omnia verba perfectam habentia declinationem et
aequalem vel in o desinunt vel in 'or'. Et in o
quidem terminantia duas species habent, activam et
neutralem. Et activa quidem semper actum significat
et facit ex se passivam absque duobus verbis, 'metuo'
et 'metuor' . . ." (Keil, ed., Grammatici Latini,
2:373).
34. See Vorlat, The Development, pp. 285-89, and
Padley, Grammatical Theory, pp. 47-48.
35. See Michael, English Grammatical Categories,
pp. 92-97, and Vorlat, The Development, pp. 277-82.
The term verbum neutrum is discussed in detail by
Priscian (Keil, ed., Grammatici Latini, 2:375-76),
who keeps it separate from the verbum impersonale
(2:413-14, 424).
36. Schottelius adds in a note: "Et haec verba
auxiliaria originem & fontem nullibi nisi in Celtica
Lingua habent, linguas ergo reliquas quae inflexione
auxiliarium utuntur, Celticae seu Teutonicae originis
in fundo & genio ipso esse, extra dubium est posi-
tum . . ." (Ausführliche Arbeit, p. 550).
37. See Jellinek, Geschichte, 2:345-46. Michael,
English Grammatical Categories, pp. 439, 549, mentions
a manuscript grammar, "De Analogia Anglicani Sermonis

Liber Grammaticus," by Thomas Tomkis (floruit ca.
1599) in which this same reduction to two conjugations
is found.

38. Jónsson first lists what he calls the verba anomala:
vera, hafa, vilja, eiga, and skulu (in the conjugation
of which he also includes munu and ætla). He then
gives the conjugations: (1) weak verbs, class II;
(2) strong verbs, class III; weak verbs, classes I and
III; strong verbs, class VII, of the type heita;
(3) strong verbs, class VII, of the type snúa;
(4) strong verbs, classes V, I, and IV, of the type
fela; class III of the type finna; class VI; (5) strong
verbs, classes IV and V of the type lesa. These modern equivalents, however, are only a rough guide to
the contents of each conjugation; Jónsson's approach
is ultimately as unsatisfactory as that of Hickes.

39. It is clear that Bosworth paid only minimal attention to what Rask had written: "De [Gjerningsordene]
dele sig her, som i alle gotiske Sprog, i tvende
Böjningsmaader; i den förste er Datidsformen flersta-
velset, og endes paa -de eller -te, den lidende Til-
lægsf[ormen]. paa d eller t; i den anden er Datiden
enstavelset med Omlyd, og den lidende Til[lægs]f[or-
men]. endes paa en eller n" (Rask, Angelsaksisk
Sproglære, pp. 52-53).

40. Her paragraphs at the bottom of this page are taken
from Hickes's 1703 edition, Institutiones, chapter 1,
sections 4-5, pp. 2, 4 (vowels), and section ii, p. 2
(punctuation).

41. Shook, "Ælfric's Latin Grammar," p. 39.

The Rediscovery of Old English Poetry
in the English Literary Tradition

Richard C. Payne

Most readers who have not studied Old English poetry
approach the subject with at least a few preconceptions.
Common, for example, is the notion that Beowulf--perhaps
encountered in a survey course translation--is a rambling
monster tale, or that heroes, battles, and incessant
blood-feuds dominate the Old English literary landscape.
Tone is expected, but it is likely to be one of murky but
stoical Teutonic pessimism. This popular view of Old
English poetry is probably impossible for scholars to
change (and not altogether necessary), but students of
the discipline can profit by investigating some basic
historical determinants of the popular commonplaces: how
and when did the popular view arise, what were the literary and critical influences that combined to shape it,
and what has been its own influence on popular and scholarly conceptions of the nature of the literature?

The indebtedness of the popular view to the later
nineteenth century is well-known and has been the subject
of several recent studies.[1] But the real roots of the
tradition are far deeper, and its seminal period is in
fact the late eighteenth century and the early decades of
the nineteenth. During this period, for the first time,
a distinctly literary interest became the driving force
behind Anglo-Saxon scholarship in England, replacing English nationalism, the study of law, and ecclesiastical
controversy, which had motivated students of the discipline since its beginnings in the English Reformation.[2]
During this period also, it was the poetry that came to
the fore of Anglo-Saxon studies, meriting the critical
applications of the canons of literary taste. What occurred, then, in the period between 1750 and 1830 was the
"rediscovery" of Old English poetry in the English literary tradition. Two discrete influences interacted to

produce the literary context for this discovery. One was
the tradition of Anglo-Saxon scholarship that the period
inherited from the age of Hickes and Wanley;[3] the other
was the literary and intellectual interests of the later
eighteenth century, particularly the interest in the art
and literature of the nonclassical past familiar to students of English romantic poetry. The rediscovery itself
can be examined in the works of the two greatest scholars
of the period, Sharon Turner and John Josias Conybeare.

The legacy of scholarship bequeathed to the new generation of Old English scholars after 1750 was an impressive one indeed. Interest in the literature had already
been aroused; the history of the period had been probed
extensively;[4] usable Anglo-Saxon grammars had been produced, along with William Somner's Dictionarium Saxonico-
Latino-Anglicum;[5] and Humfrey Wanley's monumental catalog
recorded valuable information on every Old English manuscript known to be held by a British library.[6] Many
texts had been published also, although the entire canon
of Old English poetry that we know today was long from
finding its way into print.

Acting upon this scholarly inheritance was the intellectual climate of the early romantic period. It was,
after all, the age of Percy, Tyrwhitt, and Ritson, and
the beginnings of the study of medieval literature as a
viable intellectual interest. It was also the age of
Macpherson, Gray, Coleridge, and Scott, when the old bot-
tles of medieval forms were filled with the new wine of
romantic literature.[7] In the later eighteenth century,
interest in Old English poetry was in fact strongest in
purely literary circles, and when this interest passed to
more scholarly authors like Turner and Conybeare in the
early nineteenth century, the indelible mark of romantic
literary theory remained.

The most immediately relevant intellectual phenomenon
was the explosion of interest in Celtic and Norse poetry
that took place in England just after the middle of the
eighteenth century. Although interest in the pre-Roman
culture of the Celts and "Goths" (as the ancient Teutons
were called) had been evolving steadily for a century and
a half--notably in the works of Verstegan, Sheringham,
and Hickes himself[8]--Paul Henri Mallet's Introduction à
l'histoire de Dannemarc (1755) and his Monuments de la
mythologie et de la poésie des Celtes, et particulèrement
des anciens Scandinaves (1756) brought the Northern culture before the English popular and literary consciousness as never before. Mallet was not content with the
traditional confounding of the various branches of the

"Septentrional" (northern or Germanic) peoples, but compounded the error by insisting that the "Goths" and the
Celts were one and the same.[9] The coincidental rise of
the Ossianic materials and the romantic ideal of the
Celtic bard undoubtedly abetted this confusion, even as
it set the stage for a new literary use of the Septentrional materials, which had previously been the exclu-
sive property of ecclesiastics and university men.

In 1763 Thomas Percy published his Five Pieces of
Runic Poetry, a translation of some of the texts that had
appeared in the second volume of Mallet. In 1768 Thomas
Gray published The Fatal Sisters and The Descent of Odin,
two adaptations of Norse materials that ignited the English literary world. There followed a virtual torrent
of translations and adaptations from the Norse, with more
than fifty titles appearing in England between the appearance of Percy's Five Pieces and 1814.[10] Typical of
the best of these is James Johnstone's scholarly translation of "The Death Song of Ragnar" that appeared in 1782
under the title Lodbrokar-Quida. Johnstone's introduction describes the qualities that fired the romantic
imagination:

> the poet [reading this work] is entertain'd
> with the singularity of its composition.
> Even the Christian may learn a lesson from
> the arctic Tyrtaeus. When he reflects on
> the natural ferocity of the human mind; its
> dark conception of the Deity; and the gross
> notions which it forms of future happiness,
> he will be the more inclinable to set a just
> value on the discoveries of revelation.[11]

The relevance of these apparently tangential developments may be appreciated by glancing at some of the
lesser-known English literary works of the period, works
which link these developments with Anglo-Saxon studies.[12]
Among them is Richard Hole's Arthur, or The Northern En-
chantment, a Poetical Romance in Seven Books (1789), a
Chattertonian opus. Its plot is summarized by Frank
Farley as follows:

> The plot turns on the contention between
> the Saxons and the Britons for the sover-
> eignty of England. Arthur and Merlin are
> arrayed against Hengist and the "Northern
> Parcae." Arthur and Hengist are rivals for
> the hand of Inogen, Merlin's daughter.
> Ultimately Arthur wins, Hengist is slain,
> and the Parcae are banished to Hecla.[13]

Strikingly similar plots appear in two works printed in
1801, John Thelwall's The Fairy of the Lake and William
Taylor's Wortigerne, a Playe, the latter evidently intended as a parody of neo-Chattertonian poetry. The only
improvement of Hole's plot in these works is Rowena,
daughter of Hengist, who becomes a love-interest for
Arthur (although Thelwall depicts her as a sorceress, an
evil rival of Guenevere).[14] These three works and many
others like them include various anachronistic materials
as well. Their Arthur is the refined, chivalric Arthur
of Malory; the Saxons are the "Goths" of popular conception; Merlin and other figures provide a "Celtic" coloring; and the whole story, at least in two of the three
instances cited, is couched in an idiom which the popular
culture of the age regarded as "Chaucerian." Indeed,
this concatenation of diverse materials can hardly be
considered fortuitous, for each of them constitutes a
particular interest of eighteenth-century medievalism.[15]
By employing such plots, eighteenth-century authors
could economically exploit these interests and in the
process provide dramatic contexts for original poetic
compositions placed in the mouths of Celtic "bards" and
Gothic "scalds."

Turning from the larger cultural context to the specific discussions of Old English poetry in the later
eighteenth century, we find many of the same concerns
reflected. By far the most influential of these discussions was that in Bishop Percy's "Essay on the Ancient
Minstrels in England," prefixed to his Reliques of
Ancient English Poetry, first published in 1765. Percy's
essay, instrumental in determining popular and literary
notions, documents many of the eighteenth-century commonplaces with learned footnotes and other scholarly apparatus. The intrinsic similarity between Celtic bards and
"Gothic" scalds, for example, is stressed, as is the continuity between the Saxon scald and the medieval minstrel
who was held to be responsible for the ballads that
Percy's anthology contained.[16] Citing Norse sources as
authority, Percy goes on to say that the Teutonic people,
in particular "all the Danish tribes" (including the continental ancestors of the Anglo-Saxons), regarded poetry
as a gift of Woden, to be admired with superstitious awe.
With the civilizing influence of Christianity, he con-
tinues, the role of the (literary) poet became distinct
from that of the "minstrel," who was the heir to the old
tradition.[17] Tantalizingly unspecific about particular
texts, he adds, "But although some of the larger metrical
Romances might come from the pen of monks or others, yet
the smaller narratives were probably composed by the
Minstrels, who sang them."[18]

Percy was considerably more circumspect than many who followed him: he allowed that "many of the most popular rhimes were composed amidst the leisure and refinement of the monasteries,"[19] but his overall emphasis on the illiterate Saxon "minstrel" had a profound effect on the conception of Old English poetry and its cultural context, not only in popular circles, but also among the learned.[20] For example, in a paper read before the Society of Antiquaries on February 19, 1778, William Drake remarked,

> The Anglo-Saxon and Icelandic poetry . . . will be allowed to be in all respects congenial, because of the great affinity between the two languages, and between the nations who spoke them. They were Gothic tribes, and used two not very different dialects of the same Gothic language. Accordingly we find a very strong resemblance in their versification, phraseology, and poetic allusions; the same being in a great measure common to both nations.[21]

Assertions of this kind became more firmly entrenched as commonplaces as the eighteenth century drew to a close. By 1801 George Ellis could glibly declare that Old English poetry "in its spirit and character, seems to have resembled the Runic odes so admirably imitated by Mr. Gray."[22] In the scant thirty-five years that separated Percy's Reliques from the second edition of Ellis's Specimens of the Early English Poets, a "myth" had developed in the English literary world concerning the character and background of Old English poetry.

The emergence of this myth begs the question of just how common the reading of actual Old English poetic texts was in England during this period. The answer seems to be that it was not very common at all. The posthumous publication of Edward Lye's Anglo-Saxon dictionary in 1772 testifies to the continued study of Old English texts in the original language,[23] but it appears that most Englishmen were motivated, like the American Thomas Jefferson, by the study of the law, or by the other traditional areas of historical interest.[24] Other than Tyrwhitt, few English literary scholars were proficient in coping with Old English texts in the original. Men like Percy, Gray, and the others almost certainly had no more than a limited acquaintance with either Old English or Old Norse.[25] Indeed, the notable absence of work with original-language texts left this period neglected by historians of Anglo-Saxon studies.[26]

The explanation for this apparent ano aly lies, I believe, in the character of the published canon of Old
English poetry, which had remained constant since Hearne's
publication of The Battle of Maldon in 1726.[27] The literary interest in Old English and other Northern poetry
centered, as we have seen, on the primitive "Gothic"
scald and the picturesque heathen poetry typified by the
Norse Death Song of Ragnar. The men who wrote about this
poetry in the eighteenth century generally assumed that
Old English poetry of this kind had existed either in the
pre-Christian period or in the later, neo-scaldic activity of the "minstrels." None of the Old English texts
published in England before 1800, however, even remotely
resembled the kind of poetry that the prevailing literary
mythology led one to expect.[28] Certainly the poetry of
the Alfredian Boethius did not qualify as scaldic;
Caedmon's Hymn and the poems of Junius 11 (generally attributed to Caedmon)[29] were patently religious and were
presumed to be monastic; Judith and the minor religious
poems like Durham were also obviously written by clerics
or monks; and Maldon and the Chronicle poems, though they
dealt with the traditional "Gothic" subjects of kings and
battles, seemed to be the work of monastic chroniclers.
Thus, we can hardly be surprised that Percy allowed for
some composition of poetry in the early English monasteries. Almost any text known in his day could have been
composed nowhere else. Although the idea of Old English
poetry had captivated literary men in the later eighteenth century, a corresponding interest in the individual texts known in England before 1800 had not emerged.

What is striking to present-day students of Old
English is that Beowulf and the poems of the Exeter and
Vercelli codices were entirely unknown to the English
literary world before 1800. The discovery of the
Vercelli manuscript by Friedrich Blume in 1822 during his
research on Roman law, was, of course, pure serendipity;
the contents of the manuscript did not become generally
known in England until 1843, when John M. Kemble published his edition of the poems in the manuscript.[30]
Beowulf and the Exeter Book, however, lay in English
libraries and had even been described in the magnificent
catalog compiled by Wanley in 1705.[31] In view of the
rising interest in northern antiquities, the discovery of
these two monuments of Old English poetry by the literary
establishment was inevitable. Moreover, the discovery
added new force and substance to the previous generation's
literary interest in a hypothetical type of Old English
poetry.

The credit for drawing the attention of the English public to Beowulf and the Exeter Book clearly belongs to two individuals, Sharon Turner and John Josias Conybeare. They brought to the previous generation's interest in Old English poetry a level of scholarship reminiscent of Hickes's period. With the work of Turner and Conybeare, the rediscovery of Old English in the English literary tradition was at last achieved, for their works applied the newly evolved literary theory to specific Old English poetic texts.

Few scholarly works have appeared at a more propitious juncture than Sharon Turner's monumental History of the Anglo-Saxons, published between 1799 and 1805. Turner's work, as readable as a Walter Scott novel, brought the outlines of Anglo-Saxon political and cultural history before an unprecedented following among the English public. His stirring account of Alfred's struggle against the Danes, the climax to the first part of the work, must have been especially keen to Englishmen engaged in the struggle against Napoleon; and Turner's History apparently influenced works as far removed from Anglo-Saxon studies as Wordsworth's Ecclesiastical Sonnets.[32] In the emphases and prejudices evident in the historical narrative, we can perceive a curious ambivalence. On one hand, we see the traditional picture of Anglo-Saxon culture that developed through the eighteenth century. On the other hand, we see the pattern being set for Turner's nineteenth-century successors. Interest in Arthur, Hengist, Horsa, and King Alfred; interest in pre-Christian Germanic culture and its picturesque mythology; and an extreme dislike for monastic institutions--all are examples of this tendency.[33]

Of particular interest is the twelfth book of the History, devoted to the literature, arts, and sciences of the Anglo-Saxons. In his chapter on "Their Native or Vernacular Poetry," which contains among other things the seminal account of Beowulf,[34] the same ambivalent character appears. As a prelude to this chapter he deals with the "mythical" Old English poetry that had so fascinated the later eighteenth century. The now-obligatory citation of Tacitus aside,[35] Turner mentions the existence of "ancient songs" among the pre-Christian Saxons, and he avers that such songs were cultivated as late as the tenth century; but he cautions that "none of those have survived to us . . . [because] the poets of barbarous ages usually confine the little effusions of their genius to the care of oral tradition."[36] Having made this gesture to Percy and company, Turner proceeds to a discussion of specific Old English texts, a novel practice.

Even so, the intellectual climate of the early nineteenth century and the influence of creative antiquaries like Percy and Ritson leave their mark.

The impact of contemporary literary theory is notable in Turner's description of the basic genres of Anglo-Saxon poetry:

> The history of the Saxon poetry, and, indeed, of all modern European poetry, in its ruder state, may be divided into three heads: songs or ballads; the lengthened narrative poems, or romances; and that miscellaneous kind which, if we term it lyric, it is more for the convenience of using a short generic word, than for the exact appropriation of its meaning.
>
> (History 2:286-87)

Turner's opinion of the "historical songs," the first class of Saxon poetry, which he attributed to popular oral tradition, was not very high.[37] But narrative poetry, "From these poems, of Beowulf, Judith, and Cædmon, it is clear that the Anglo-Saxons had begun to compose long narrative poems, full of fancy, which seem to be justly entitled to the name of metrical romances, unless the higher term of heroic poem be more appropriate" (History 2:316). In both opinions he appeals to the same criteria of romantic taste: he condemns "historical songs" because they lack the naive simplicity of the ballads printed by Percy; yet he praises the "long narrative poems" because they seem to anticipate, albeit imperfectly, the narrative art of Chaucer and the later "metrical romances" printed by Percy, Ritson, and others.[38] The canons of taste here are as predictable as they are attuned to the literary sensibilities of the period.

The publication of Turner's History at the beginning of the nineteenth century coincided with another event which boosted enormously Anglo-Saxon studies in England: the establishment of the Rawlinson professorship of Anglo-Saxon at Oxford. The third holder of the four-year appointment, the Reverend John Josias Conybeare, continued the rediscovery begun with Turner. Conybeare became the Rawlinson professor in 1809 and subsequently served as professor of poetry at Oxford. His major work, Illustrations of Anglo-Saxon Poetry, was published posthumously in 1826,[39] but much of his research had been shared with the English scholarly establishment in the preceding fifteen years. His "Account of a Saxon Manuscript preserved in the Cathedral Library at Exeter," for example, was read before the Society of Antiquaries on November 5, 1812, and was published in volume 17 of *Archaeologia* (1814). Many other discoveries of his were disseminated in the same way.

The preface to Conybeare's *Illustrations* contains a complete record of known poetic texts in Old English--an unprecedented list which attests to the rising literary interest in these poems. The list is arranged by genre, and the eight generic headings into which he divides the corpus are interesting from two points of view. First, we can see here, as in Turner's generic divisions, a clear reflection of romantic literary theory. Second, today's student of Old English will be struck by how similar Conybeare's list is to that of a modern literary historian. The eight categories or genres are (1) "Narrative Poetry, derived from Historical or Traditional Sources," (2) "Narrative Poetry derived from Scriptural Sources," (3) "Narrative Poetry founded on the Lives of Saints," (4) "Hymns and other minor Sacred Poems," (5) "Odes and Epitaphs," (6) "Elegiac Poetry," (7) "Moral and Didactic Poetry," and (8) "Miscellaneous." This list appears similar to Turner's less detailed, three-fold division, although the discovery of the Exeter Book poems suggested the larger number of Conybeare's categories. "Elegiac Poetry" and "Narrative Poetry founded on the Lives of Saints" never would have occurred to Turner, simply for the want of examples. The discovery of the Exeter Book, like that of *Beowulf* before it, also made possible the scrutiny of actual Old English texts which seemed to reflect the "Gothic" poetry of the scalds--the poetry that had so gripped the popular imagination.

We see this effect at various points in the *Illustrations*. The history of scholarly interest in *Widsith*, for example, begins here.[40] We can also see the interest in Germanic antiquities in Conybeare's treatment of *Beowulf*, which is considerably more extensive (and more accurate) than Turner's.[41] Conybeare agreed with Thorkelin that the poem was probably a redaction of some earlier work derived from pre-Christian antiquity. With a genuine sense of longing, he comments on the *Beowulf* poet:

> Whatever his age, it is evident that he was
> a Christian, a circumstance which has per-
> haps rendered his work less frequent in al-
> lusions to the customs and superstitions of
> his pagan ancestors, and consequently some-
> what less interesting to the poetical anti-
> quary than if it had been the production of
> a mind acquainted only with that wild and

157

picturesque mythology which forms so peculiar and attractive a feature of the earlier
productions of the Scandinavian muse.[42]

Reflection of the "Gothic" proclivity in Conybeare's
aesthetic judgments also appears in his summary of the
Exeter Book's contents (Illustrations, pp. 201-82).
Christ I draws only censure for its lapse in poetic
taste. Predictably, Christ III, Guthlac A and B,
Azarias, Juliana, and the short poems between The Gifts
of Men and Widsith--which constitute a major sectional
division in the manuscript--receive only the most per-
functory notice. By contrast, "The Exile's Complaint"
(The Wife's Lament) and "The Ruined Wall-Stone" receive
more attention, with obvious aesthetic approval. The
first of these poems, characterized as an "elegiac ballad," Conybeare considers especially interesting because
it appears to allude "to the adventures and misfortunes
of some hero once familiar to the Scaldic Muse," and as
such constitutes "one of those interesting links which
connect the remains of Anglo-Saxon literature with that
of their continental brethren of the same great family of
nations" (Illustrations, p. 245). The Ruin, however,
most clearly satisfies the canons of contemporary poetic
taste. It was, said Conybeare,

> superior, both in picturesque description
> and in the tone of moral feeling which
> pervades it, to the great mass of Saxon
> poetry. . . . The reader will be reminded,
> in the contrast between past grandeur and
> actual desolation thus presented by the
> ancient Scald, of the more elaborate de-
> lineation of a modern author, the celebrated
> description of Dinevor Castle in Dyer's
> "Grongar Hill"; but a still more interest-
> ing parallel, because drawn from the poetry
> of a period equally remote and imperfectly
> civilized, will be found among the early
> bards of Wales. . . .
>
> (Illustrations, p. 250)

The work of Conybeare brought to fruition the intellectual interests stimulated by Mallet and Percy, and
firmly established the rediscovery of Old English poetry
in the English literary tradition. At the same time,
developments on the Continent emphasized even more
sharply the Germanic aspects of the literary interest in
Old English, to give new force to what Eric Stanley has
called "the search for Anglo-Saxon paganism" (see note 1).
Thorkelin's transcripts of Beowulf, Jakob Grimm's work on

comparative Teutonic mythology and grammar, and other works by founders of the "New Philology" soon had a profound impact on the direction of Anglo-Saxon scholarship in England.[43] After 1830 men like Thorpe and Kemble who had been trained on the Continent brought a new standard of learning and professionalism to the English scholarly establishment; but they also brought with them the intellectual interests and prejudices that had developed abroad. New views made unfashionable, if not unpalatable, ideas like Turner's suggestion that <u>Beowulf</u> had been influenced by the learned literary tradition of the early medieval epic.[44]

The rediscovery of Old English poetry was, both chronologically and intellectually, a phenomenon of the romantic period. The same texts that influenced the revival of Old English also generated the creative aspects of romantic medievalism. Conversely, the literary taste, theory, and practice of the period are clearly reflected in the writings of the scholars and critics of Old English poetry. Almost exactly contemporary with the "rediscovery" in the efforts of Conybeare, the study of Old English poetry became an academic discipline, and the locus of Anglo-Saxon studies shifted quickly to the universities, both in England and elsewhere. Whether this coincidence resulted in the literary interests and attitudes attuned to the romantic sensibility, one "fossilized" in the scholarly lore of the discipline, I leave for others to judge. In any event, the distance between the attitudes of 1830 and attitudes now current is not nearly so great as many would suggest.

Notes

1. See E. G. Stanley, <u>The Search for Anglo-Saxon Paganism</u> (Totowa, N.J.: Rowman & Littlefield, 1975).
2. See Eleanor N. Adams, <u>Old English Scholarship in England from 1566-1800</u> (1917; reprinted. Hamden, Conn.: Archon Books, 1970), p. 70 et passim.
3. For a convenient summary of achievements in Anglo-Saxon studies during these years, see David C. Douglas, <u>English Scholars, 1660-1730</u>, 2d ed. (London: Eyre and Spottiswoode, 1951).
4. Ibid. See also Adams, <u>Old English Scholarship</u>, pp. 11-84, and Robin Flower, "Laurence Nowell and the Discovery of England in Tudor Times," <u>Proceedings of the British Academy</u> 21 (1935): 47-70.
5. The seminal grammar of Old English is George Hickes's <u>Institutiones Grammaticae Anglo-Saxonicae et Moeso-Gothicae</u> (Oxford: Oxford University Press,

1689). This grammar reappeared in revised form in
Hickes's Linguarum Vett. Septentrionalium Thesaurus
Grammatico-Criticus et Archaeologicus (Oxford: Oxford
University Press, 1703) and was the basis of a shorter
redaction by Hickes's pupil Edward Thwaites in 1711.
Thwaites's work was in turn the basis of Elizabeth
Elstob's The Rudiments of Grammar for the English-
Saxon Tongue (London: Bowyer, 1715), the first Anglo-
Saxon grammar written in English. Somner's Dictio-
narium had been published in Cambridge in 1659.
6. Humfrey Wanley, Antiquae Literaturae Septentrionalis
Liber Alter seu Humphredi Wanleii Librorum Vett. Septentrionalium, qui in Angliae Bibliothecis extant, nec
non multorum Vett. Codd. Septentrionalium alibi extan-
tium Catalogus Historico-Criticus (Oxford: Oxford
University Press, 1705). On the influence and scope
of Wanley's catalog, see Douglas, English Scholars,
pp. 113-17, and N. R. Ker, Catalogue of Manuscripts
Containing Anglo-Saxon (Oxford: Clarendon Press,
1957), pp. xiii ff.
7. On the creative aspects of eighteenth-century
medievalism, see Arthur Johnson, Enchanted Ground
(London: Athlone Press, 1964).
8. Richard Verstegan's Restitution of Decayed Intelligence (Antwerp: Bruney, 1605) set out to prove that
the true (i.e., Germanic) pedigree of the English nation was as noble as the spurious derivation from
"Brutus" provided by Geoffrey of Monmouth and other
medieval authors. A similar nationalistic motive
seems to have prompted Robert Sheringham's De Anglorum
Gentis Origine Disceptatio (Cambridge: J. Hayes,
1670). Sheringham's work, a monograph of some four
hundred pages, is astounding in its erudition, as it
collects virtually every demographic comment made by
classical and medieval authors, in Greek, Latin, and
the Northern vernaculars, and brings them to bear on
the problem of tracing the origins of the English
nation. Heavily indebted to Sheringham for its historical materials, Hickes's Thesaurus likewise tended
to show a great interest in the prehistoric common
origins of the "Septentrional" peoples. By including
in his great work his own descriptive grammars of
Gothic, Old High German, and Old English, as well as
Runolph Jones's grammar and glossary of Icelandic, and
by pointing out the obvious relationships not only
among the cognate languages, but also among such
things as the runes, Hickes strengthened the conception of a unified Northern culture.
9. This mistaken identification, which was repeatedly
corrected by the more learned of the English scholars,
obviously persisted in the popular consciousness until

it was finally put to rest by Jakob Grimm in the next
century. For evidence of the persistence of this mis-
identification in England, see, e.g., Archaeologia 9
(1789): 332-33 and 16 (1812): 95-121. One of those
who knew better was Thomas Percy, who published a
translation of Mallet's two volumes in 1770 under the
title Northern Antiquities and pointed out the French
scholar's error in his preface to the translation.
Percy's fastidiousness in ethnic identification did
not seem to extend to the various branches of the
Germanic family, however. Although Mallet's work is
drawn exclusively from Norse sources, Percy's subtitle
reads, "A Description of the Manners, Customs, Religion, and Laws of the Ancient Danes, Including Those
of our own Saxon Ancestors." For a general discussion
of Mallet's influence, see Frank Edgar Farley, Scandinavian Influences in the English Romantic Movement,
Harvard Studies and Notes in Philology and Literature,
vol. 9 (Boston: Ginn, 1903), pp. 30-39.

10. Farley, Scandinavian Influences, pp. 229-31.
11. James Johnstone, Lodbrokar-Quida (Copenhagen:
Stein, 1782), p. 93. We may illustrate the point
further by quoting some of the "gross notions" set
forth in the poem, in Johnstone's translation: "But
still, there is a never-failing consolation for my
spirit--the board of BALDER's sire stands open to the
brave. Soon from the foe's capacious scull we'll
drink the amber beverage. Departed heroes know no
griefs when once they enter the palace of dread
FIOLNER--I'll not approach the courts of VITHRIS with
the faltering voice of fear" (p. 29). The fascination
that this sort of poetry held for the Romantic imagination is amply demonstrated by the fact that this
poem, which was incidentally one of the Five Pieces
published by Percy in 1763, was translated or "imitated" by no fewer than six other English writers (not
including Johnstone) between that year and 1804. See
Farley, Scandinavian Influences, pp. 67-76.
12. For a more comprehensive view of these works, see
Farley, Scandinavian Influences, pp. 90-189.
13. Ibid., p. 110.
14. Ibid., pp. 140-42, 151. Rowena was not, of course,
the invention of Thelwall and Taylor, but is a traditional figure employed by creative historians as early
as Geoffrey of Monmouth (Historia Regum Britanniae
4:12).
15. See Johnson, Enchanted Ground, pp. 1-59.
16. Thomas Percy, Reliques of Ancient English Poetry
(London: Dodsley, 1765), pp. xv-xvi.
17. Ibid., p. xvi. In a footnote to later (1794) versions of the essay, Percy remarks that the two-fold

division that he posits between Anglo-Saxon "poets" and "minstrels" is reflected in their terminology, the words sceop and leoðwyrta being reserved for the learned, literary "poet," while the terms gligman and hearpere were applied to the "minstrels." Elsewhere in his notes (p. lxviii), Percy remarks that the Anglo-Saxon clergy, and in particular the monks, were antithetical to the art of the "minstrels," who represented a neo-paganism directly descendant from that of the scalds.

18. Ibid., p. xvi.
19. Ibid.
20. A sole dissenting voice was that of the Reverend Samuel Pegge, who read a paper before the Society of Antiquaries on May 29, 1766, in which he opined that "we cannot reasonably argue from the modes and customs of the Britons or Danes to those of the Saxons." Pegge took particular aim at Percy's credulity in adducing as evidence for the existence of "minstrels" the testimony of William of Malmesbury that Alfred had disguised himself as a harper to spy upon the Danish camp; see Archaeologia 3 (1786): 310.
21. William Drake, Archaeologia 5 (1779): 385.
22. George Ellis, Specimens of the Early English Poets, To Which is Prefixed an Historical Sketch of the Rise and Progress of the English Poetry and Language, 2d ed. (London: Washbourne, 1801), p. 11.
23. Edward Lye, Dictionarium Saxonico- et Gothico-Latinum (London: E. Allen, 1772). On other studies at this time, see Adams, Old English Scholarship, pp. 106-13.
24. Thomas Jefferson, An Essay Towards Facilitating Instruction in the Anglo-Saxon and Modern Dialects of the English Language (New York: Trow, 1851), p. 4. Jefferson might also serve as an example of the mechanics of eighteenth-century study of the Old English language. Hickes's Thesaurus was of course available to anyone wishing to take the trouble to read it; and Thwaites's redaction of Hickes's grammar in Latin and Elizabeth Elstob's English redaction of Thwaites were also available to those who might be intimidated by the formidable bulk of the Thesaurus. All three books are mentioned by Jefferson, who says that he acquired his knowledge of Old English from them (p. 14). The depth of his knowledge of the language, as revealed in his Essay, is most charitably described as "gentlemanly," and this degree of competency probably represented the norm among those Englishmen who attempted to acquire the language through perusal of published grammars.

25. Farley, Scandinavian Influences, pp. 32-35, 214.
Tyrwhitt displayed considerable command of Old English
grammar in his monumental edition of Chaucer (London:
Payne, 1775-78), and his knowledgeable critique of
Hickes's analysis of Old English metrics in that edition generated much discussion during the period.
See, e.g., Ellis, Specimens, pp. 11-13.
26. The only one of the discussions mentioned above
which includes an actual Old English text is Ellis's
Specimens, which prints The Battle of Brunanburh under
the title "An Ode on Athelstan's Victory." The
facing-page "literal" translation is so inaccurate as
to bear eloquent witness to the shallowness of Ellis's
knowledge of Old English; and Samuel Henschall's ren-
dition of the poem into Chattertonian rhyming couplets,
which Ellis appends, is best passed over in silence.
Brunanburh is the only Old English text to appear in
print, in England during this period, other than the
twelfth-century poem on the saints of Durham (Anglo-
Saxon Poetic Records, 6:27), which was printed in a
translation of a German work published in 1798 in
London (J. C. Adelung, Three Philological Essays,
trans. A. F. M. Willich).
27. Johannis confratris et monachi Glastoniensis
Chronica, ed. Thomas Hearne (Oxford: Oxford University Press, 1726), pp. 570-77.
28. The sole exception to this generalization is the
Finnsburh Fragment, which was printed in Hickes's
Thesaurus and which, for reasons difficult to fathom,
received no critical attention. Perhaps the most
likely explanation of this anomaly is that it testifies to the superficial way in which Hickes's monumental work was read by those who revived the literary
interest in Old English poetry.
29. The identification of the Junius Manuscript poems
with Caedmon had originated with Francis Junius himself in the editio princeps of the texts, Caedmonis
Monachi Paraphrasis Poetica Genesis ac praecipuarum
Sacrae paginae Historiarum (Amsterdam: By the Author,
1655). Although Hickes, among others, expressed
reservations about this attribution (Thesaurus 1:133),
it seems to have flourished among eighteenth-century
scholars.
30. See Kenneth R. Brooks, ed., Andreas and the Fates
of the Apostles (Oxford: Clarendon Press, 1961),
pp. xiii-xiv.
31. Wanley, Antiquae Literaturae, pp. 218-19, 279-81.
32. For a nearly contemporary witness of Turner's
History, see John Petheram, An Historical Sketch of
the Progress and Present State of Anglo-Saxon

Literature in England (London: Lumley, 1840), p. 118.
See also Stanley, The Search, p. 22.
33. Reminiscent of the interest sparked by Mallet is
book 7, "The Manners of the SAXONS in their Pagan
State." In introducing this section Turner remarks,
with characteristic honesty: "as we have no Runic
spells to call the pagan warrior from his grave, we
can only see him in those imperfect sketches which
patient industry may collect from the passages that
are scattered in the works which time has spared,"
Sharon Turner, History of the Anglo-Saxons, 2d ed.
(London: Longman, 1807), 2:2. Perhaps the best example of Turner's contempt for "monkish" institutions
is his vilification of St. Dunstan and the Benedictine
Reform movement of the tenth century (1:372-407).
These and the other interests mentioned in the text
are common to a number of earlier historians and are
ultimately derived from the works of Verstegan and
Sheringham. Among the more important of these his-
torical works are Aylett Sammes, Britannia Antiqua
Illustrata (London: Roycroft, 1676), William Guthrie,
A General History of England (London: Knox, 1744),
and John Pinkerton, "A Dissertation on the Origin and
Progress of the Goths, Being an Introduction to the
Modern History of Europe," in vol. 2 of his Enquiry
into the History of Scotland (London: G. Nicol,
1789).

Turner's account of Beowulf brought the attention
of the English literary world to the poem for the
first time, and his treatment of the poem was so
prominent that it could hardly be overlooked. He comments that Beowulf "is the most interesting relic of
the Anglo-Saxon poetry which time has suffered us to
receive" (History 2:294), and spends a great deal of
time on the poem, printing translations of parts of
the first eight fits, interspersed with summaries of
the action to cover the parts not translated (2:294-
303). Turner's translations are highly inaccurate,
and his understanding of the action of the poem is
imperfect at best--understandable perhaps because he
was working with a difficult poem in manuscript (see
below) and probably did not get through much more of
the poem than the "specimen" that he translated.
35. The venerable history of quoting Tacitus (De
Moribus Germaniae, chap. 2) on this subject may be
adduced as a sort of microcosm of the "mythographic"
evolution described in this essay, and like most other
aspects of this phenomenon, it is ultimately derived
from Verstegan and Sheringham. Verstegan, in comment-
ing on the warlike nature of the ancient Germans, says:
"They go singing to the warres, and haue certain verses

by singing of which they encowrage themselues"
(Restitution, p. 48). Sheringham quotes the entire
passage from Tacitus: "Celebrant carminibus antiquis
(quod unum apud illos memoriae et annalium genus est)
Tuistonem deum terra editum, et filium Mannum, originem gentis, conditoresque (De Anglorum, p. 166). In
these two highly learned works, the citation of
Tacitus here is simply one of a large number of references to classical and medieval authorities on history and demography, but this one example was seized
upon and wrenched from the larger context by an age
hungry for the elusive poetry of the "Goths." Among
others, the chain of works leading from Sheringham to
Turner includes: Sammes, Britannia (1676), p. 438;
Sir William Temple, Essays of Heroic Virtue, Of Poetry
3d ed. (London: Chiswell, 1692), p. 65; and of course
Percy, Reliques (1794 ed.), p. xxii.
36. Turner, History, 2:30.
37. Ibid., 2:292. "These historical songs have none of
the story, nor the striking traits of description which
interest us in the ballads of a subsequent age. In the
Saxon songs we see poetry in its rudest form, before
the art of narration was understood." Specific examples of this genre given by Turner include the Chronicle poems Brunanburh and The Death of Edgar.
38. See Johnson, Enchanted Ground, pp. 195-218, in which
much of the same terminology employed by Turner is
explained.
39. William Conybeare, ed., Illustrations of Anglo-
Saxon Poetry (London: Harding and Lepard, 1826).
40. Ibid., pp. 9 ff. The influence of the eighteenth
century is revealed in the terminology employed in
Conybeare's introduction: "The poem . . . owes its
origin in all probability to a period yet more remote
[than that of Caedmon's Hymn], and to an author of a
very different cast, a Scald or Minstrel by profession."
41. Ibid., pp. 30-172. Conybeare shows great restraint
and a charitable nature in correcting Turner's errors,
which notably included the view that "the subject is
the expedition of Beowulf to wreak the fæthe, or
deadly feud, on Hrothgar for a homicide which he has
committed" (Turner, History, 2:294). Conybeare points
out (p. 30) that Turner was misled by a misbound manuscript leaf, the correct placement of which was determined by Thorkelin in preparing his printed edition
and Latin translation of the poem, De Danorum Rebus
Gestis Secul. III & IV (Copenhagen: Rangel, 1815).
42. Conybeare, Illustrations, pp. 33-34. Conybeare
considers highly dubious Thorkelin's fanciful suggestion that Beowulf was originally composed in Danish at

the time of the poem's action and was translated into
Old English at the command of King Alfred. Conybeare
remarks that "the only point in which Thorkelin's
hypothesis appears to [Conybeare] to be borne out by
the language and aspect of the poem, is the probability
that it may be a translation or rifaccimento of some
earlier work. . . ." (p. 30).

43. On the influence of "the New Philology" on later
English scholarship, and a comparison of its charac-
teristics with those of the tradition that it sup-
planted, see Hans Aarsleff, The Study of Language in
England, 1780-1860 (Princeton: Princeton University
Press, 1967), passim.

44. Turner, History, 2:317-20. With formidable erudition, Turner goes through a long list of authors:
Victorinus, Juvencus, Prudentius, Sedulius, Claudius
Marius Victor, Sidonius, Paulinus, Alcinus Avitus,
Arator, Fortunatus, Petrus Apollonius, and Bede. He
adds, "From the epic poems of antiquity and their imitations, the Anglo-Saxons, as well as the Franks, and
the Goths in Spain, learnt the art of constructing and
carrying on an epic fable. The first imitations were
in Latin, by those who knew the language and loved its
poetry. But that men arose who cultivated poetry in
their native tongue, as well as in the Latin language,
we may learn from the example of Aldhelm . . . and
from [such men the art of narration] probably descended to the Scop, or professional poet" (2:320).

J. M. Kemble and Sir Frederic Madden: "Conceit and Too Much Germanism"?

Gretchen P. Ackerman

The subjects of this essay were undoubted titans in the world of early English scholarship as it evolved in the opening decades of the Victorian period. They had strikingly different backgrounds, and they marked out different areas of medieval study in which to exercise their considerable scholarly powers. Because of his notable career in Germany, Kemble commands the greater international prominence. His broad scholarly output has been masterfully reviewed by Bruce Dickins, and biographer Raymond A. Wiley has just provided us with a full life of Kemble, with particular emphasis on his Anglo-Saxon activity.[1] Madden's fame, on the other hand, was more exclusively English. He had a solid professional base in the British Museum, where he served for forty years as keeper of manuscripts while completing many scholarly projects of his own.[2] Much of his life is known to interested scholars through his magnificent 43-volume diary, an unpublished treasure of social history for the years 1819-73.[3] It is unabashed in revealing the personality of its author--scholarly genius and zeal, devotion to wife and children, and a private nature marred by egotism, pettiness, and snobbery. It is largely in this diary, along with public exchanges in the Gentleman's Magazine, that Madden reveals his special vision of his contemporary and rival John Mitchell Kemble. Kemble's widely known and documented arrogance was precisely suited for exasperating a man like Madden, hypersensitive to the point of paranoia in professional matters.

One astute and sympathetic observer of the Kembles, Thackeray's daughter Anne, describes the family: "The Kembles strike one somehow as a race apart. They seem divided from the rest of us by more dominant natures, by

more expressive ways and looks; one is reminded of those
deities who once visited the earth in the guise of shep-
herds, as wanderers clad in lion skins, as muses and
huntresses, not as Kembles only."[4] Oddly enough, the
life of one member of this impressive clan was transformed by the publication of Jakob Grimm's Grammar in
1819. That date is crucial to this study, which is obviously limited, too, by Kemble's life span, 1807-57, and
to a lesser extent by Madden's dates, 1801-73. Chronologically important here is the year 1864, the founding
date of the Early English Text Society. Madden, unlike
Kemble, lived to pay dues as a charter member, and to enjoy the friendship of his younger, admiring colleague
Walter Skeat, though later diary entries reveal flashes
of the old acrimony, like the allusion to "foolish
Furnivall."[5]

In old age Madden probably had scant reason to remember his role in a scholarly quarrel instigated by Kemble
in the Gentleman's Magazine of 1834. Since the 1830s
were major years in the evolving careers of both men, it
is important to look briefly at Kemble's early life, and
the twisted road which brought him to early fame with the
publication of his Beowulf in 1833.

Although John Mitchell Kemble's choice of a career
must have proved a surprise to his intimate associates,
the Goddess Fortuna seemed to smile at his birth, and to
promise future greatness. Born to a family long famous
on the British stage, he inherited a handsome face from
his father and an unpredictable, versatile intelligence
from his Swiss-French mother, Marie Thérèse de Camp.
Kemble's aunt was the great Mrs. Siddons, and his sister
the actress-abolitionist Fanny Kemble, deservedly the
subject of at least six full-length biographies.[6] At
Trinity College, Cambridge, he was noted for a good singing voice, athletic skills, and a taste for unconven-
tional behavior, confirmed by the belated degree he
earned in 1830. The college authorities held back until
he reluctantly met minimal requirements in the knowledge
of Locke and Paley. The good voice which he and his sister Fanny inherited from their mother remained a constant
motif in the Kemble family. John and Fanny's sister
Adelaide studied singing in Italy and returned to England,
where she won sufficient fame as an opera singer to earn
her own entry in the Dictionary of National Biography.
Years later, John Kemble's daughter Gertrude married Sir
Charles Santley (1834-1922), famous English baritone, who
published a book about his rich musical career.[7]

Our present concern, however, lies with Kemble's student years at Cambridge. He studied law, apparently in unsystematic fashion, but with some stirrings of interest in the antiquarian past of his native land. As a Trinity man of obvious but still as yet undefined gifts, he became a member of the Apostles, thereby claiming friendship with some of the master-spirits of the coming age: Charles Buller, Arthur Hallam, Frederick Denison Maurice, Richard Chenevix Trench, Alfred Tennyson. Among Tennyson's juvenilia is a sonnet titled "To J. M. K.," a poem good enough to suggest the future greatness of its author, fascinating in what it suggests of Kemble's compelling personality: "thou wilt be," says Tennyson, "a latter Luther and a soldier-priest."[8]

In 1828 Kemble had indeed committed himself to becoming an Anglican priest. During the summer of that year he traveled abroad, to Heidelberg and Munich, where meetings with scholars like Massmann awakened his interest in Saxon languages. A less profitable trip took place in the autumn of 1830; Kemble and some of his Cambridge friends tried to join a band of Spanish rebels who opposed Ferdinand VII, but succeeded only in reaching Gibraltar. After taking his M.A. at Cambridge in 1833, Kemble went to Göttingen. There the "soldier-priest" saluted by Tennyson found his true calling. Kemble published his first major work, the Beowulf, in 1833. His dedication credits Jakob Grimm for "all the knowledge I possess, such as it is"; and he goes on to call him "the founder of that school of philology which has converted etymological researches, once a chaos of accidents, into a logical and scientific system." Kemble offers his book to Grimm as a "tribute of admiration and respect from perhaps the first Englishman who has adopted and acted upon his views."[9]

Sir Frederic Madden's apprenticeship differed vastly from Kemble's. Madden spent his early years in Portsmouth, as one of the younger children in a family of decent lineage but scanty funds. Unlike his military and squirearchical relatives, young Madden showed precocious talent for languages, which he first exercised by deciphering Hebrew headstones in the Jewish cemetery of his native town. He escaped from the provinces to London, and worked on the preservation of Old and Middle English manuscripts under the direction of Henry Petrie. This led to a brief career at Oxford, where he progressed only so far as his responsions or "little go," owing to his need for self-support. Madden eventually won appointment as keeper of manuscripts at the British Museum, along with acclaim lasting from his time to our own for his editions of such key medieval texts as Syr Gawayne and the Grene Knyght (1839), Layamon's Brut (1848), and the Wycliffite Bible (1850).

Kemble's greatness arises from his Poems of Beowulf (1833), and his later, more definitive edition containing translation, glossary, and notes (1837). Frederic Madden also proved himself as scholar-editor in the same decade. After his pioneer edition of Havelok the Dane (1828), a "lost" romance he had rediscovered at the Bodleian Library, he then published a modest but charming treatise, The Privy Purse Expenses of the Princess Mary (1831). His edition of William and the Werwolf (1832), reedited in 1867 by Madden's protégé Skeat, was more important. In 1824 Madden had been fortunate enough to meet J. J. Conybeare and visit his magnificent private library at Batheaston. Conybeare showed him a transcription of "a very curious Saxon poem relating to the Danes and published in 1815 by Thorkelin"; he also lent him copies of Elstob and Thwaites.[10] Madden was inspired to begin his own collation of materials in Cotton Vitellius A. xv; but more important to his career was Conybeare's copy of the Gesta Romanorum, which he studied and finally published in 1838. To close the decade, Madden's Gawayne anthology was issued by the Bannatyne Club in 1839.

The 1830s brought Madden and Kemble together in collaboration and conflict. The collaboration was unsought; Kemble and Madden worked together under Richard Taylor, an editor, on corrections and notes for a new edition of Warton's History of English Poetry, finally published in 1840. In a passing reference to Beowulf Madden referred to Kemble as an "able scholar."[11] Kemble's published remarks on Madden took a different line. In an impressive article "On English Praeterites" for the Philological Museum, a Cambridge publication, he expressed dismay at the choice of Madden as editor of the Brut. Though Madden was, in Kemble's words, "a laborious and praiseworthy enquirer into the middle period of our language, [he] is unfortunately a stranger to Anglo-Saxon, and the language of Layamon must be descended upon, not risen to."[12] Kemble complained with some justice about "glossatorial" errors Madden had made in his edition of the Havelok, and he condemned as well a translated portion of Beowulf, which he concluded must have come to Madden "from the hand of some injudicious friend."[13] Kemble was famous for his arrogant personality, which discouraged prospective students at Cambridge and may have played some role in alienating his German-born wife.[14] Madden in turn was hot-tempered and hypersensitive. The Madden diary not surprisingly reflects outrage at the tone and

substance of Kemble's remarks. More important, Madden
the diarist confessed that the Kemble critique "aroused
me to a sense of what was due to Layamon."[15] Nearly two
years later, in December 1834, Kemble credited himself
with Madden's enhanced stature as a scholar, remarking in
the Gentleman's Magazine on "the great improvement which
I see in his Saxon, since he wrote the notes to
Havelok."[16]

Writing to Grimm on New Year's Day, 1838, Kemble remembered with satisfaction the stern strictures he had
given the editor of the Havelok. The delayed appearance
of Madden's Layamon, he thought, was perhaps a good sign,
since "when it appears, [it] will be much the better for
the dressing I gave its editor four or five years ago.
He has been working hard ever since, and will probably
have much improved his production."[17] On October 12,
1833, soon after his original censuring of Madden,
Kemble reported to Grimm that he had "given Sir Frederick
Madden a sharp blow over the fingers; he is utterly
abominable: conceited, jealous, backbiting & ignorant."
He went on, "it was not a month after I made this awful
exposure of Sir Frederick Madden, that the King knighted
him for his Teutonic learning! This is so comical one
can hardly help laughing aloud when one thinks of it."[18]
Though Kemble speaks of "laughing," readers of this passage must agree, it combines jealousy and malice in a
fashion all too typical of flawed humanity. William IV
had indeed conferred upon Madden a knighthood of the
Hanoverian Guelphic order; but Madden had sought the
knighthood with unbecoming eagerness by modern standards.
This touch of worldly success was symbolic of what Kemble
himself failed to achieve in later life, when suitable
appointments and deserved honors eluded him with curious
perversity.

In 1834 Kemble capitalized on his fame as first English
editor of Beowulf by opening a scholarly controversy in
the pages of the Gentleman's Magazine.[19] His avowed purpose was to praise his friend Benjamin Thorpe's Analecta
Anglo-Saxonica, an Old English grammar based on a Danish
grammar of Old English by Rask. Thorpe had trained himself in the Germanic virtues of thoroughness, exactitude,
and system. Kemble's combative temper transformed his
review into an opening offensive in a philological quarrel which almost immediately involved James Ingram, retired professor of Anglo-Saxon at Oxford, his younger
colleague Thomas Wright, the middle-aged Joseph Bosworth,
and the thirty-three-year-old Frederic Madden. One of
the best chroniclers of this controversy is the late
Arthur G. Kennedy, a latter-day product of the Germanic

school and a professor of English philology at Stanford.
Kennedy finds that only metaphors drawn from the American
West are adequate for describing the quarrels sparked by
the Kemble review. It was, as he writes, "one of those
red-blooded, two-fisted philological arguments such as
our ancestors were privileged to witness when men were
men and English philology was in its untrammeled and
sturdy youth." Later in this same article he refers to
"that wild and western two-gun spirit which . . . pre-
vailed upon the philological frontiers."[20] Kennedy's
wild-western imagery is more apt than we might think;
Kemble had a grandnephew named Owen Wister, author of The
Virginian.

The de haut en bas tone of Kemble's reference to
Madden in 1833, galling to any victim, especially to one
with Madden's sensitivity, has already been noted. When
writing on Thorpe, Kemble digresses from his chief sub-
ject--the content and method of the Analecta--in order to
heap gratuitous insult on scholars who lack his special-
ized advantages. He writes with the narrow fervor of a
convert who has seen the true light and accordingly de-
fames outsiders in a spirit of self-righteous wrath. The
incompetent scholars of the gentlemanly Oxford school, he
says,

> "have entirely forgotten what they did when
> they first began Greek and Latin; viz., that
> they first learned the grammar of these
> tongues; and then by means of the Dictionary
> and the Authors have become competent schol-
> ars, ventured or not, according as their
> humour led them, upon editing books them-
> selves. This process, our Saxonists
> hitherto, with extremely few exceptions,
> have dramatically reversed; most have begun
> by editing books which they could not hope
> to understand; and though some may have
> succeeded during the progress of their work
> in picking up a little of the grammar, the
> great majority certainly have not."

Kemble may exaggerate when he says, "had it not been for
the industry of Danes and Germans, and those who drew
from the well-heads of their learning, we might still be
where we were, with idle texts, idle grammars, idle dictionaries, and the consequences of all these--idle and
ignorant scholars."[21]

The title Gentleman's Magazine seems curiously unsuited
to the subsequent controversy. James Ingram of Oxford

wrote promptly for the next issue, chiefly to express
hurt feelings and to promise a rebuttal (which never
appeared).[22] Thomas Wright, then twenty-four years old,
took up the cause of the "old" or Oxonian philology by
citing a list of worthies to whom we should all still
wish to pay homage: Sharon Turner, J. J. Conybeare,
Joseph Bosworth, Richard Price. As for Kemble himself,
Wright declares that he "is so dependent upon the leading
strings of Danes and Germans, that he ventures not a step
without them."[23] Wright then finds fault with Thorpe's
Analecta (chiefly for its meagre glossary) and with
Kemble's Beowulf, impregnated with "palpable darkness,"
"gloomy ideas," and "mysticism," which have given us "no
longer Anglo-Saxon, but German Saxon."[24]

In the October issue of the same magazine a correspondent known only as "M. N." censured the Ingram-Wright
faction for appearing both "querulous" and "peevish."
Instead of proving the case for native English scholarship, Wright erred by an uninformed attack on both
Thorpe's Analecta and Kemble's Beowulf; their scholarship
enhanced these works in a way exactly contrary to Wright's
intention.[25]

It is not surprising that Sir Frederic Madden re-
sponded, too, in the Gentleman's Magazine, a periodical
to which he contributed short, speculative articles (like
the one signed "Nauticus," which deals with naval costume
at the time of Elizabeth and James I).[26] This recalls the
gentlemanly antiquarianism that Kemble had by implication
disparaged in favor of the new "science" of philology.
Any serious student of Madden's work should heed an early
article, written for the Gentleman's Magazine in 1825,
when he was only twenty-four.[27] Signed "Ritsonianus," it
took the unpopular but ultimately right side in a scholarly controversy involving Joseph Ritson. Ritson had
bitterly censured Warton's History of English Poetry for
"habitual blunders," and had been censured in turn by
Warton's editor Richard Price, who was too laudatory and
defensive toward Warton to give Ritson his due. Young
Madden briefly and effectively defended Ritson's philosophy of scholarship, which embodied the scientific method
of its day. Ten years later, Madden's judgment again
triumphed over his temperament when he joined the quarrel
initiated by Kemble in defense of the new Germanism.

In his article of November 1834 entitled "On the
Progress of Anglo-Saxon Literature in England,"[28]
Madden revealed his large-mindedness and magnanimity,
tributes to his scholarly perspective as well as a welcome contrast to the spite and spleen so prevalent in his

private journal. He began with a plea consistent with his calling as master-librarian, urging a continued search for those "treasures which still lie hid in the libraries of our Colleges and Cathedrals, as well as in the private collections of individuals" (p. 483). His close association with collectors like Sir Thomas Phillipps underlies this statement as does his own youthful triumph in rediscovering the "lost" romance of Havelok. Madden's tone is that of a man of the world. He calls the controversy between "old and Modern Schools of Saxonists" "amusing, indeed, but profitless to those who look quietly on the disputants." He is not content, however, to remain above the battle; he takes sides: "I confess I have but little cause to be partial to Mr. Kemble--yet my own study and reading in Saxon literature convinces me that he is in the right, and that the old school of Saxonists, from the time of Hickes to Bosworth, did not study the language on those sound principles of grammar and analogy which have recently been pointed out to us by the Northern philologists." As for Thorpe's Analecta, Madden discreetly suggested that Kemble had overpraised the book for his own proselytizing purposes.

One of its deficiencies, observes Madden, is the defective indexing of the glossary. Glossaries, we might note, were peculiar problems in the early period of English philological studies, before the existence of works like Bosworth's dictionary. The glossary of Madden's Havelok evoked special censure.[29] Tyrwhitt's glossary to Speght's Chaucer and Sir Walter Scott's glossary to Sir Tristrem, error-laden as they were, remained major sources before better tools appeared. In his journal Madden complained about both works, and tried single-handedly to provide a more accurate word-list for Sir Tristrem, a task later achieved by one of the great Germanists, Eugen Kölbing.[30]

At this point Madden seems the noblest Roman of them all. It is surely a fine moment when he declared himself in effect a Kemble partisan; by doing so he had to transcend the memory of Kemble's patronizing comments and to embrace a new philological discipline alien to his own tradition. Even so, Madden could not resist using the last part of his article to defend himself against Kemble's charge that he was unfit to edit the Brut. He presented an inaccurate rendering of a Layamon passage from the hand of Sharon Turner, and then provides his own superior version of the same passage (p. 485).

In December 1834 Madden published in the Gentleman's Magazine his "Remarks on Thorpe's Anglo-Saxon Glossary."[31]

Here he returned to a discussion of the Analecta, the innocent, even admirable work which Kemble used as a stick for beating the unsystematic Oxford antiquarians. Madden continued to take a lofty line, pointing out specific errors in Thorpe's citations from Layamon, making it clear that these observations "are not intended as an attack on Mr. Thorpe's work, nor do they at all lessen its general accuracy and value; but are only drawn up to show that a mere knowledge of Saxon is not sufficient to ensure an editor of Layamon from occasional mistakes, whatever Mr. Kemble may think to the contrary" (p. 594). Madden claimed kinship with scholars like Thorpe; in working on authors difficult of access, "with so few and feeble guides to help us understand them, . . . no one would be more ready to confess an error, or be more grateful for correction, if offered in a proper manner, than myself." Obviously, Madden was defending himself against Kemble's charges of incompetence and striving for a courteous tone of the sort Kemble spurned.

This same issue of the Gentleman's Magazine contained a "letter" from Kemble written to the putative editor "Sylvanus Urban," and entitled "Oxford Professors of Anglo-Saxon."[32] Kemble ignored Madden's role in the dispute, and addressed himself instead to Thomas Wright: "His ignorance would have obtained for him the pity of my learned German friends, and of myself; his malice, so happily tempered with impotence, has given him a juster title to that which he has obtained, our contempt" (p. 603). Kemble had obvious gifts for vitriolic combat. He accused his Oxford enemies of opposing not only his Germanic system, but his background as a "Cambridge man" and a "Whig" (p. 601).

Kemble's Whiggery deserves a further word. The fruitful friendships of his university days among the Apostles were to shape the emerging world of Victorian England. Moreover, he tried ineffectually to join a Spanish revolt against royal tyranny, and there is evidence for his sympathetic interest in the Utilitarianism of Bentham and Mill. In a letter to Jakob Grimm, Kemble discussed English and foreign affairs, his profound dislike for Palmerston at home and Metternich abroad, and his gratified response to the French Revolution of 1848.[33] As we shall see, his later publications suggest wider concerns than the technical expertise of his chosen field.

Madden, unlike Kemble the Whig, was a conservative who regarded all factions with disfavor. When hit by a brickbat on a London street he solemnly remarked to his diary, "This is what comes of elevating the lower classes

175

and giving them holidays."[34] Sworn in as special con-
stable at the time of Chartist agitation in 1848, Madden
was amused by the atypical role thrust on him by the
Wellington government. Since he frequently used phrases
like "dirty Whigs and radicals,"[35] his contempt for the
Charter and its implications were apparent. Profession-
ally admirable always, he gave primary concern to the
safety of the Museum library in this period of threatened
unrest. Madden and Kemble could not have conversed with
profit on politics, though Madden continued to be a reasonably close student of Kemble's scholarly writings.

On August 24, 1839, Madden looked at one of the early
volumes of Kemble's Latin charters; this later became
part of the Codex Diplomaticus Aevi Saxonici, published
seriatim 1839-48, during the same period that Madden was
engaged on the long and laborious editing of the Brut.
"Kemble," says Madden, "with all his pretentions, is
ignorant of the charters of Offa, Edgar, etc." On December 13 of that year, Madden made a more extensive diary
entry: "Read Kemble's Preface to Vol. I of Saxon charters. Some talent but with conceit and too much Germanism." In 1840 each man remained outwardly civil to the
other. Madden, as we know, called Kemble an "able
scholar" in the 1840 edition of Warton.[36] In a diary
entry for March 28, 1840, Madden notes noncommittally
that Kemble has sent him a paper on Anglo-Saxon runes.
Madden writes more testily on May 1, 1841: "Read Kemble's
preface to Beowulf which contains some useful rules expressed with his usual arrogance. Much of it occupied in
correcting himself." Kemble would not have found this
last comment insulting, since his letters to Grimm reveal
his hopes for bringing out a third, improved edition of
the Beowulf.

The letters to Grimm are especially rich and numerous
from 1840 till 1849, when Kemble returned to England from
Germany. In 1840 Kemble and his growing family had taken
up residence in a Surrey cottage at Chapelfields near
Addlestone. Friends had secured his appointment as
examiner of plays in England, a post formerly held by his
father for the same reason--relief of financial distress.
Teaching and university lecturing had proved uncongenial.
Kemble was happier with the editorship of the British and
Fortnightly Review, a post he held from 1836 till 1844.
The Surrey dialect of his Chapelfields retreat fascinated
him, and as late as 1854 he published an article called
"Surrey provincialisms," one of the transactions of the
Philological Society for that year.[37]

Although Kemble wrote amiably to Grimm about the births of his two younger children, a letter of 1849 describes a broken marriage and impending divorce, which necessitated Kemble's removal to Hanover.[38] The archaeological interests awakened during the Surrey years flourished after his return to Germany. He engaged in field work near Lüneburg, and was sponsored by a committee in Manchester to collect and document Celtic and Roman antiquities. Just as the "gentlemanly" Oxford school had originated in antiquarian collections, then progressed through careful examination of old texts to a working concept of literary scholarship, so Kemble reversed the process, coming to antiquarianism at the end of a road which began with the bracing blast of Grimm's philological method. For Kemble, antiquarianism became archaeology, a more sophisticated examination of realia than that of the eighteenth-century gentleman-collector; the latter served as a prototype for young Frederic Madden, the proud collector of Roman coins in his youth, who was saluted in later years as a "ripe scholar and antiquary"[39] by William Carew Hazlitt. There is some irony, perhaps, in the title of the last paper Kemble wrote, "On the Utility of Antiquarian Collections as Throwing Light on the Prehistoric Annals of European Nations"; here Kemble supplied a motto which might have united the partisans who quarreled so bitterly over Thorpe's Analecta in 1834.

Bitter partisanship was an ugly quality shared by both sides, Germanists and anti-Germanists alike, and it continued to affect the Kemble-Madden relationship. In 1856 Sir Henry Ellis retired from his post as chief librarian at the British Museum. Ellis quite properly had no authority to name his successor, though he hoped that the post might go to John Kemble. Madden, himself an obvious candidate, was chagrined by the thought of this particular rival: "A greater coxcomb and a more infamous, withal, than Kemble does not exist," he wrote in his diary for March 4, 1856. But Madden and Kemble were passed over in favor of Antonio Panizzi, called by his biographer "prince of librarians";[40] Madden never found a term more admiring than the "gorilla," and complained to his diary of working "in a house of bondage run by a blackguard Italian."[41] He fulminated on this subject until his retirement from the Museum in 1867, though he commented once more informally on John Kemble.

Early in 1857, Kemble wrote his article "On the Utility of Antiquarian Collections" in nearly festive circumstances. He delivered this paper as a speech to the Society of Antiquaries in Dublin, but caught a bronchitic cold which, to the surprise of all who knew him, proved

swiftly fatal. He died at the Gresham Hotel on March 26,
1857, just before his fiftieth birthday. The news soon
reached Madden in London, where his diary entry is dated
March 28: "I was informed of the death of Mr. Kemble at
Dublin! All are surprised at it, and he is certainly a
loss in some branches of literature. His overwhelming
estimate of himself was the rock of offense on which he
fell, and his language toward those who disagreed with
him was quite unbearable." This is not the perfect epitaph for Kemble whose "arrogance" may have been based on
a true sense of rare abilities frequently frustrated by
bad luck. Perhaps the last lines of Tennyson's early
sonnet suggest the quality of a gifted man whose inner
life has for so long eluded us. "Thou from a throne /
Mounted in heaven will shoot into the dark / Arrows of
lightnings. I will stand and mark."

Among the Apostles Richard Chenevix Trench was des-
tined for an eminent career in the church, first as dean
of Westminster, finally as Anglican archbishop of Dublin.
In his ecclesiastical dignity Trench was disconcerted by
the revived tale of his youthful escapade with Kemble
plotting against the Spanish monarchy. But there are
better reasons to remember him now. In the year of
Kemble's death Trench made two speeches before the London
Philological Society. He declared that a lexicographer
must record not only the "good" words, but all words,
good or bad.[42] In 1857 this was correctly considered a
brave stand for antiprescriptivism, a prelude, indeed, to
the noble enterprise of the Oxford English Dictionary,
issued first in 1888 and in itself a refutation of
Kemble's unkind suggestion that nothing good could come
out of Oxford. The OED, partially envisaged by the en-
lightened Cambridge man, Richard Trench, is symbolic of
reconciliation, and of renunciation of antipathy, controversy, and resentment, the three ugly goddesses who often
marred the Kemble-Madden relationship. Neither Kemble
nor Madden lived to see the OED or even to glimpse the
possibility of its existence, but it would have won deserved approval from Oxford antiquarian and Cambridge
Whig alike.

Kemble's legacy lies not only in the pioneering scholarship, but in the special meaning his crusade for Germanic system brings to Klopstock's words: "Nie war gegen
das Ausland ein andres Land gerecht wie du."[43] The early
explorations of workers and visionaries like Grimm,
Grundtvig and Grein, and later scholars like Luick,
Kölbing, Zupitza, ten Brink, Sievers, Jespersen, and
Klaeber, have helped us recapture our early English heritage, as did ardent natives like Kemble and Madden.

Notes

1. Bruce Dickins, "John Mitchell Kemble and Old
English Scholarship," Proceedings of the British
Academy 25 (1939): 51-84; Raymond A. Wiley, "Anglo-
Saxon Kemble: the Life and Works of John Mitchell
Kemble, 1807-1857 . . .," Anglo-Saxon Studies in
Archaeology and History (Oxford: British Archaeological Reports, 1979), 1:165-273.
2. See Robert W. and Gretchen P. Ackerman, Sir
Frederic Madden: A Biographical Sketch and Bibliog-
raphy (New York: Garland, 1979).
3. Sir Frederic Madden's diary is preserved in
Bodleian MS hist. C 140-182. Subsequent citations
herein are by day, month, and year only.
4. Quoted by Margaret Armstrong, Fanny Kemble, a Pas-
sionate Victorian (New York: Macmillan, 1938), p. 5.
5. Madden diary, May 15, 1872.
6. Armstrong, noted above; Dorothie Bobbé, Fanny
Kemble (New York: Minton Balch, 1931); Leota S.
Driver, Fanny Kemble (Chapel Hill: University of
North Carolina Press, 1933); Henry Gibbs, Affection-
ately Yours, Fanny (London: Jarrolds, 1948); Dorothy
Marshall, Fanny Kemble (New York: St. Martin's,
(1978); Fanny Kemble Wister, ed., Fanny the American
Kemble: Her Journals and Unpublished Letters
(Tallahassee: South Pass Press, 1972).
7. Sir Charles Santley, Reminiscences of My Life
(London: Pitman, 1909).
8. "To J.M.K.," The Works of Alfred Tennyson (New
York: Macmillan, 1907), p. 24.
9. Quoted by Ewald Flügel, "The History of English
Philology," The Flügel Memorial Volume (Stanford:
Stanford University Press, 1916), p. 25. John
Kemble's 51-page review of Grimm's Deutsche Grammatik
was in fact so adulatory that Grimm prevented its publication in the Foreign Quarterly Review. The typeset
copy, which has been deposited in Cambridge University
Library, has now been published in Facsimile, with a
preface by Raymond A. Wiley, as volume 6 of Old
English Newsletter Subsidia (Binghamton, N.Y.: SUNY
at Binghamton, 1981).
10. Madden diary, June 17, 1824.
11. Thomas Warton, The History of English Poetry, ed.
Richard Taylor (London: Thomas Tegg, 1840), 1:2,
note d.
12. John Kemble, "On English Praeterites," Philological
Museum 2 (1833): 381-82.
13. Ibid.
14. Raymond A. Wiley, ed., John Mitchell Kemble and
Jakob Grimm: A Correspondence, 1832-1852 (Leiden:

Brill, 1971), p. 284. See also Wiley's biography of
Kemble, noted above.
15. Madden diary, August 20, 1833.
16. Kemble, "Oxford Professors of Anglo-Saxon,"
Gentleman's Magazine 2, n.s. 2 (December 1834): 602.
17. Wiley, ed., Correspondence, p. 159.
18. Ibid., pp. 41-42.
19. Kemble, "On Thorpe's Analecta," Gentleman's Magazine 1, n.s. 1 (April 1834): 391-93.
20. Arthur G. Kennedy, "Odium Philologicum, or, A Century of Progress in English Philology," Stanford Studies in Language and Literature, ed. Hardin Craig
(Stanford: Stanford University Press, 1941),
pp. 11-12.
21. Kemble, "On Thorpe's Analecta," p. 392.
22. Kennedy, "Odium Philologicum," p. 14.
23. Wright, "Anglo-Saxon Scholars and Literature"
Gentleman's Magazine 2, n.s. 2 (September 1834): 260.
24. Ibid., p. 259.
25. Gentleman's Magazine 2, n.s. 2 (October 1834): 362.
26. [Madden], Nauticus, "Naval Costume temp. Elizabeth
through James I," Gentleman's Magazine n.s. 101
(October 1831): 293.
27. [Madden], Ritsonianus, "Vindications of the Late
Joseph Ritson," Gentleman's Magazine 137 (June 1825):
486-88.
28. Madden, "On the Progress of Anglo-Saxon Literature
in England," Gentleman's Magazine 2, n.s. 2 (November
1834): 483-86.
29. Kemble, "On English Praeterites," pp. 373-88.
30. Madden diary, September 10, 1829, May 25, 1871, and
October 20, 1871. See also Madden's splendid article
"On Sir Walter Scott's 'Sir Tristrem,'" Gentleman's
Magazine 154 (October 1833): 307-12.
31. Madden, "Remarks on Thorpe's Anglo-Saxon Glossary,"
Gentleman's Magazine 2, n.s. 2 (December 1834): 591-94.
32. See note 15 above.
33. Wiley, ed., Correspondence, pp. 266-68. In 1837
Kemble had written an anonymous pamphlet attacking
church establishment, entitled A Few Historical Remarks upon the Supposed Antiquity of Church Rates, and
the Three-fold Division of Tithes.
34. Madden diary, April 15-16, 1860.
35. Madden diary, August 18, 1867.
36. Wiley, ed., Correspondence, p. 284. In a recent
letter to me, Wiley refers to three letters from Kemble
to Madden in the British Library (MSS Egerton 2842-
2844), dated November 1, 1839, November 21, 1844, and
December 13, 1848. All three deal with technical details concerning Anglo-Saxon charters, and Wiley describes their tone as uniformly "cordial and friendly."

37. See Wiley, ed., Correspondence, p. 16.
38. Ibid., p. 16.
39. Thomas Warton, History of English Poetry, ed.
William Carew Hazlitt (London: Reeves and Turner,
1871), 1:xiv.
40. Edward Miller, Prince of Librarians: the Life and
Times of Antonio Panizzi of the British Museum
(London: Deutsch, 1967).
41. Madden diary, September 10, 1857.
42. See Kennedy, "Odium Philologicum," p. 20. Trench's
lecture of this year was entitled "On Some Deficiencies
in Our English Dictionaries."
43. Quoted by Flügel, "The History," p. 28.

Select Bibliography:
Secondary Studies of Anglo-Saxon Scholarship

General

Adams, Eleanor N. Old English Scholarship in England
from 1566-1800. Yale Studies in English, 55. New
Haven: Yale University Press, 1917. Reprinted
Hamden, Conn.: Archon Books, 1970.

Chadwick, H. M. The Study of Anglo-Saxon. 2d ed.
Cambridge: Heffer, 1955.

Clubb, Merrel D. "Junius, Marshall, Madden, Thorpe--and
Harvard." In Studies in Language and Literature in
Honour of Margaret Schlauch. Edited by Mieczysław
Brahmer et al. Warsaw: Państwowe Wydawnictwo Naukowe,
1966. Reprinted New York: Russell and Russell,
2971, pp. 55-70.

Dictionary of National Biography. 63 vols. London:
Smith, Elder, 1885-1900. Supplements. London:
Oxford University Press, 1901-1960.

Douglas, David C. English Scholars, 1660-1730. 2d ed.
London: Eyre and Spottiswoode, 1951.

Greenfield, Stanley B., and Robinson, Fred C. A Bibliography of Publications on Old English Literature to the
End of 1972. Toronto: University of Toronto Press,
1980.

Horsman, Reginald. "Origins of Racial Anglo-Saxonism in
Great Britain before 1850." Journal of the History of
Ideas 37 (1976): 387-410.

Kenyon, Christine. "The Study of Old and Middle English
in the Universities of the United Kingdom: An Historical Survey." Bulletin des Anglicistes Médiévistes
1 (1972): 4-17.

Ker, N. R. Catalogue of Manuscripts Containing Anglo-
Saxon. Oxford: Oxford University Press, 1957.
Supplement in Anglo-Saxon England 5 (1976):121-31.

Sisam, Kenneth. Studies in the History of Old English
Literature. Oxford: Clarendon Press, 1953.

Stanley, E. G. The Search for Anglo-Saxon Paganism.
Cambridge: Brewer; Totowa, N.J.: Rowman and
Littlefield, 1975.

Steeves, Harrison Ross. Learned Societies and English
Literary Scholarship in Great Britain and the United
States. New York: Columbia University Press, 1913.
Reprinted New York: AMS Press, 1970.

Tuve, Rosemond. "Ancients, Moderns, and Saxons." ELH 6
(1939): 165-90.

Walters, H. B. The English Antiquaries of the Sixteenth,
Seventeenth and Eighteenth Centuries. London:
E. Walters, 1934.

Whitelock, Dorothy. Changing Currents in Anglo-Saxon
Studies: an Inaugural Lecture. Cambridge: Cambridge
University Press, 1958.

Sixteenth and Seventeenth Centuries

Black, Pamela M. "Laurence Nowell's 'Disappearance' in
Germany and Its Bearing on the Whereabouts of His
Collectanea 1568-1572." English Historical Review 92
(1977): 345-53.

Bromwich, John. "The First Book Printed in Anglo-Saxon
Types." Transactions of the Cambridge Bibliographical
Society 3 (1959-63): 265-91.

Brook, V. J. K. A Life of Archbishop Parker. Oxford:
Clarendon Press, 1962.

Buckalew, Ronald E. "Leland's Transcript of Ælfric's
Glossary." Anglo-Saxon England 7 (1978): 149-64.

Cronne, H. A. "The Study and Use of Charters by English
Scholars in the Seventeenth Century: Sir Henry
Spelman and Sir William Dugdale." In English Historical Scholarship in the Sixteenth and Seventeenth Centuries. Edited by Levi Fox. London and New York,
1956, pp. 73-91.

Bibliography

Davies, W. T. "A Bibliography of John Bale." Oxford
Bibliographical Society Proceedings & Papers 5
(1936-39): 201-79.

Del Lungo Camiciotti, Gabriella. "Le origine della
filologia inglese nell'antiquaria del XVI secolo."
Annali dell'Istituto Universitario Orientale di Napoli
23, filologia germanica (1980): 51-100.

Dickins, Bruce. "The Making of the Parker Library."
Transactions of the Cambridge Bibliographical Society
6, pt. 1 (1972): 19-34.

_____. "William L'Isle the Saxonist and Three XVIIth-
Century Remainder-Issues." English and Germanic
Studies 1 (1947-48): 53-55.

Dunkel, Wilbur. William Lambarde, Elizabethan Jurist
1536-1601. New Brunswick, N.J.: Rutgers University
Press, 1965.

Flower, Robin. "Laurence Nowell and the Discovery of
England in Tudor Times." Proceedings of the British
Academy 21 (1935): 46-73.

Fox, Levi, ed. English Historical Scholarship in the
Sixteenth and Seventeenth Centuries. London and New
York: Oxford University Press, for the Dugdale
Society, 1956.

Gneuss, Helmut. "Englands Bibliotheken im Mittelalter
und ihr Untergang." In Festschrift für Walter Hübner.
Edited by Dieter Riesner and Helmut Gneuss. Berlin:
Schmidt, 1964, pp. 91-121.

_____. "Ergänzungen zu den altenglischen Wörterbüchern."
Archiv für das Studium der neueren Sprachen und
Literaturen 199 (1962): 17-24.

Goepp, Philip H. "Verstegan's 'Most Ancient Saxon
Words.'" In Philologica: the Malone Anniversary
Studies. Edited by Thomas A. Kirby and Henry B. Woolf.
Baltimore: Johns Hopkins University Press, 1949,
pp. 249-55.

Grant, Raymond J. S. "Laurence Nowell's Transcript of
BM Cotton Otho B.xi." Anglo-Saxon England 3 (1974):
111-24.

Greg, W. W. "Books and Bookmen in the Correspondence of Archbishop Parker." The Library 4th ser. 16 (1935-36): 243-79.

Heltzel, Virgil B. "Sir Thomas Egerton and William Lambard." Huntington Library Quarterly 11 (1947-48): 201-3.

Hetherington, M. S. "Sir Simonds D'Ewes and Method in Old English Lexicography." Texas Studies in Literature and Language 17 (1975): 75-92.

_____. The Beginnings of Old English Lexicography. Austin, Texas: By the Author, 1980.

Jones, Norman L. "Matthew Parker, John Bale, and the Magdeburg Centuriators." Sixteenth Century Journal 12, no. 3 (1981): 35-49.

Kendrick, T. D. British Antiquity. London: Methuen, 1950. Reprinted. London: Methuen; New York: Barnes and Noble, 1970.

Ker, N. R. "Oxford College Libraries in the Sixteenth Century." Bodleian Library Record 6 (1959): 459-515.

Liddell, J. R. "John Leland and King Henry VIII." The Library 3rd ser. 3 (1911): 132-49.

_____. "Leland's Lists of MSS. in Lincolnshire Libraries." English Historical Review 54 (1939): 88-95.

Liebermann, Felix. "Zu Matthaeus Parkers altenglische Studien." Archiv für das Studium der neueren Sprachen und Literaturen 92 (1894): 415-16.

McCusker, Honor. "Books and Manuscripts Formerly in the Possession of John Bale." The Library 4th ser. 16 (1935-36): 144-65.

McKisack, May. Medieval History in the Tudor Age. Oxford: Clarendon Press, 1971.

Marckwardt, Albert H. "The Sources of Laurence Nowell's Vocabularium Saxonicum." Studies in Philology 45 (1948): 21-36.

_____. "Nowell's Vocabularium Saxonicum and Somner's Dictionarium." Philological Quarterly 26 (1947): 345-51.

Bibliography

_____, ed. Laurence Nowell's "Vocabularium Saxonicum."
University of Michigan Studies in Language and Litera-
ture, vol. 25. Ann Arbor: University of Michigan
Press, 1952.

Mary Joan, R.S.M., Sister. "Minsheu's Guide into the
Tongues and Somner's Dictionarium." Mediaeval Studies
24 (1962): 375-77, ill.

Murphy, Michael A. "John Foxe, Martyrologist and 'Editor'
of Old English." English Studies 49 (1968): 516-23.

_____. "Abraham Wheloc's Edition of Bede's History in
Old English." Studia Neophilologica 39 (1967): 46-59.

_____. "Methods in the Study of Old English in the Six-
teenth and Seventeenth Centuries." Mediaeval Studies
30 (1968): 345-50.

_____. "Religious Polemics in the Genesis of Old English
Studies." Huntington Library Quarterly 32 (1969):
241-48.

Page, R. I. "Anglo-Saxon Texts in Early Modern Transcripts." Transactions of the Cambridge Bibliographical Society 6 (1972-76): 69-85.

[_____]. Matthew Parker's Legacy: Books and Plate.
Cambridge: Corpus Christi College, 1975.

Pearce, E. C. "Matthew Parker." The Library 4th ser.
6 (1925-26): 209-28.

Piggott, Stuart. "Antiquarian Thought in the Sixteenth
and Seventeenth Centuries." English Historical Scholarship in the Sixteenth and Seventeenth Centuries.
Edited by Levi Fox. London and New York: Oxford
University Press, For the Dugdale Society, 1956,
pp. 93-114.

_____. "William Camden and the Britannia." Proceedings
of the British Academy 37 (1951): 199-217.

Powicke, Maurice. "William Camden." Essays and Studies
n.s. 1 (1948): 67-84.

Rosier, James L. "Lexicographical Genealogy in Old
English." Journal of English and Germanic Philology
65 (1966): 295-302.

_____. "A New Old English Glossary: Nowell upon Huloet." Studia Neophilologica 49 (1977): 189-94.

_____. "The Sources and Methods of Minsheu's Guide into the Tongues." Philological Quarterly 40 (1961): 68-76.

_____. "The Sources of John Joscelyn's Old English-Latin Dictionary." Anglia 78 (1960): 28-39.

Schoeck, Richard J. "Early Anglo-Saxon Studies and Legal Scholarship in the Renaissance." Studies in the Renaissance 5 (1958): 102-10.

Sharpe, Kevin. Sir Robert Cotton, 1586-1631: History and Politics in Early Modern England. London and New York: Oxford University Press, 1979.

Shirley, F. J. Elizabeth's First Archbishop. London: SPCK, 1948.

Skeat, T. C. "Two 'Lost' Works by John Leland." English Historical Review 65 (1950): 505-8.

Sledd, James. "Nowell's Vocabularium Saxonicum and the Elyot-Cooper Tradition." Studies in Philology 51 (1954): 143-48.

Steensma, Robert C. "'So Ancient and Noble a Nation': Sir William Temple's History of England." Neuphilologische Mitteilungen 77 (1976): 95-107.

Strongman, Sheila. "John Parker's Manuscripts: An Edition of the Lists in Lambeth Palace MS 737." Transactions of the Cambridge Bibliographical Society 7, pt. 1 (1977): 1-27.

Swanton, Michael J. "Eine wenig bekannte Fassung von Ælfrics Glossar." Archiv für das Studium der neueren Sprachen und Literaturen 213 (1976): 104-7.

Timmer, B. J. "De Laet's Anglo-Saxon Dictionary." Neophilologus 41 (1957): 199-202.

Tite, Colin G. C. "The Early Catalogues of the Cottonian Library." British Library Journal 6 (1980): 144-57.

Towers, Terence. "Smith and Son, Editors of Bede." In Famulus Christi. Edited by Gerald Bonner. London: SPCK, 1976, pp. 357-65.

Bibliography

Turner, Alberta. "Another Seventeenth-Century Anglo-Saxon Poem." Modern Language Quarterly 9 (1948): 389-93.

Utley, Francis L. "Two Seventeenth-Century Anglo-Saxon Poems." Modern Language Quarterly 3 (1942): 243-61.

Van Norden, Linda. "Sir Henry Spelman on the Chronology of the Elizabethan College of Antiquaries." Huntington Library Quarterly 13 (1949-50): 131-60.

Warnicke, Retha M. "The Laurence Nowell Manuscripts in the British Library." British Library Journal 5 (1979): 201-02.

——. "Note on a Court of Requests Case of 1571." English Language Notes 11 (1974): 250-56.

——. William Lambarde, Elizabethan Antiquary 1536-1601. Chichester: Phillimore, 1973.

Wood, D. N. C. "Elizabethan English and Richard Carew." Neophilologus 61 (1977): 304-15.

Woolf, Henry B. "John Cleveland's 'West Saxon Poet.'" Philological Quarterly 30 (1951): 443-47.

——. "The Earliest Printing of Old English Poetry." English Studies 34 (1953): 113-15.

Wormald, Francis, and Wright, C. E., eds. The English Library before 1700: Studies in Its History. London: University of London, Athlone Press, 1958.

Wright, C. E. "The Dispersal of the Monastic Libraries and the Beginnings of Anglo-Saxon Studies. Matthew Parker and His Circle: a Preliminary Study." Transactions of the Cambridge Bibliographical Society 1 (1949-53): 208-37.

——. "Sir Edward Dering: a Seventeenth-Century Antiquary and His 'Saxon' Charters." In The Early Cultures of North-West Europe. Edited by Cyril Fox and Bruce Dickins. Cambridge: Cambridge University Press, 1950, pp. 369-93.

Yerkes, David. "Dugdale's Dictionary and Somner's Dictionarium." English Language Notes 14 (1976): 110-12.

Eighteenth and Early Nineteenth Centuries

Aarsleff, Hans. The Study of Language in England, 1780-1860. Princeton: Princeton University Press, 1967.

Ackerman, Robert W., and Ackerman, Gretchen P. Sir Frederic Madden: a Biographical Sketch and Bibliography. New York and London: Garland, 1979.

Ashdown, Margaret. "Elizabeth Elstob, the Learned Saxonist." Modern Language Review 20 (1925): 125-46.

Beauchamp, Virginia Walcott. "Pioneer Linguist: Elizabeth Elstob (1683-1756)." Papers in Women's Studies (University of Michigan) 1, no. 3 (1974): 9-43.

Bennett, J. A. W. "Hickes's Thesaurus: a Study of Oxford Book-Production." Essays and Studies n.s. 1 (1948): 28-45.

Birrell, T. A. "The Society of Antiquaries and the Taste for Old English, 1705-1840." Neophilologus 50 (1966): 107-17.

Calder, Daniel G. "The Study of Style in Old English Poetry: A Historical Introduction." In Old English Poetry: Essays on Style. Edited by Daniel G. Calder. Berkeley: University of California Press, 1979, pp. 1-65.

Cooley, Franklin D. "Early Danish Criticism of Beowulf." ELH 7 (1940): 45-67.

Dickins, Bruce. "John Mitchell Kemble and Old English Scholarship." Proceedings of the British Academy 25 (1939): 51-84.

Gardner, William Bradford. "George Hickes and His Thesaurus." Notes and Queries n.s. 2 (1955): 196-99.

Garmonsway, G. N. "Anna Gurney, Learned Saxonist." Essays and Studies 8 (1955): 40-57.

Halsall, Maureen. "Benjamin Thorpe and the Vercelli Book." English Language Notes 6 (1969): 164-69.

Hargreaves, Henry. "Hickes's Institutiones Grammaticae: An 'Ex dono authoris' Copy." Aberdeen University Review 46 (1975): 53-55.

Heyworth, P. L. "Humfrey Wanley and 'Friends' of the Bodleian, 1695-98." Bodleian Library Record 9 (1976): 219-30.

Hughes, S. F. D. "Mrs. Elstob's Defense of Antiquarian Learning in Her Rudiments of Grammar for the English-Saxon Tongue (1715)." Harvard Library Bulletin 27 (1979): 172-91.

Kennedy, Arthur G. "Odium Philologicum, or, A Century of Progress in English Philology." In Stanford Studies in Language and Literature. Edited by Hardin Craig. Stanford: Stanford University Press, 1941, pp. 11-27.

Kinghorn, A. M. "Warton's History and Early English Poetry." English Studies 44 (1963): 197-204.

Malone, Kemp. "Conybeare and Thorkelin." English Studies 50 (1969): i-xi.

Munby, A. N. L. Connoisseurs and Medieval Miniatures, 1750-1850. Oxford: Clarendon Press, 1972.

Murphy, Michael A. "The Elstobs, Scholars of Old English and Anglican Apologists." Durham University Journal 58 (1966): 131-38.

Savage, David J. "Grundtvig: a Stimulus to Old English Scholarship." In Philologica: the Malone Anniversary Studies. Edited by Thomas A. Kirby and Henry B. Woolf. Baltimore: Johns Hopkins University Press, 1949, pp. 275-80.

Sisam, Kenneth. "Humfrey Wanley." In Studies in the History of Old English Literature. Oxford: Clarendon Press, 1953, pp. 259-77.

Toldberg, Helge. "Grundtvig og de Engelske Antikvarer." Orbis Litterarum 5 (1947): 258-311.

Wiley, Raymond A. "Anglo-Saxon Kemble: the Life and Works of John Mitchell Kemble, 1807-1857, Philologist, Historian, and Archaeologist." Anglo-Saxon Studies in Archaeology and History. British Archaeological Reports, British Series, vol. 72. Oxford: British Archaeological Reports, 1979. 1:165-273.

_____, ed. John Mitchell Kemble and Jakob Grimm: a Correspondence, 1832-1852. Leiden: Brill, 1971.

_____. "Four Unpublished Letters of Jakob Grimm to John Mitchell Kemble, 1832–1840." Journal of English and Germanic Philology 67 (1968): 475–84.

Wright, C. E. "Humfrey Wanley: Saxonist and Library-Keeper." Proceedings of the British Academy 46 (1960): 99–129.

Index

Copyediting directed by Ara Salibian.
Designed by Jack Schwartz.
Calligraphy by Fred Welden.
Produced by Cathy Carpenter.
Camera-ready copy typed by Geraldine Kline
     on an IBM Selectric with Advocate font.
Printed and bound by Braun-Brumfield, Inc.,
          of Ann Arbor, Michigan.